Asset Analytics

Performance and Safety Management

The main aim of this book series is to provide a floor for researchers, industries, asset managers, government policy makers and infrastructure operators to cooperate and collaborate among themselves to improve the performance and safety of the assets with maximum return on assets and improved utilization for the benefit of society and the environment.

Assets can be defined as any resource that will create value to the business. Assets include physical (railway, road, buildings, industrial etc.), human, and intangible assets (software, data etc.). The scope of the book series will be but not limited to:

- Optimization, modelling and analysis of assets
- Application of RAMS to the system of systems
- Interdisciplinary and multidisciplinary research to deal with sustainability issues
- Application of advanced analytics for improvement of systems
- Application of computational intelligence, IT and software systems for decisions
- Interdisciplinary approach to performance management
- Integrated approach to system efficiency and effectiveness
- Life cycle management of the assets
- Integrated risk, hazard, vulnerability analysis and assurance management
- Adaptability of the systems to the usage and environment
- Integration of data-information-knowledge for decision support
- Production rate enhancement with best practices
- Optimization of renewable and non-renewable energy resources

More information about this series at http://www.springer.com/series/15776

Reggie Davidrajuh

Petri Nets for Modeling of Large Discrete Systems

Springer

Reggie Davidrajuh
Department of Electrical Engineering
and Computer Science
University of Stavanger
Stavanger, Norway

ISSN 2522-5162 ISSN 2522-5170 (electronic)
Asset Analytics
ISBN 978-981-16-5205-9 ISBN 978-981-16-5203-5 (eBook)
https://doi.org/10.1007/978-981-16-5203-5

This Springer imprint is published by the registered company Springer Nature Singapore Pte Ltd.
The registered company address is: 152 Beach Road, #21-01/04 Gateway East, Singapore 189721, Singapore

This book is dedicated to my family:

my wife Ruglin

and

my daughter Ada

Foreword

It gives me great pleasure to write a "foreword" for this wonderful book on Petri nets and an innovative approach to handling huge Petri net models using distributed computing so as to enable them to be fast enough for real-time control applications. Petri nets are handy for modeling discrete event systems. However, they suffer from some weaknesses, e.g., massive size, huge state space, and slow simulation. Due to the enormous state space, model checking a Petri net is difficult. Also, Petri nets are difficult to be used for real-time applications due to the slowness in simulation. Thus, this book suggests modular Petri nets as a way of overcoming these difficulties.

In modular Petri nets, modules are designed, developed, and run independently. Also, the modules communicate with each other via inter-modular connectors. Hence, the bottom-up approach is suggested (starting with the modules and then combining them after thorough testing) for developing newer Petri net models. However, many Petri net models of real-life systems exist (legacy models), which are enormous and non-modular. These legacy models cannot be discarded as large amounts of time, effort, and money were spent developing these legacy models. In this case, the top-down approach is the only solution, which starts with the existing legacy models, decomposing them into modules, and then joining them together after testing them individually. This book presents both approaches centering around modules (known as "Petri modules"). Petri modules are well defined for inter-modular collaboration.

This book aims to introduce a methodology in which Petri nets are moved to a new level. In this new level, large Petri net models are made of Petri modules that are independent and run on different computers. Also, Petri modules communicate with each other using the inter-modular components (e.g., TCP/IP sockets). Thereby, the compact Petri modules run faster and, thus, become suitable for supervisory control of real-time systems.

This book focuses on Petri modules. This book presents the literature study on modular Petri nets and definitions for the newer Petri modules. Also, algorithms for extracting Petri modules and algorithms for connecting Petri modules and applications are given in this book. The ideas and algorithms proposed in this book are implemented in the software General-purpose Petri net Simulator (GPenSIM, developed by the author of this book). Hence, real-life discrete event systems could be modeled, analyzed, and performance-optimized with GPenSIM.

I congratulate Prof. Davidrajuh for bringing out this highly technical book in a very lucid manner and welcome this book as a valuable addition to the Springer series on "Asset Analytics".

Ajit Kumar Verma
Professor (Technical Safety) and Series Editor,
Asset Analytics-Performance and Safety
Management, Western Norway University
of Applied Sciences, Haugesund, Norway

Preface

Cyber-physical systems involve hardware and software that are highly interconnected and complex. Unexpected failures in these systems can cause material damages, cost a lot of money and reputation, and can risk human lives too. The correct way of avoiding unexpected failures is to make a mathematical model of the system and to perform exhaustive analysis on it. Also, mathematical models are inevitable for performance analysis of the systems (e.g., finding throughput and bottlenecks) and to plan for extensions (e.g., measuring cost over performance factor).

Petri net, since its inception in 1962, has been used for modeling and performance analysis of discrete event systems. In the 1970s and 80s, Petri net was tried out on modeling smaller discrete manufacturing systems like flexible manufacturing systems with a handful of CNC machines and robots. Very soon, it became apparent that even for smaller systems, the Petri net models become huge. Also, the state spaces generated from the models become too big to handle (the problem of state explosion). Of course, for a large Petri net model of a real-life discrete system, the state space is enormous, and analysis of it is not a possibility.

Also, simulations take too much time, as the simulation of a Petri net means tracking the movement of tokens as they pass through places and transitions. For a large Petri net with hundreds of places and transitions, monitoring the movements of all those tokens makes the simulations slower. The slow simulations also make Petri net not suitable for real-time control. If faster execution of Petri net is possible, then Petri net could become an ideal candidate for supervisory control of real-time systems.

Finally, researchers and engineers agree that model checking is the only systematic way of finding and fixing errors in industrial systems before they go into production. For Petri net models of discrete event system, model checking verifies whether the state space satisfies a given property specification. Here too, due to the enormous size of the state space, model checking is either difficult or not possible at all.

Some Petri net slicing methods are proposed in the literature to make the Petri net smaller so that the resulting state space also becomes smaller. However, for real-life discrete even systems (especially for manufacturing systems), the proposed Petri net slicing methods fail to produce any slice at all, as the systems are strongly connected.

In some cases, the slicing methods provide slices; however, the resulting state spaces remain as huge as before.

For all these problems mentioned above (massive Petri net models resulting in enormous state spaces, slowness in simulation, and unsuitability for real-time control), this book presents the modular Petri net as the solution. Although in the literature, modular Petri net has been proposed as a solution, this is the first time modular Petri net is given a full focus. In this book, starting with a historical perspective (literature study), a clear and well-defined Petri module is designed and analyzed. Also, the toolbox of the General-purpose Petri net Simulator (GPenSIM) is extended to support modules, so that modular Petri net models of real-life discrete event systems can be developed and tested.

It is must be emphasized that the modular Petri net presented in this book is designed and developed as a general solution to many problems that are discussed above. In particular, the theory, design, and implementation of modular Petri net presented in this book provide four benefits:

1. Fast and Flexible model development: Modelers can independently design, develop, and test modules that make up a modular Petri net model.
2. Faster simulation: The modules can be hosted on different computers so that they can run faster, and these modules can communicate through TCP/IP sockets, exchanging tokens (messages, status, and control policies as tokens).
3. Real-time control: A module can receive data from sensors that are attached to the computer that is hosting the module. Also, a module can control actuators that are also attached to the computer.
4. Departmental cost calculation: Since GPenSIM supports cost calculation, activity-based departmental cost calculation is possible as modules represent different departments of a manufacturing system and the transitions inside a module represent different activities of a department.

The Structure of This Book

This book consists of four parts. Part-I "Petri nets and GPenSIM" is the introductory part consisting of four chapters:

- Chapter 1 "Introduction to Petri nets" starts with formal definitions of the key terms used in this book.
- Chapter 2 "Introduction to GPenSIM" introduces the software known as the General-purpose Petri net Simulator (GPenSIM). Only the basics of GPenSIM are given in this chapter. GPenSIM defines a Petri net language on the MATLAB platform. GPenSIM is also a simulator with which Petri net models can be developed, simulated, and analyzed. GPenSIM is developed by the author of this book.
- Chapter 3 "Models of Real-Life Systems" presents some Petri net models of typical manufacturing systems. The reason behind this chapter is to clearly show

the major difficulties in using Petri nets for modeling of real-life discrete event systems generally and manufacturing systems especially.

- Chapter 4 "GPenSIM for Monolithic Petri nets" presents the software GPenSIM, focusing on the transitions and their visibility. Chapter 4 is essential as the knowledge of how GPenSIM supported the development of monolithic Petri nets will help understand the extensions that are added to GPenSIM to support modules.

Part-II "Design of Modular Petri Nets" consists of the following four chapters:

- Chapter 5 "Literature Review on Modular Petri Nets" presents an extensive literature study on modular Petri nets. The conclusions drawn from the literature study are the basis for the new design of Petri net modules presented in this book.
- With the conclusion from the literature study, Chap. 6 "Toward Developing a New Modular Petri net" takes the first attempt to design a modular Petri net. This chapter introduces the main elements of a modular Petri net (such as Petri modules and Inter-Modular Connectors (IMC)) and also the input and out ports (IO ports) of a module.
- Chapter 7 "Design of a New Modular Petri Nets" presents complete details about modular Petri nets, providing the formal definitions to all the elements. An application example on modular Petri net is also given.
- Chapter 8 "GPenSIM support for Petri Modules" presents the extension to GPenSIM to support developing modular Petri nets. This chapter discusses the programming constructs provided by GPenSIM for the development.

Part-III "*Legacy* Petri Nets" is about transforming legacy models into Modular Petri nets. Part-III consists of the following two chapters:

- Chapter 9 "Module Extraction": Modularization of a monolithic model starts with identifying the modules (or segments or groups of elements) of the model that can decompose the model into a set of connected independent modules. Once the modules are identified, how can the modules be carved out of the model so that these modules individually adhere to the formal definition of modules? The module extraction algorithm is described in this chapter. Also, this chapter presents an analysis of the preservation of structural properties by modularization.
- Chapter 10 "Activity-Oriented Petri nets (AOPN)": Sometimes, it may not be possible to modularize a legacy model, due to its crisscrossing connections. For example, the modularization techniques described in Chap. 9 may not be successful. In this case, AOPN could be a remedy.

The final part (Part-IV) is about "Collaborating Modules", allowing the modules to collaborate to perform larger jobs. Part-IV consists of the following five chapters:

- Chapter 11 "Discrete Systems as Petri Modules" is about putting the modules together in a modular Petri net. This chapter consists of three groups of sections. In the first group of sections, nine blocks are introduced as the basic building blocks of a discrete system. The second group of sections introduces five matrices, such as adjacency, reachability, Rader's, connection, and component matrices. The third group of sections introduces the spanning tree and connected components

of a graph. All the material introduced in this chapter will be used in the newer algorithms developed in Chap. 12.
- Chapter 12 "Algorithms for Modular Connectivity" presents five new algorithms for analyzing the network connectivity in the modular Petri net models. The algorithms are designed with Industry 4.0 in mind; this means the modules are intelligent enough to choose with whom they may communicate, in case some of the modules are not collaborating.
- Chapter 13 "Model Checking for Collaborativeness" focuses on the property of collaborativeness. Collaborativeness is a property of a module, indicating whether the module is willing or be able to participate in collaboration with the other modules. This chapter applies the theories and techniques developed in this book to solve the problem of model checking for collaborativeness. The literature study suggests the use of external tools, off-line, for model checking of collaborativeness. However, Chap. 13 proposes using a novel online technique that is tailor-made for the GPenSIM environment.
- Chapter 14 "Generic Petri Module" presents a generic three-layered architecture for Petri modules that can participate in collaboration while performing some useful functions on their own. This chapter starts with a crude structure for Petri modules and discusses the necessity of using colored Petri net. Finally, the generic architecture is presented.

Companion Website

Companion Website for this book is
http://www.davidrajuh.net/gpensim/book-II/.

This Companion website presents the GPenSIM code for some of the examples given in this book.

Acknowledgement

The book is a result of my teaching and research at two institutions. I work as a Professor of informatics at the Department of Electrical Engineering and Computer Science (IDE), University of Stavanger. I give two courses for master students in Computer Science, "DAT530 Discrete Simulations" and "DAT600 Algorithm Theory". My experiences from these two courses are instrumental in writing this book. I am also a Visiting Professor at the Department of Engineering Processes Automation and Integrated Manufacturing Systems (RMT2), Silesian University of Technology, Gliwice, Poland. In Gliwice, I give a variety of short courses to master students in Mechanical Engineering. A part of the book is written during my stays in Gliwice, benefiting from my discussions with my colleagues there. My sincere thanks go to these two institutions (IDE and RMT2) for offering me ample time and research facilities to complete this book.

Dr. Damian Krenczyk (Silesian University of Technology, Gliwice, Poland), has tirelessly read the full draft version of the book and gave very useful suggestions for improvement. I am indebted to Dr. Krenczyk for all the help and advice I received from him.

From the publisher Springer's side, I would like to thank the "Asset Analytics" series editor Prof. Ajit Verma Kumar, for encouraging me to submit the book to the series and for the speedy and qualitative review process. Prof. Ajit Verma was also kind enough to write the foreword of this book. My thanks also go to Ms. Kamiya Khatter—the receiving editor at Springer Nature India. Ms. Kamiya patiently answered my numerous emails to her.

I am also thankful to my wife Ruglin and my daughter Ada for tolerating my frequent absence in their daily lives.

Stavanger, Norway
May 2021

Reggie Davidrajuh

Contents

About the Author

Reggie Davidrajuh has a Bachelor's study in Physics, a Master's degree in Control Systems, and a Ph.D. in Industrial Engineering (awarded by the Norwegian University of Science and Technology). Also, he has a D.Sc. (habilitation) degree in Information Science (AGH University of Science and Technology) and one more Ph.D. in Mechanical Engineering (Silesian University of Technology). He is presently a professor of Informatics at the University of Stavanger, Norway, and holds a visiting professor position at the Silesian University of Technology, Poland.

Dr. Davidrajuh is an editor of the journal "International Journal of Business and Systems Research". Also, he serves on the editorial committees of many journals that include "Expert Systems with Applications" (Elsevier) and "Archives of Control Sciences" (a Quarterly of Polish Academy of Sciences). Dr. Davidrajuh has published over 150 publications in diverse areas such as supply chain, e-commerce, e-government, modeling and simulation, discrete event systems, green power generation, etc. His three papers won the best paper awards: "Modeling humanoid robot as a discrete event system" at the IEEE Third International Conference on Artificial Intelligence, Modeling, and Simulation (AIMS2015), in December 2015, in Kuala Lumpur; "GPenSIM for Performance Evaluation of Event Graphs" at the International Scientific and Technical Conference on Manufacturing (Manufacturing 2017), in October 2017, in Poznan, Poland; "Measuring Network Centrality in Petri Nets" at the 2018 IEEE International Conference on Advanced Manufacturing (ICAM), in November 2018, in Yunlin, Taiwan.

He has organized over 60 international conferences and has given keynote speeches in four conferences. His current research interests are "Modeling, simulation, and performance analysis of discrete-event systems", Algorithms, and Graph Theory. He is a senior member of IEEE and a Fellow of the British Computer Society. He is also a member of the Norwegian Academy of Technical Sciences.

Nomenclature

λ_2	Algebraic Connectivity: the second eigenvalue of a Laplacian matrix
β	Self-loop strength (arc weight of an arc that is directed from a node to itself)
$\bullet p$	Input transitions of place p
$\bullet t$	Input places of transitions t
δ	Value for step-wise reduction of the self-loop strength
$\overrightarrow{t_i}$	Firing transition t_i
Φ	State formula (in CTL)
ϕ	Path formula (in CTL)
Φ_i	Petri module
Ψ_i	Inter-Modular Connector
A	Adjacency Matrix (N, N) of a graph, consisting of N nodes
A	CTL path quantifier for "all paths"
A	Incidence Matrix (m, n) of a Petri Net, m places and n transitions
A	Set of arcs (directed connections) of a Petri Net
AOPN	Activity-Oriented Petri Nets
a or a_i	Arc of a Petri Net
a or a_{ij}	Element of an adjacency matrix or incidence matrix
C	Connection Matrix
C_{m_i}	Collaborativeness of a Petri module
CTL	Computation Tree Logic
D	Rader's Matrix, Diagonal matrix
E	(Number of) edges of a graph $G = (V, E)$
E	CTL path quantifier for "there exist some paths"
F	CTL temporal modality for "in future" or "eventually"
FMS	Flexible Manufacturing System
G	CTL temporal modality for "always" or "globally"
GPenSIM	General-purpose Petri Net Simulator
IMC	Inter-Modular Connector
L	Laplacian Matrix
LFN	Leader-Followers Networking
LTS	Labeled Transition System (*aka* the Kripke Structure)

M	Marking (state) of a Petri Net
$M(p)$	Marking of (the number of tokens in) place p
$M[t_i\rangle$	Enabled transition t_i in the marking M
M_0	Initial marking (initial state) of a Petri Net
$M_\dashv$	Terminal state of a state space
$M_0[\rangle$	All the markings that are reachable from M_0
$M_0[t_1\rangle M_1$	M_1 is directly reachable from M_0 due to the firing of t_1
MPN	Modular Petri Net, consisting of one or more Petri modules and zero or more Inter-Modular Connectors
MSF	Main Simulation File (in GPenSIM)
N	CTL temporal operator for "Next"
N	Natural numbers
N^+	Natural numbers, excluding zero
NPN	Negotiating-Peers Networking
P	Set of Places of a Petri Net
p	Atomic property (in CTL)
$p\bullet$	Output transitions of place p
PDF	Petri net Definition File (in GPenSIM)
PTN	Place–Transition (P/T) Petri Net
p or p_i	Place of a Petri Net
R	Reachability Matrix
R	Real numbers
R^+	Positive real numbers, greater than zero
RG	Reachability Graph (State Space)
$SCEG$	Strongly Connected Event Graph
SMN	Steiner-Mode Networking
T	Set of Transitions of a Petri Net
$t\bullet$	Output places of transitions t
$t_\dashv$	Terminal transition of a state space
$t_i\rangle$	Enabled transition t_i
T_{m_i}	Timing of a Petri module
tI	Input port(s) of a Petri module
$tINV$	Transition for inviting the other modules for collaboration
$tMCC$	Transition for model checking for collaborativeness
tO	Output port(s) of a Petri module
TPN	Timed Petri Net
t or t_i	Transition of a Petri Net
U	CTL temporal operator for "Until"
V	(Number of) vertices of a graph $G = (V, E)$
$W(p_i, t_j)$	Weight of the arc between the place p_i and the transition t_j
Z	Integers

List of Figures

List of Tables

List of Algorithms

Part I
Petri Nets and GPenSIM

Chapter 1
Introduction to Petri Nets

This chapter introduces the basic concepts of Petri nets. This chapter starts with the formal definitions of some of the key concepts (such as P/T Petri nets, enabled transitions, and state space). The state equation and the structural properties (P-invariant and t-invariant) are introduced. Also, a short introduction to strongly connected event graphs and timed Petri nets is given.

1.1 Petri Nets

This chapter gives only a brief introduction to Petri nets. For a formal study of Petri nets, interested readers are referred to the standard textbooks on Petri nets. For an introduction to Petri nets, Reisig [12] is recommended. Peterson [11] is the first textbook on Petri nets, and it is still useful. For a summary of Petri nets, Murata [10] is recommended.

Petri nets have been used for modeling, simulation, and performance analysis of discrete event systems. The wide acceptance of Petri nets is due to their well-known properties such as graphical (visual) representation that closely resemble real-life objects and formal and well-defined semantics. Petri net has a simple mathematical background (limited to linear algebraic techniques and graph theorems) that enables thorough system analysis (such as state space analysis, performance bottlenecks, and deadlock avoidance) [11].

A large number of Petri net software tools are also available, some of them for specific purposes and some for general simulations (e.g., CPN and GPenSIM). Several Petri net extensions are also available, some of them increase the modeling power while preserving its analytical power (e.g., Colored Petri nets), while some other extensions make a trade-off (e.g., state machines and marked graphs increase the analytical power while slightly reducing the model power) [11].

R. Davidrajuh, *Petri Nets for Modeling of Large Discrete Systems*, Asset Analytics,
https://doi.org/10.1007/978-981-16-5203-5_1

The recent research topics on Petri nets are on supervisory control (Petri net-based control of discrete and hybrid systems), and modular Petri nets (partitioning Petri net models into modules for ease of model building and ease of analysis). This book is also on the latter topic.

Some basic definitions are given in the following section. These definitions are not complete in the sense that the definitions are provided only to those issues that are relevant to the topics discussed in this book. For a thorough study on Petri nets, the following textbooks are suggested [1, 5, 7, 9, 14].

1.2 Formal Definitions

Since its inception, Petri nets have gone through many versions (extensions and subclasses) mainly to incorporate time and to increase its modeling power [11].

1.2.1 P/T Petri Nets

Definition 1.1 The Place–Transition Petri net (P/T Petri net, for short) is defined as a four-tuple:

$$PTN = (P, T, A, M_0),$$

where

- P is a finite set of places, $P = \{p_1, p_2, \ldots, p_{n_p}\}$.
- T is a finite set of transitions, $T = \{t_1, t_2, \ldots, t_{n_t}\}$. $\mathrm{P} \cap \mathrm{T} = \emptyset$.
- A is the set of arcs (from places to transitions and from transitions to places). $A \subseteq (P \times T) \cup (T \times P)$. The default arc weight W of a_{ij} ($a_{ij} \in A$, an arc going from p_i to t_j or from t_i to p_j) is one, unless noted otherwise.
- M is the row vector of markings (tokens) on the set of places. $M = [M(p_1), M(p_2), \ldots, M(p_{n_p})] \in N^{n_p}$, M_0 is the initial marking. Due to the markings, a $PTN = (P, T, A, M)$ is also called a **marked P/T Petri net**. □

Example 1.1 (P/T Petri net) Figure 1.1 shows a simple Petri net that consists of three places and three transitions, connected by six arcs. The initial marking M_0 on the Petri net is one token on the places p_1. Thus, $M_0 = [1, 0, 0]$.

Figure 1.1 also shows that the transition t_1 is enabled and can fire, as the net has enough input tokens for t_1.

Definition 1.2 (*Enabled Transition*) t_i is enabled in a marking M if

$$\forall p \in P, \quad W(p, t_i) \le M(p)$$

. □

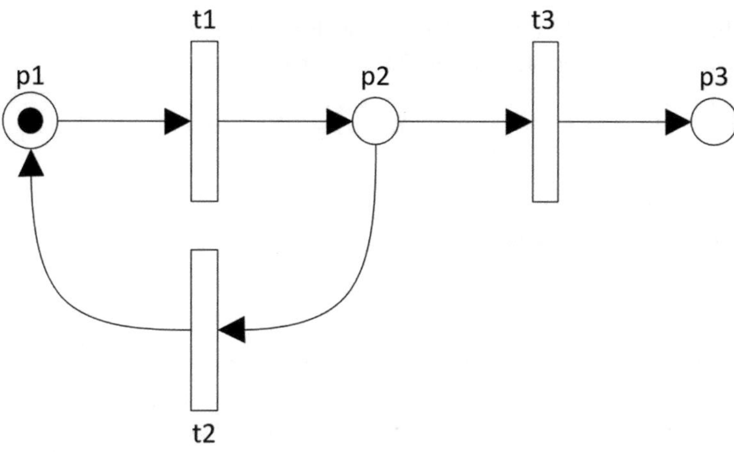

Fig. 1.1 A simple P-T Petri net

An enabled transition t_i is denoted by $\boldsymbol{t_i}\rangle$. An enabled transition t_i in a marking M is denoted by $\boldsymbol{M[t_i}\rangle$.

In simple words, according to the Definition 1.2, a transition is enabled only if all the input places of it have a number of tokens that are at least equal to the respective arc weights.

Example 1.2 (Enabled transition) In Fig. 1.1, only t_1 is enabled, as it has enough tokens in its input place. If t_1 starts firing, it consumes one token from the input place p_1. When t_1 completes firing, it deposits one token into the output place p_2.

Definition 1.3 (*Input Places and Output Places*) The input places of a transition t, denoted by $\bullet t$, is the set of all places that are directly input to t:

$$\forall p \in \ \bullet t, \quad W(p, t) \neq 0.$$

Likewise, the output places of a transition t, denoted by $t\bullet$, is the set of all places to which t has a direct outward connection:

$$\forall p \in \ t\bullet, \quad W(t, p) \neq 0.$$

□

Similarly, the set of input transitions and the output transitions of places (denoted $\bullet p$ and $p\bullet$, respectively) are defined.

If t_1 fires in Fig. 1.1, the new marking M_1 due to the firing of transition t_1 from the previous marking M_0, denoted by $\boldsymbol{M_0[t_1\rangle\ M_1}$ (in other words, M_1 is directly reachable from M_0 due to the firing of t_1), is defined by the following definition. Whereas $\boldsymbol{M_0[\rangle}$ denotes all the markings that are reachable from M_0.

Definition 1.4 (*New Marking*) When an enabled transition t_i fires, the new marking M_{j+1} obtained from the previous marking M_j is given by

$$\forall p_i \in P, \quad M_{j+1}(p_i) = M_j(p_i) - W(p_i, t_i) + W(t_i, p_i).$$

□

A firing transition t_i is denoted by $\overrightarrow{t_i}$.

1.2.2 State Space (aka Reachability Graph)

The state space generated from a marked Petri net is also known as the *Reachability Graph (RG)*. In literature, the state space is also referred to the *Labeled Transition System (LTS)* and the *Kripke Structure*.

Definition 1.5 The State Space (RG) of a marked Petri net $PTN = (P, T, A, M_0)$ is defined as a three-tuple:

$$RG = (R, T_l, L),$$

where

- $R = M_0[\rangle$ is the set of all reachable markings from M_0.
- T_l is the set of transitions that created R:
  $\forall t \in T_l, \ \exists (M_i[t\rangle M_j) \ | \ M_i, M_j \in R$.
- L is a set of labeled transitions,
  $L = \{(M_i, t, M_j), \ M_i, M_j \in R, t \in T_l \ | \ M_i[t\rangle M_j\}$. □

Example 1.3 (State space) Figure 1.2 shows the state space of the marked Petri net shown in Fig. 1.1. In this state space, there are three unique states such as {p1}, {p2}, and {p3}. The state highlighted in yellow color is a duplicate state. The state {p3} is also a terminal state (the system is deadlocked or terminated in this state), thus highlighted in red color.

1.2.3 State Equation and the Incidence Matrix

Definition 1.6 The Incidence Matrix (A) of a Petri net with n_p places and n_t transitions is given by

$$A_{(n_p \times n_t)} = [a_{ij}],$$
$$\text{where } a_{ij} = W(t_j, p_i) - W(p_i, t_j).$$

□

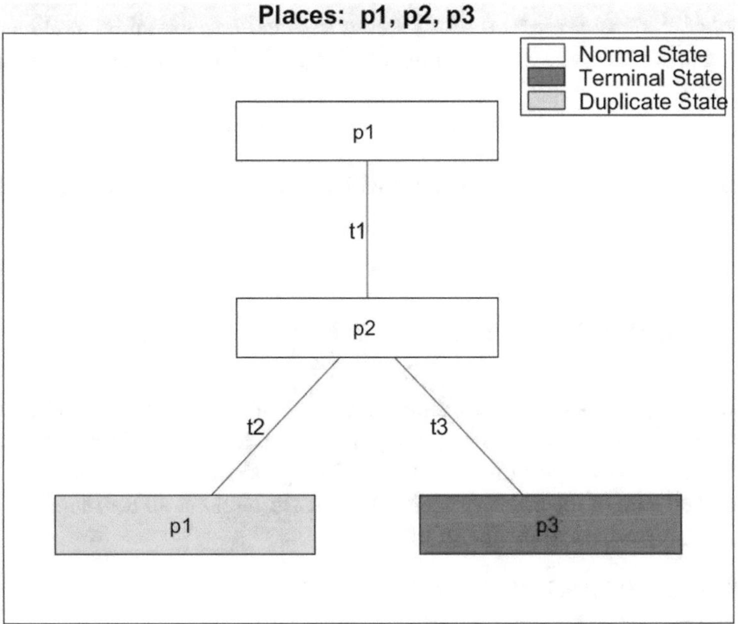

Fig. 1.2 State space of the marked Petri net shown in Fig. 1.1

Example 1.4 (Incidence Matrix) Following the definition given above, the incidence matrix A of the P/T Petri net that is shown in Fig. 1.1 becomes

$$A = \begin{bmatrix} -1 & 1 & 0 \\ 1 & -1 & -1 \\ 0 & 0 & 1 \end{bmatrix}.$$

Definition 1.4 on New Markings presents an equation for the change in the markings when a transition fires. When a series of transitions fires, $f(t) = (t_j, t_k, t_l, \ldots)$, the new markings can be obtained from the state equation. $f(t)$ is known as the Parikh vector.

Definition 1.7 The State Equation of a marked P/T Petri net $PTN = (P, T, A, M_0)$ presents the new markings M' due to the firing of a Parikh vector $f(t)$:

$$M' = M_0 + A \times f(t),$$

where A is the incidence matrix. □

State M' generated by the state equation due to the series of firing $f(t)$ from the initial state M_0 is denoted by the following operator: $M_0[f(t) \gg M'$.

Example 1.5 **(The State Equation)** Let us say that from the initial marking $M_0 = [1\ 0\ 0]$, transition t1 fires. Representing the firing of t1 by the vector [1 0 0], the new marking M' is

$$M' = M_0 + A \times [1\ 0\ 0] = [0\ 1\ 0],$$

meaning in the the new marking, there will be token only in p2, and that will be a single token.

1.2.4 Structural Property: P-Invariant

P-invariants (Place-invariants) represents the structural (invariant) relationships that exist for the token distribution among the places, regardless of the initial tokens.

A p-invariant is a vector of weights (set of integers) attached to each place so that the weighted sum of the tokens remains constant throughout all the markings of the state space, regardless of the initial marking.

Definition 1.8 **P-invariant** of a marked P/T Petri net $PTN = (P, T, A, M_0)$ is defined as

$$\forall p_i \in P,\ \ \exists w_i \in \mathbb{Z}, k \in \mathbb{Z},\ \ |\ \sum (w_i \times M(p_i)) = k.$$

□

From the state equation, if the weighted markings remain constant for the p-invariant:

$$X^T M' = X^T M_0 \quad \Longrightarrow X^T A = 0,$$

where A is the incidence matrix. The non-trivial solutions of $X^T A = 0$ is the p-invariant. As p-invariant represents the the linearly dependent places, there will be $(n_p - r)$ number of basic p-invariant, where r is the rank of the incidence matrix A [10].

Example 1.6 **(P-Invariant)** In the P/T Petri net shown in Fig. 1.1, the initial token in p1 only vanishes when t1 fires, and the firing deposits a new token into p2. Thereafter, either t2 or t3 can fire, consuming the token in p2 and depositing a new token either into p1 or p3, respectively. Thus, in any marking, the summation of tokens in p1, p2, and p3 will be equal to one. In other words, the places p1, p2, and p3 are a p-invariant.

1.2.5 Structural Property: T-Invariant

Definition 1.9 T-invariant of a marked P/T Petri net $PTN = (P, T, A, M_0)$ is defined as

$$\forall t_i \in T, \ \exists x_i \in \mathbb{N} \mid M_0 = M_0 + A \times X$$
$$\text{if such as } X \text{ exists, then } f(t) = X \text{ is the T-invariant,}$$
$$\text{where } x_i \text{ is the number of times } t_i \text{ fired to make } M_0[f(t) \gg M_0.$$

□

To make the transformation $M_0[X \gg M_0$ happen,

$$M_0 = M_0 + A \times X \quad \Longrightarrow \quad A \times X = 0$$

Hence, T-invariants are the linearly dependent columns of A, and thus, there will be $(n_t - r)$ number of T-invariants, where r is the rank of A [10].

Example 1.7 **(T-Invariant)** As the example on p-invariant depicts, firing of t1 and t2 consecutively will bring the system back to the initial state. Hence, the transitions t1 and t2 are a t-invariant.

1.2.6 Timed Petri Nets

P/T Petri nets do not involve time. Hence, P/T Petri nets are insufficient to model engineering systems as these systems usually involve time. **Timed Petri net** (TPN) is an extension to P/T Petri net to incorporate time. There are three different ways to include time into Petri nets:

1. Add time to transitions [15].
2. Add time to places [8].
3. Add time to places and transitions [13].

In this book, time is only attached to transitions, as the way it is done in the software GPenSIM too [6]. Adding time to transitions is also more logical as transitions represent activities (such as technological, transport, and auxiliary operations), which do take time (whereas places represent passive elements like buffers).

Definition 1.10 Timed Petri net (TPN, for short) is defined as a five-tuple:

$$TPN = (P, T, A, M_0, FT),$$

where

- (P, T, A, M_0) is a marked Petri net,
- FT is a mapping of T into $\mathbb{R}^+$:
  $\forall t \in T, \;\; FT(t) \in \mathbb{R}^+, \;\; FT(t) > 0.$ □

Note that $FT(t)$ that is known as the **firing time** of the transitions is defined to be greater than zero. As activities, doesn't matter how fast they are (inclusive so-called "immediately firing" ones), do take time, perhaps close to zero, but not zero. Though literature allows zero-timed transitions, GPenSIM strictly enforces firing times with non-zero values ("*strictly* positive values"). This enforcement is for the numerical algorithm that runs the simulation iterations to converge.

1.2.7 Strongly Connected Event Graphs (SCEGs)

Many of the real-world discrete event systems are Strongly Connected Event Graphs (SCEGs). Thus, the following definitions are given to introduce SCEG, and the properties of SCEG are also given.

Definition 1.11 Event Graph (EG) is a P/T Petri net

$$EG = (P, T, A)$$

in which each place has exactly one input and one output transition; that is, the sets of input and output transitions of each place have only one member: $| \bullet p_j| = |p_j \bullet| = 1$. □

Definition 1.12 Strongly Connected Graph is a graph G,

$$G = (V, E),$$

where V is the set of vertices (*aka* nodes) and E is the set of edges (*aka* arcs or connections), and for any two vertices $v_i, v_j \in V$, there is a path from v_i to v_j and from v_j to v_i. □

Example 1.8 (Event Graph and Strongly Connected Graph) The graph shown in Fig. 1.3 is strongly connected as if any two nodes that are taken are connected in both directions. For example, considering the nodes t1 and t3, t1 has at least one outward connection to t3, such as t1-p1-t2-p3-t3, and t3 has an outward connection to p1 such as t3-p4-t1. Also, every place (p1 to p4) in the graph has exactly one input transition and one output transition. Hence, the graph shown in Fig. 1.3 is a strongly connected event graph.

The graph shown in Fig. 1.4 is not an event graph. Though the places p1 and p4 satisfy the event graph property ($| \bullet p_j| = |p_j \bullet| = 1$), p2 has two input transitions,

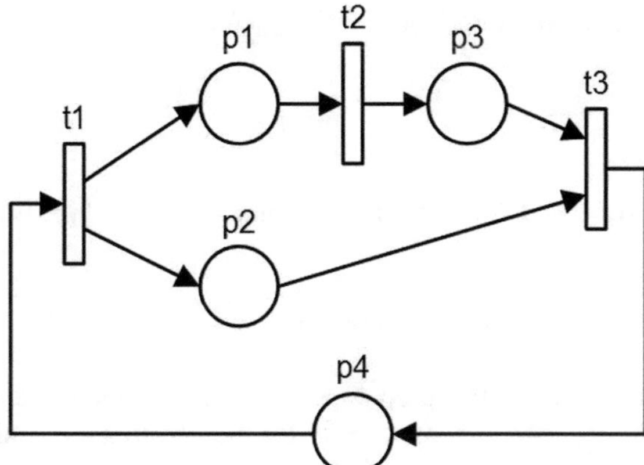

Fig. 1.3 A Strongly Connected Event Graph (SCEG)

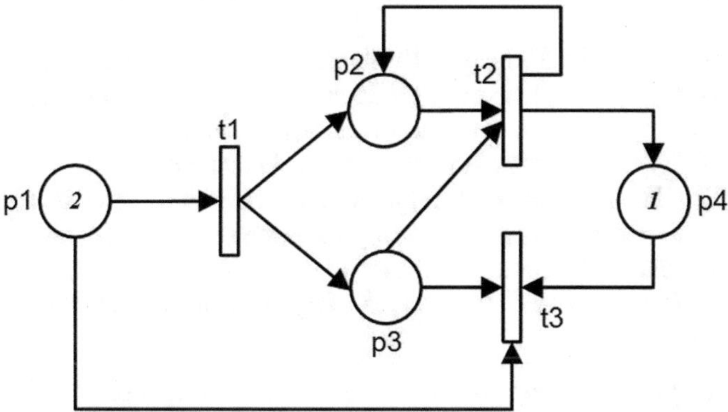

Fig. 1.4 A graph that is neither strongly connected not an event graph

whereas p3 has two output transition. Also, this graph is not strongly connected as p4 is not outwardly connected to p1 (however, p1 has an outward connection to p4).

Though a graph is not strongly connected, there could be components (sub-graphs) that are strongly connected. In the graph shown in Fig. 1.4, the only strongly connected component that has more than one node is {p2, t2}.

Chapter 12 "Network Algorithms for Modular Connectivity" discusses how strongly connected components of a graph can be found, with the aim of connecting and synchronizing the modules.

Definition 1.13 (*Elementary Circuit*) In a strongly connected graph, there will be cycles (circuits). An elementary circuit in a strongly connected graph is a directed path that starts at one node and comes back to the same node, while no other node is repeatedly visited in the path. □

Example 1.9 (Elementary Circuit) The graph shown in Fig. 1.3 possesses two elementary circuits:

1. t1-p1-t2-p3-t3-p4-t1.
2. t1-p2-t3-p4-t1.

The graph shown in Fig. 1.4 also has an elementary circuit, which is p2-t2-p2.

1.2.7.1 Properties of Strongly Connected Event Graphs

Given below are some of the properties of Strongly Connected Event Graphs (SCEGs). These properties are very useful for the performance evaluation of discrete event systems. In an SCEG,

- Property 1: The number of tokens in an elementary circuit is invariant, meaning that the number of tokens does not change with the firings of the transitions [4, 11].
- Property 2: Performance is bounded by its critical circuit [3, 11]. The critical circuit is the elementary circuit that has the lowest flowrate r, $r^* = min[\sum(M(p_n))/\sum(dt_i)]$, where $\sum(dt_i)$ is the sum of the firing times of the transitions in the circuit and $\sum(M(p_n))$ is the sum of all tokens in that circuit.
- Property 3: Under the assumption that a transition fires as soon as it is enabled, the firing rate of each transition in steady state (the same as the current token flow rate at any point in the circuit) is given by $r = r^*$ [3].
- Property 4: Deadlock-free if, and only if, every elementary circuit contains at least one token [11].

Based on the properties mentioned above, there are many tools available for the performance evaluation of SCEG. However, the General-purpose Petri net Simulator (GPenSIM) is considered as the ideal tool for working with event graphs [2]. GPenSIM is presented in the next chapter (Chap. 2).

References

1. Bause F, Kritzinger PS (1998) Stochastic Petri nets: an introduction to the theory. ACM SIGMETRICS Perform Eval Rev 26(2):2–3
2. Cameron A, Stumptner M, Nandagopal N, Mayer W, Mansell T (2015) Rule-based peer-to-peer framework for decentralised real-time service oriented architectures. Sci Comput Program 97:202–234
3. Chretienne P (1984) Controlled execution of timed Petri nets. Technol Sci Inform 3(1):19–26
4. Commoner F, Holt AW, Even S, Pnueli A (1971) Marked directed graphs. J Comput Syst Sci 5(5):511–523
5. David R, Alla H (2005) Discrete, continuous, and hybrid Petri nets, vol 1. Springer
6. Davidrajuh R (2018) Modeling discrete-event systems with GPenSIM. Springer International Publishing, Cham

7. Haas PJ (2006) Stochastic Petri nets: modelling, stability, simulation. Springer Science & Business Media
8. Lee DY, DiCesare F (1994) Scheduling flexible manufacturing systems using Petri nets and heuristic search. IEEE Trans Robot Autom 10(2):123–132
9. Marsan MA, Balbo G, Conte G, Donatelli S, Franceschinis G (1994) Modelling with generalized stochastic Petri nets. Wiley
10. Murata T (1989) Petri nets: properties, analysis and applications. Proc IEEE 77(4):541–580
11. Peterson JL (1981) Petri net theory and the modeling of systems. Prentice Hall PTR
12. Reisig W (2012) Petri nets: an introduction, vol 4. Springer Science & Business Media
13. Sifakis J, Yovine S (1996) Compositional specification of timed systems. In: Annual symposium on theoretical aspects of computer science. Springer, pp 345–359
14. Wang J (2012) Timed Petri nets: theory and application, vol 9. Springer Science & Business Media
15. Zuberek WM (1991) Timed Petri nets definitions, properties, and applications. Microelectron Reliab 31(4):627–644

Chapter 2
Introduction to GPenSIM

This chapter introduces the General-purpose Petri net Simulator (GPenSIM). Only the basics of GPenSIM are given in this chapter; for a detailed study of GPenSIM, [9] is recommended. The development of GPenSIM is influenced by [27]. GPenSIM defines a Petri net language for modeling and simulation of discrete event systems on the MATLAB platform. GPenSIM is also a simulator with which Petri net models can be developed, simulated, and analyzed. Also, GPenSIM can be used as a real-time controller.

In this chapter, Sect. 2.1 discusses the aspect of time in GPenSIM. Section 2.2 discusses the issue of atomicity and how it is handled with virtual tokens. Section 2.3 presents the layered architecture of GPenSIM. The basics of modeling with GPenSIM is presented in Sect. 2.4. And Sect. 2.5 presents a simple example of using GPenSIM for creating a Petri net model.

GPenSIM is being used by many researchers around the world for its "flexibility" [4] and extensibility [23]. GPenSIM is freely available [16]. GPenSIM supports many Petri nets extensions, such as inhibitor arcs, transition priorities, enabling functions, and color extension. Also, it provides a collection of functions for performance analysis. Because of its flexibility, it is also easy to implement many other Petri net extensions with GPenSIM, e.g., Attributed Hybrid Dynamical net [19] and Cohesive Place-Transition Nets with inhibitor arcs [14].

2.1 Time in GPenSIM

With GPenSIM, a discrete system can be modeled and implemented either as

- An untimed Petri net: firing times are not assigned to any of the transitions, meaning all the transitions are *primitive* [29]; or
- A Timed Petri net: firing times are assigned to all the transitions, meaning all the transitions are *non-primitive* [28].

R. Davidrajuh, *Petri Nets for Modeling of Large Discrete Systems*, Asset Analytics,
https://doi.org/10.1007/978-981-16-5203-5_2

In GPenSIM, it is not acceptable to assign firing times to some of the transitions and let the other transitions take zero value; very small values close to zero can be assigned, but not zero [9]. GPenSIM interprets a Timed Petri net in the following manner [7, 9]:

- No variable firing time: the transitions representing events are assigned a firing time beforehand. The pre-assigned firing time can be deterministic (e.g., firing time $dt_i = 5$ TU) or stochastic (e.g., firing time dt_i is normally distributed with mean value 10 TU and standard deviation 2 TU). However, variable firing times are not possible.
- Maximal-step firing policy: The Timed Petri net operates with the maximal-step firing policy. This means if more than one transition is collectively enabled and they are not in conflict with each other at a point of time, then all of these transitions fire at the same time.
- Enabled transition starts firing immediately: enabled transition can start firing immediately as long as there is no (forcibly) induced delay between the time a transition became enabled and the time it is allowed to fire.

Being a MATLAB toolbox, GPenSIM supports all the probability distributions (e.g., Gaussian, Uniform, Poisson, etc.) that are supported by MATLAB. For example, the firing time of a transition can be taken as Normal distribution, "(e.g., firing time dt_i is normally distributed with mean value 10 TU and standard deviation 2 TU)".

The P/T Petri net is untimed, and all the transitions take zero time for firing. Hence, the transitions cannot represent any real-world activities, as activities in the real world do take time. The Timed Petri net was extended from the untimed Petri net based on the assumptions (interpretations) stated above. Timed Petri nets are needed to model real-world discrete event systems as the firing time of a transition represents the time taken by the activity, and the (virtual) tokens inside a transition represent the work-in-progress; virtual tokens are described in the following subsection.

2.2 Automicity and Virtual Tokens

Figure 2.1 explains how non-primitive transition t_i of a Timed Petri net (firing time of the transition is not zero) can be understood in terms of primitive (firing time is zero) transitions of P/T Petri nets. As Fig. 2.1 shows, each non-primitive transition in the Timed Petri net can be considered as an assembly of four elements. It has two primitive transitions *starter* and *stopper* and a *virtual place* between them. In addition, there is a place *pme* with an initial token (pme: the place to impose mutual exclusion) in order to make sure that once the starter has fired, it will not fire again until the stopper is fired.

Figure 2.2 explains the firing of t_i. Whenever t_i is ready to fire, *starter* fires immediately and passes the input tokens into the virtual place; the input tokens will stay in the virtual place for an amount of time (delay) equal to the firing time of t_i. At the completion of the delay, the stopper fires immediately, consuming all the virtual

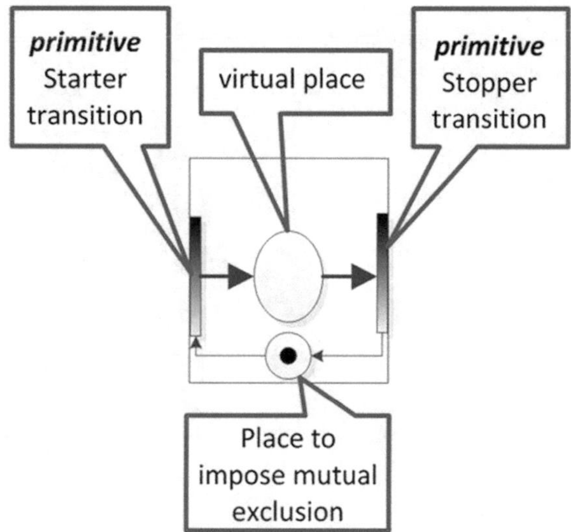

Fig. 2.1 Composition of a non-primitive transition

tokens and depositing newer output tokens into the output places. The firing mechanism described above makes sure that the tokens are accountable (do not disappear) anytime during the firing of the non-primitive transition t_i. Thus, the ***atomicity*** property is upheld.

2.3 Layered Architecture

GPenSIM is designed using the well-proven paradigms in software engineering such as layered architecture, modular components, and natural language interface.

GPenSIM is built following three-layer architecture, as shown in Fig. 2.3. The bottom layer deals with the token game; this layer computes newer states with the help of linear algebraic equations and matrix manipulations. The middle layer adds more high-level functionality such as stochastic timing, coloring of tokens, and user-defined conditions ("guard-conditions" in some literature). The top layer offers applications such as building a Petri net-based model, running simulations, determining reachability graph, and printing the simulation results.

The layered architecture allows the application of GPenSIM to solve diverse problems. Figure 2.4 shows how a modeler can develop a specific layer for solving his problem. For example, the layer FishSIM [22] was developed for modeling the fish supply chain and ScheduleSIM [15] for scheduling of jobs in grid computing. Also, ElevatorSIM [10] for modeling of elevator operations.

Fig. 2.2 Maintaining the "atomicity" property during the firing of a non-primitive transition

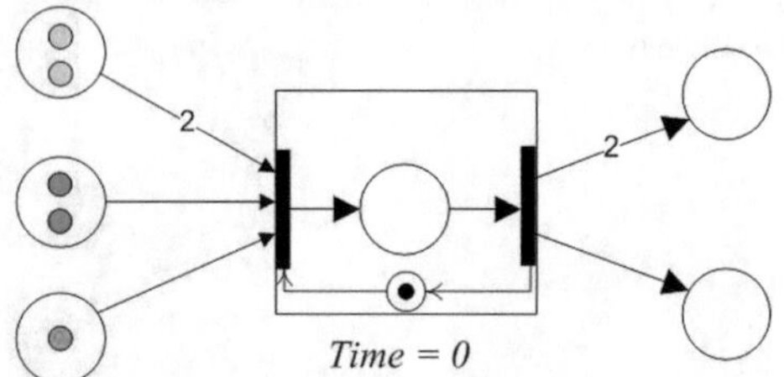

(a) Non-primitive transition is enabled and about to fire

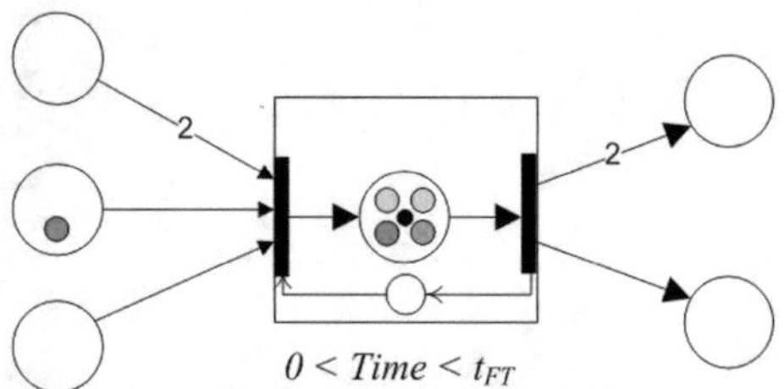

(b) Non-primitive transition starts firing: primitive starter fires instantly, removing the tokens from the input place and placing them as virtual tokens inside the virtual place

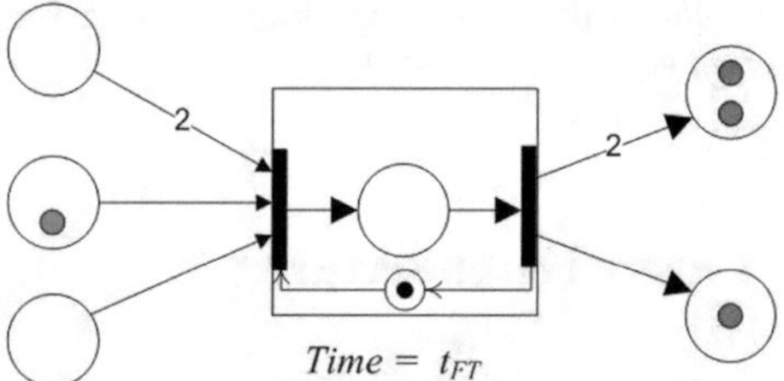

(c) Non-primitive transition completes firing: primitive stopper transition fires instantly, removing the virtual tokens from the virtual place and depositing output tokens into the output place

2.4 Modeling with GPenSIM: The Basics

This section introduces the basic aspects of modeling discrete event systems with GPenSIM.

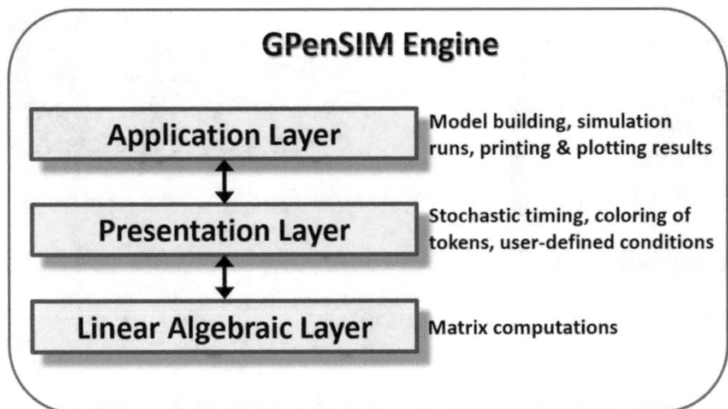

Fig. 2.3 Layered architecture of GPenSIM

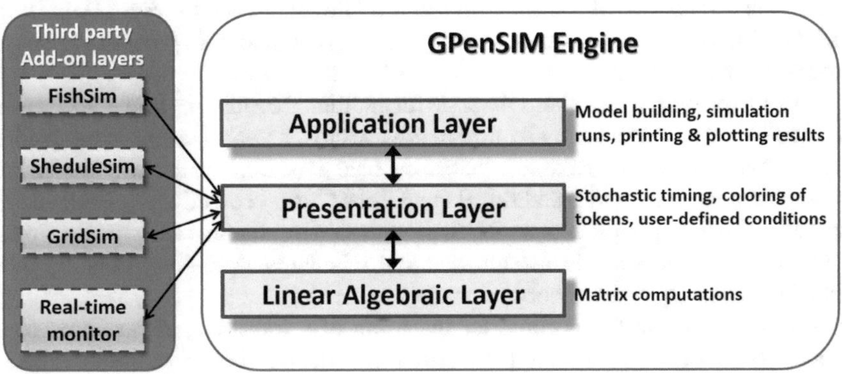

Fig. 2.4 Third-party toolboxes built on top of GPenSIM

2.4.1 Separating the Static and Dynamic Details

GPenSIM advocates a clear separation of the static and the dynamic details. The definition of a Petri net graph (static details) is given in the **Petri net Definition File** (**PDF**). There may be a number of PDFs if the Petri net model is divided into many modules, and each module is defined in a separate PDF. While the PDF has the static details, the **Main Simulation File** (**MSF**) contains the dynamic information (such as initial tokens in places and firing times of transitions) of the Petri net (Fig. 2.5).

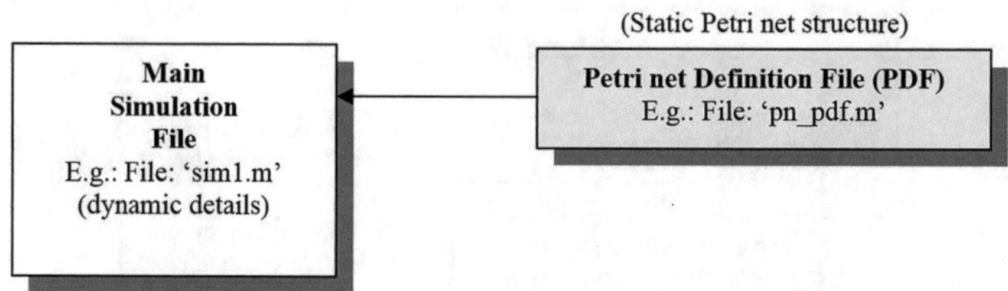

Fig. 2.5 Separating the static and the dynamic details

2.4.2 Processor Files

In addition to these two files (**Main Simulation File** (**MSF**) and **Petri net Definition File** (**PDF**)), there can be a number of pre-processors and post-processors. These processors define the run-time dynamic details of the model.

A **pre-processor** file contains the code for additional conditions to check whether an enabled transition can actually fire; in other words, a pre-processor is run before firing a transition, just to make sure that an enabled transition can actually start firing depending upon some other additional conditions ("firing conditions"). Further, we can write separate pre-processors for each transition or combine them into a single common pre-processor. It is also allowed to use individual pre-processors together with the common pre-processor.

A **post-processor** file is run after the firing of a transition. A post-processor contains code for actions that has to be carried out after a certain transition completes firing. Just like pre-processors, post-processors can be specifically for individual transitions or combined into one common post-processor.

2.4.2.1 Using Pre-processor and Post-processor

According to the Petri net theory, a transition can fire ("enabled transition") when there are enough tokens in the input places. However, an event representing a transition can have additional restrictions for firing; for example, if two events (event-1 and event-2) are competing for a common resource and if they both are enabled, then event-2 is *allowed to fire* if event-2 possesses higher priority than event-1. In the GPenSIM literature, these additional conditions are called "firing conditions".

The firing conditions for firing a transition are coded in a pre-processor file. *After a transition completes firing*, there may be some book-keeping that need to be done or some other activities that need to be performed; these can be coded into a post-processor file.

Note that the names of the processor files must follow a strict naming policy, as they will be chosen and run automatically. For example, the specific pre-processor

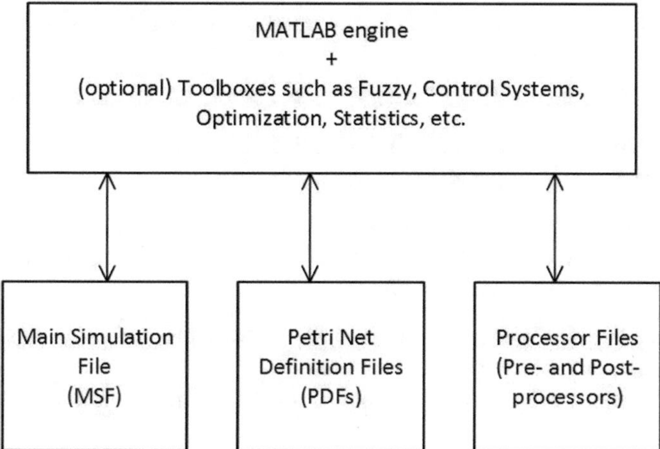

Fig. 2.6 Integrating with MATLAB environment

for the transition "trans1" must be named "trans1_ pre.m"; similarly, the specific post-processor for the transition "trans1" must be named "trans1_post.m".

2.4.3 *Global Info*

The different files (Main Simulation File MSF, Petri net Definition Files PDFs, and pre-processor and post-processor files) can access and exchange global parameter values through a packet called "**global**_info". If a set of parameters is needed to be passed between different files, then these parameters are added to the global_info packet. Since global_info packet is visible in all the files, the values of the parameters in the packet can be read and even changed in different files.

2.4.4 *Integrating with MATLAB Environment*

One of the most important reasons for developing GPenSIM and the most advantage of it is its integration with the MATLAB environment so that we can harness diverse toolboxes available in the MATLAB environment; see Fig. 2.6. For example, by combining GPenSIM with the Control System Toolbox, we can experiment hybrid discrete–continuous control applications.

2.5 Creating a Simple Petri Net Model with GPenSIM

The methodology for creating a Petri net model consists of the following three steps:

- Step-1. Defining the Petri net graph in a Petri net Definition File (PDF): This is the static part. This step consists of three substeps:

  1. Identifying the passive elements of a Petri net graph: the places,
  2. Identifying the active elements of a Petri net graph: the transitions, and
  3. Connecting these elements with arcs.

- Step-2. Coding the firing conditions in the relevant pre-processor files and post-firing activities in the post-processor files.
- Step-3. Assigning the initial dynamics of a Petri net in the Main Simulation File (MSF):

  – The initial markings on the places, and The firing times of the transitions.

After creating a Petri net model, simulations can be done.

2.5.1 Creating a Simple Petri Net Model: An Example

Example 2.1 (Creating a simple Petri net Model):

As the first example of creating a simple Petri net model with GPenSIM, we will create a P/T Petri net. The three steps are explained below, using the sample Petri net shown in Fig. 2.7.

Figure 2.7 shows a Petri net model of a production facility where three robots are involved in sorting products from an input buffer to output buffers. The three robots are represented by the transitions Robot-1 to Robot-3 and the buffers by the places

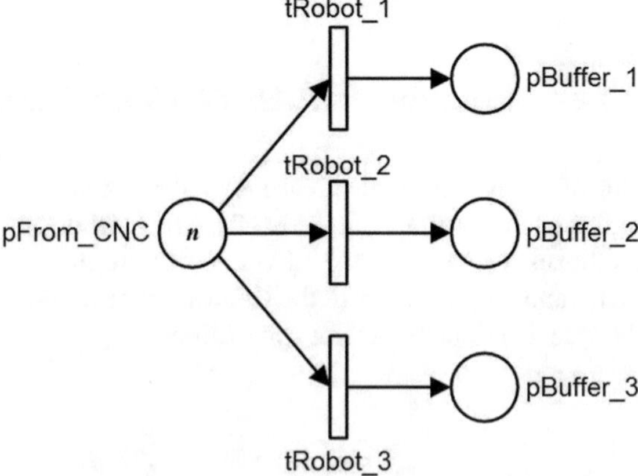

Fig. 2.7 Petri net model of a production facility

```
% file: PDF: production_pdf.m
function [pns] = production_pdf()

pns.PN_name = 'A PN model of a production facility';
pns.set_of_Ps = {'pFrom_CNC','pBuffer_1','pBuffer_2',...
                  'pBuffer_3'};
pns.set_of_Ts = {'tRobot_1','tRobot_2','tRobot_3'};
pns.set_of_As = {'pFrom_CNC','tRobot_1',1, ...
    'pFrom_CNC','tRobot_2',1, 'pFrom_CNC','tRobot_3',1,...
    'tRobot_1','pBuffer_1',1, 'tRobot_2','pBuffer_2',1,...
    'tRobot_3','pBuffer_3',1};
```

Fig. 2.8 The Petri net Definition File (PDF)

Buffer-1 to Buffer-3. Let us assume that the three robots take 10, 5, and 15 time units per operation.

Let us add some conditions for firing:

1. The output buffers have limited capacity: Buffer-1, Buffer-2, and Buffer-3 can accommodate a maximum of 2, 3, and 1 machined parts (tokens), respectively.
2. The robots should be operated in a manner that, at any time, Buffer-2 should have more parts than Buffer-1 and Buffer-1 should have more parts than Buffer-3.

The firing conditions stated above shall be coded in the pre-processor files.

Creating M-Files :
In this example, the following M-files are created in the three steps:

- Step-1: Creating the PDF file.
- Step-2: Creating the pre-processors for the three transitions. This is because there are firing conditions attached to the transitions. Since there are no post-firing actions defined, there is no need for any post-processor files.
- Step-3: Creating the MSF: Assigning the initial dynamics (initial markings and firing times) and running the simulations.

Step-1: PDF: Defining the static Petri net graph
Let us call the PDF for the Petri net in Fig. 2.7 as "production_pdf.m". The PDF is shown in Fig. 2.8.

The first line assigns a name (or label) to the model ("A PN model of a production facility"). The second line declares the set of places, and the third line the set of transitions. Finally, the arcs are also declared.

Step-2: Pre-processor files
We will need three pre-processor files, one for each transition: Pre-processor "tRobot_1_pre": tRobot_1 will fire only if the number of tokens (machined parts) already put in output pBuffer_1 is less than 2. Also, number of tokens in pBuffer_1 should be less than that of pBuffer_2; coding these two firing conditions into the pre-processor for tRobot-1 is shown in Fig. 2.9. As the name of the transition is"tRobot_1", this pre-processor must be named "tRobot_1_pre.m".

```
function [fire, transition] = tRobot_1_pre(transition)

n1 = ntokens('pBuffer_1'); % number of tokens in pBuffer-1
n2 = ntokens('pBuffer_2'); % number of tokens in pBuffer-2
fire = and(lt(n1, n2), lt(n1, 2));
```

Fig. 2.9 The pre-processor of tRobot_1 ("tRobot_1_pre.m")

```
function [fire, transition] = tRobot_2_pre(transition)

n2 = ntokens('pBuffer_2');  % number of tokens in pBuffer-2
fire = lt(n2, 3);
```

```
function [fire, transition] = tRobot_3_pre(transition)

n1 = ntokens('pBuffer_1');   % number of tokens in pBuffer-1
n3 = ntokens('pBuffer_3');   % number of tokens in pBuffer-3
fire = and(gt(n1, n3), lt(n3, 1));
```

Fig. 2.10 The pre-processors of tRobot_2 and tRobot_3 ("tRobot_2_pre.m" and "tRobot_3_pre.m")

Similarly, the pre-processor files for tRobot_2 and tRobot_3 are created, satisfying the given firing conditions. Figure 2.10 shows the pre-processor files for tRobot_2 and tRobot_3:

Again, post-processor files are not needed as there are no post-firing actions.

Step-3: MSF: Assigning the initial dynamics and running simulations

Figure 2.11 shows the Main Simulation File ("production.m"). In the MSF, first we indicate the static Petri net graph, by passing the name of the PDF ("production_pdf") to the function "**pnstruct**". Then, the initial dynamics (such as the initial markings of the places and the firing times of the transitions) are assigned. (Note that for untimed Petri net, there will not be any firing times added to the transitions). After stuffing the initial dynamic details into a packet (e.g., "dyn" in this example), this packet is passed to the function "initialdynamics", which combines the static Petri net structure with the initial dynamics, creating the initial Petri net dynamic structure.

Function "gpensim" takes the initial Petri net dynamic structure and starts the simulations. Once the simulations are complete, the output (results) of the function gpensim can be used to print and plot the results.

Function "prnss" (stands for "print state space") will print the state space changes as a text output. Whereas, function "plotp" (stands for "plot places") gives a graphical output, showing how the tokens changed in the given places (Fig. 2.12).

```
% MSF: 'production.m'
global global_info
global_info.STOP_AT = 60; % stop after 60 time units

pns = pnstruct('production_pdf');

dyn.m0 = {'pFrom_CNC',8}; % initial tokens
dyn.ft = {'tRobot_1',10, 'tRobot_2',5,...  % firing times
          'tRobot_3',15};
pni = initialdynamics(pns, dyn); % combine stats & dynamics

sim = gpensim(pni);  % start and run simulations

prnss(sim);  % print results
plotp(sim,{'pBuffer_1','pBuffer_2','pBuffer_3'}); % plot res.
```

Fig. 2.11 The main simulation file (MSF, "production.m")

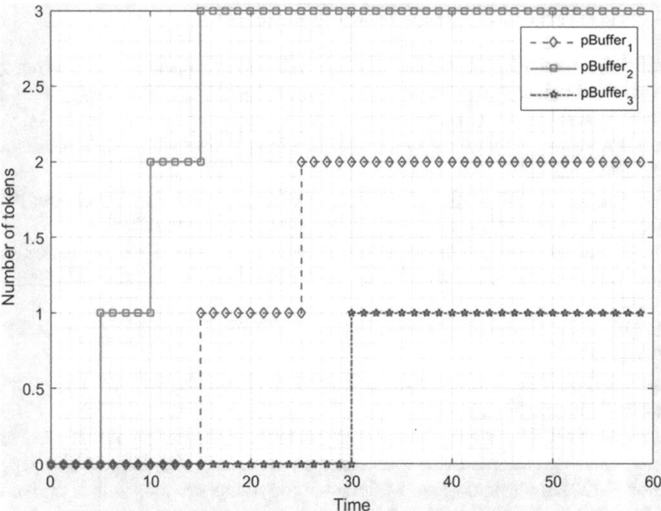

Fig. 2.12 Simulation results, showing how the tokens in places changed during the simulation

2.6 GPenSIM and Its Applications

Though GPenSIM is relatively new, it is being used by some universities around the world, for modeling and simulating large discrete event systems (e.g., [1, 2, 4, 5, 17, 18, 20, 23, 26]). The reasons for the acceptance of GPenSIM are the simplicity of learning and using, its flexibility to incorporate newer functionality, and its ability to control (model-based control) of external hardware and software [4, 23].

Since GPenSIM is realized as a toolbox on the MATLAB platform, diverse toolboxes that available in the MATLAB environment (such as Fuzzy Logic Toolbox,

Control Systems Toolbox, and Advanced Statistics) can be used in the Petri net models that are developed with GPenSIM. The ability to call different functionalities provided by the other toolboxes enables the creation of hybrid models, e.g., Fuzzy Petri net models. With GPenSIM, many industrial large-scale discrete problems were modeled and solved. For example, repetitive production processes [31], airport capacity expansion [12], Atlantic fish supply chain in Norway [22], process mining [30], flexible manufacturing system [18], Game play analysis [5], modeling service-oriented architecture [4], Power systems modeling [1, 25], Marine-Motor control [26], Restaurant Management [17], Business Process Modeling [24], Warehouse processes [3, 21], Bluetooth communication [6], Slicing algorithms [11, 13], modeling of elevators [10], Automated Manufacturing Systems With Unreliable Resources [2, 20], and supervisory control [2, 8, 19, 20].

References

1. Abbaszadeh A, Abedi M, Doustmohammadi A (2018) General stochastic Petri net approach for the estimation of power system restoration duration. Int Trans Electr Energy Syst 28(6):e2550
2. Al-Ahmari A, Kaid H, Li Z, Davidrajuh R (2020) Strict minimal siphon-based colored Petri net supervisor synthesis for automated manufacturing systems with unreliable resources. IEEE Access 8:22411–22424
3. Behzad B, Farzad M, Davidrajuh R (2020) Understanding the ikea warehouse processes and modeling using modular Petri nets. Int J Simul–Syst, Sci Technol 21(2)
4. Cameron A, Stumptner M, Nandagopal N, Mayer W, Mansell T (2015) Rule-based peer-to-peer framework for decentralised real-time service oriented architectures. Sci Comput Program 97:202–234
5. Chang H (2015) A method of gameplay analysis by Petri net model simulation. J Korea Game Soc 15(5):49–56
6. Davidrajuh R (2007) Exploring the use of bluetooth in building wireless information systems. Int J Mobile Commun 5(1):1–10
7. Davidrajuh R (2008) Developing a new Petri net tool for simulation of discrete event systems. In: 2008 second Asia international conference on modelling simulation (AMS), pp 861–866
8. Davidrajuh R (2012) Designing fault-tolerant autonomous systems with adaptive supervisory control. In: 2012 Sixth UKSim/AMSS European symposium on computer modeling and simulation. IEEE, pp 185–190
9. Davidrajuh R (2018) Modeling discrete-event systems with GPenSIM. Springer International Publishing, Cham
10. Davidrajuh R (2019) Developing a toolbox for modeling and simulation of elevators. Int J Simul–Syst, Sci Technol 20(S1):1.1–1.6
11. Davidrajuh R, Krenczyk D (2019) Extending gpensim for model checking on Petri nets. Int J Simul–Syst, Sci Technol 20(1)
12. Davidrajuh R, Lin B (2011) Exploring airport traffic capability using Petri net based model. Expert Syst Appl 38(9):10923–10931
13. Davidrajuh R, Roci A (2018) Performance of static slicing algorithms for Petri nets. Int J Simul Syst Sci Technol 20:15
14. Davidrajuh R, Saadallah N (2017) Implementing a cohesive pt nets with inhibitor arcs in gpensim. Int J Simul: Syst, Sci Technol 18(2)
15. Davidrajuh R, Velauthapillai D (2010) Schedsim: a test-bed for solving simple assembly line balancing problems

16. GPenSIM (2019) General-purpose Petri net simulator. Technical report. http://www.davidrajuh.net/gpensim. Accessed 20 July 2020
17. Hussein ZS (2014) Simulation of food restaurant using colored Petri nets. J Eng Sustain Dev 18(4):77–88
18. Jyothi SD (2012) Scheduling flexible manufacturing system using Petri-nets and genetic algorithm. Thiruvananthapuram, India, Department of Aerospace Engineering, Indian Institute of Space Science and Technology
19. Kaid H, Al-Ahmari A, Li Z, Davidrajuh R (2020) Intelligent colored token Petri nets for modeling, control, and validation of dynamic changes in reconfigurable manufacturing systems. Processes 8(3):358
20. Kaid H, Al-Ahmari A, Li Z, Davidrajuh R (2020) Single controller-based colored Petri nets for deadlock control in automated manufacturing systems. Processes 8(1):21
21. Krenczyk D, Davidrajuh R, kolud B (2019) Comparing two methodologies for modeling and simulation of discrete-event based automated warehouses systems. In: Advances in Manufacturing II. Springer, pp 161–175
22. Melberg R, Davidrajuh R (2009) Modeling atlantic salmon fish farming industry. In: 2009 IEEE international conference on industrial technology, pp 1–6
23. Mutarraf U, Barkaoui K, Li Z, Wu N, Qu T (2018) Transformation of business process model and notation models onto Petri nets and their analysis. Adv Mech Eng 10(12):1–21
24. Mutarraf U, Barkaoui K, Li Z, Wu N, Qu T (2018) Transformation of business process model and notation models onto Petri nets and their analysis. Adv Mech Eng 10(12):1687814018808170
25. Ortiz L, Gutiérrez LB, González JW, Águila A (2020) A novel strategy for dynamic identification in ac/dc microgrids based on arx and Petri nets. Heliyon 6(3):e03559
26. Pan XL, He G, Zhang CJ, Ming TF, Wang XC (2012) Research on modeling and simulating of discrete event system based on Petri net. In: Advanced Engineering Forum, vol 4. Trans Tech Publications, pp 80–85
27. Peterson JL (1981) Petri net theory and the modeling of systems. Prentice Hall PTR
28. Popova-Zeugmann L (2013) Time Petri nets. Springer, Time and Petri Nets, pp 31–137
29. Proth J (1993) Performance evaluation of manufacturing systems. Practice of Petri Nets in manufacturing. Springer, pp 147–183
30. Roci A, Davidrajuh R (2018) A polynomial-time alpha-algorithm for process mining. Int J Simul–Syst, Sci Technol 19(5)
31. Skolud B, Krenczyk D, Davidrajuh R (2016) Solving repetitive production planning problems. an approach based on activity-oriented Petri nets. In: International Joint Conference SOCO'16-CISIS'16-ICEUTE'16. Springer, pp 397–407

Chapter 3
Models of Real-Life Systems

This chapter presents some Petri net models of typical manufacturing systems (such as flexible manufacturing system, circular AGVs, and cyclic processes). The reason behind this chapter is to clearly show the major difficulties in using Petri nets for modeling real-life discrete event systems generally and manufacturing systems specifically. All the models described in this section are taken from the author's recent publications: The FMS example and its Petri net model are taken from [1, 2], Circular AVGs from [3], and Cyclic Processes from [4, 5].

3.1 Model-1: Flexible Manufacturing System

Note: This problem on Flexible Manufacturing System is treated as a running example in this book. This problem will be visited often, referring to Fig. 3.1 ***for the physical system and Fig.*** 3.2. ***for the Petri net model***.

A simple Flexible Manufacturing System (FMS) shown in Fig. 3.1 is for making only one type of product. The operational specifications of the FMS are as follows:

- The input raw material of type-1 arrives on the conveyor belt C1. Robot R1 picks up the raw material of type-1 and places it into the machine M1. Similarly, robot R2 picks up the raw material of type-2 from conveyor belt C2 and places it into the machine M2.
- Machine M1 makes the part P1, and M2 makes the part P2. When the parts are made by the machines M1 and M2, they are placed on the Assembly Station (AS) by the robots R1 and R2, respectively.
- Assembly Station AS is used to join the two parts P1 and P2 together to form the semiproduct. Robot R2 does the part assembly at AS.

R. Davidrajuh, *Petri Nets for Modeling of Large Discrete Systems*, Asset Analytics,
https://doi.org/10.1007/978-981-16-5203-5_3

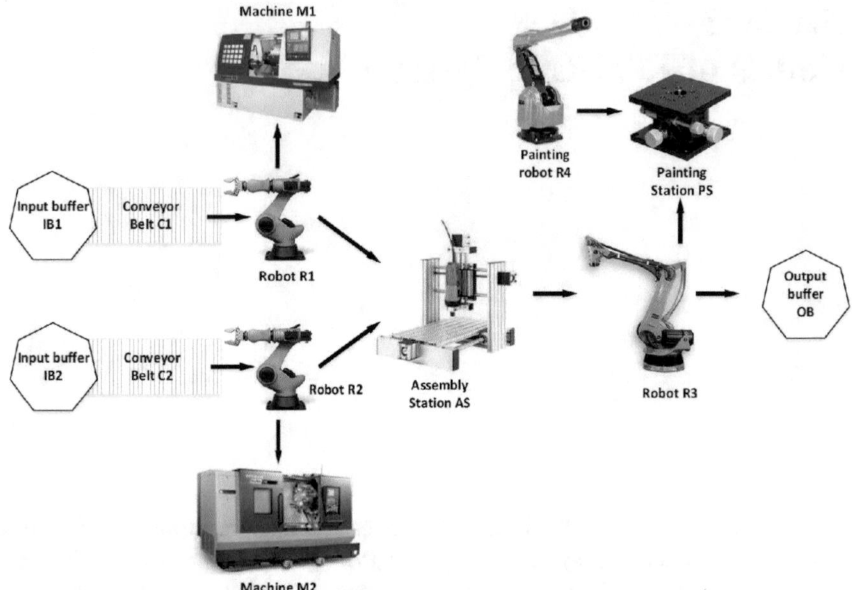

Fig. 3.1 A simple Flexible Manufacturing System (FMS)

- Robot R3 picks the product from the assembly station and places it on the Painting Station PS.
- Robot R4 performs the surface polishing and painting.
- Once the painting is completed, robot R3 picks up the completed product from the Painting Station PS and packs it into the cartridge OB.

3.1.1 The Petri Net Model

In the Petri net model shown in Fig. 3.2, the following activities represent the FMS operations ("t" stands for transition):

- tC1: conveyor belt C1 brings the input material of type-1 into the FMS.
- tC2: conveyor belt C2 brings the input material of type-2 into the FMS.
- tC1M1: robot R1 moves raw material from conveyor belt C1 and places it on M1.
- tC2M2: robot R2 moves raw material from conveyor belt C2 and places it on M2.
- tM1: machining of part P1 at machine M1.
- tM2: machining of part P2 at machine M2.
- tM1AS: robot R1 moves part P1 from M1 to the Assembly Station AS.
- tM2AS: robot R2 moves part P2 from M2 to the Assembly Station AS.
- tAS: robot R2 assembles parts P1 and P2 together at the Assembly Station AS.

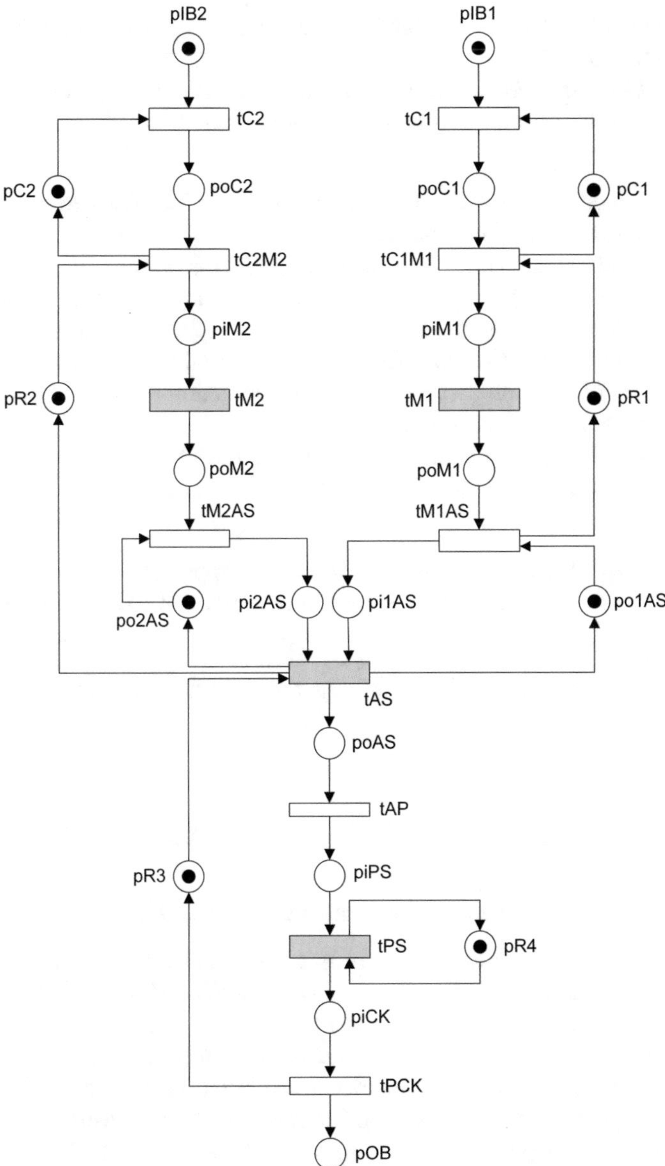

Fig. 3.2 The Petri net model of a Flexible Manufacturing System [2]

- tAP: robot R3 picks the product from the assembly station and places on the Painting Station PS.
- tPS: robot R4 performs surface polishing and painting on the product.
- tPCK: when the painting job is finished, R3 packs the product into the output cartridge.

The Petri net model of the FMS that is shown in Fig. 3.2 is obtained by connecting the activities listed above, one after the other.

The input buffers IB1 and IB2 are represented by the places pIB1 and pIB2, and the output buffer by the place pOB. These three places are for testing purposes only. These three places can be omitted in the final model, to make the Petri net a Strongly Connected Event Graph (SCEG). There exist well-established techniques for analyzing nets with SCEG property; see also the subsection on "Strongly Connected Event Graphs (SCEG)" Sect. 1.2.7.

To use the techniques for analysis of SCEG, the three buffers has to be neglected; the three buffers can be removed from the model, under the two following two assumptions:

Assumption 3.1 The raw materials are of infinite supply:
The supply of raw materials from the input buffers (IB1 and IB2) is never exhausted.

Assumption 3.2 The output buffers have infinite capacity:
The finished product will be placed into the output buffer OB that has no capacity restraints.

3.1.2 Analysis of the Petri Net Model: P-Invariants

The Petri net has a large number of p-invariants. For example:

1. Places pi1AS and po1AS are a p-invariant. If pi1AS loses its token due to the firing of tAS, tAS deposits a new token into po1AS. Similarly, pi2AS and po2AS are a p-invariant due to the firing of tAS.
2. Places pC1 and poC1 are p-invariant due to the firings of tC1 and tC1M1. Similarly, pC2 and poC2 are p-invariant due to the firings of tC2 and tC2M2.
3. Places pR1, piM1, and poM1 are a p-invariant. If tC1M1 consumes the token in pR1, then tC1M1 deposits a token into piM1. The token in piM1 will be transferred to poM1 by tM1, and finally, tM1AS puts the token back into pR1. Thus, pR1, piM1, and poM1 become a p-invariant due to the cyclic firing of tC1M1, tM1, and tM1AS.
4. pR4 is a p-invariant on its own. This is because when tPS fires, it consumes the token in pR4 and then puts it back on to it.

There are 19 p-invariants in this Petri net. All of these p-invariants are listed below.
{pR4}
{pi1AS,po1AS}

{pi2AS,po2AS}
{pC1,poC1}
{pC2,poC2}
{pR1,piM1,poM1}
{pi1AS,pi2AS,po1AS,po2AS}
{pR2,pi2AS,piM2,poM2}
{pR2,pi1AS,pi2AS,piM2,po1AS,poM2}
{pR3,piCK,piPS,poAS}
{pR3,pi1AS,piCK,piPS,po1AS,poAS}
{pR3,pi2AS,piCK,piPS,po2AS,poAS}
{pR2,pR3,pi2AS,piCK,piM2,piPS,poAS,poM2}
{pR3,pi1AS,pi2AS,piCK,piPS,po1AS,po2AS,poAS}
{pR2,pR3,pi1AS,pi2AS,piCK,piM2,piPS,po1AS,poAS,poM2}
{pIB1,pOB,pi1AS,piCK,piM1,piPS,poAS,poC1,poM1}
{pIB1,pOB,pi1AS,pi2AS,piCK,piM1,piPS,po2AS,poAS,poC1,poM1}
{pIB2,pOB,pi2AS,piCK,piM2,piPS,poAS,poC2,poM2}
{pIB1,pOB,pR2,pi1AS,pi2AS,piCK,piM1,piM2,piPS,poAS,poC1,poM1,poM2}

3.1.3 Analysis of the Petri Net Model: T-Invariants

There are no states from which a set of transition firings will bring back to the same state. Thus, there are no t-invariants.

3.1.4 Analysis of the Petri Net Model: State Space

As shown in Fig. 3.2, the initial state is assumed as one token each in the following places. Input places pIB1, pIB2, pR1 to pR4 (showing the availability of the robots R1 to R4), pC1, pC2 (showing the availability of the conveyor belts), and po1AS, po2AS. The resulting reachability graph (the state space) of the FMS is shown in Fig. 3.3.

It is important to note that there are 45 states in the reachability graph shown in Fig. 3.3. **The state space shown in Fig.** 3.3 **is incomprehensible due to overlapping of the 45 states**. Out of the 45 states, only 29 are unique states (the 16 duplicate states are highlighted in yellow color). However, this state space is only for the initial markings of one token each in pIB1 and pIB2. If the initial markings on the pIB1 and pIB2 are increased (while keeping the same one initial token in pR1 to pR4, pC1, pC2, and po1AS, po2AS), then the number of states in the reachability graph increases linearly.

Table 3.1 presents the number of states in the reachability graph when the initial tokens in pIB1 and pIB2 are increased.

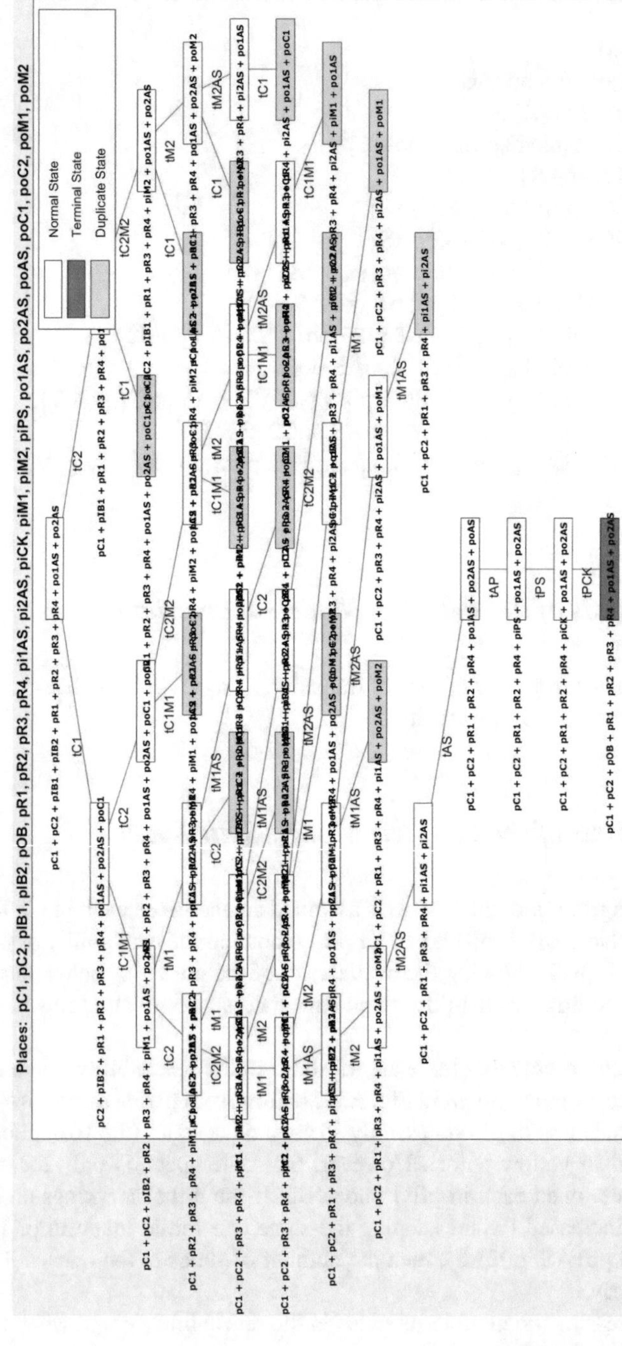

Fig. 3.3 The State Space of the Flexible Manufacturing System. *The state space is incomprehensible due to overlapping of the 45 states*

Table 3.1 Number of states in the state space versus number of initial tokens in the input buffers

Number of initial tokens in pIB1 and pIB2	Number of unique states in the reachability graph
(1, 1)	29
(2, 2)	184
(3, 3)	520
(4, 4)	904
(5, 5)	1288
(6, 6)	1672
(7, 7)	2056
(8, 8)	2440
(9, 9)	2812
(10, 10)	3208

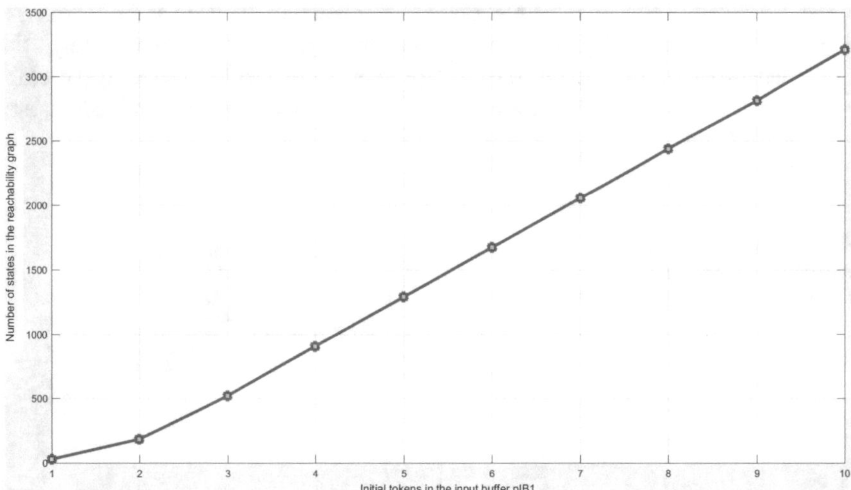

Fig. 3.4 Number of states in the state space versus number of initial tokens in the input buffers pIB1 and pIB2

Table 3.1 shows the enormous size of the state space (e.g., 184 states when there are just two tokens each in the put buffers pIB1 and pIB2). Figure 3.4 also shows a linear increase in the number of states when the initial tokens in the input buffers are increased.

3.2 Model-2: Circular AGVs

A factory transportation network is shown in Fig. 3.5 that uses Automated Guided Vehicles (AGVs) to transport raw materials and semi-products between work stations. The factory has six work stations (named WS1–WS6), and the tracks between the stations are labeled T12 to T61.

The problem is to model the factory transportation system as a Petri net model so that an optimal number of AGVs to deploy can be estimated.

The transport system can employ any number of AGVs, subject to the following conditions:

- AGVs can move in any direction, clockwise and anti-clockwise.
- As shown in Fig. 3.5, it has only one track. Hence, only one AGV can move on the trail between any two stations. However, any number of AGVs can be stationed in any station.
- An AGV cannot change the direction of movement until they are at the station $S1$.
- New AGVs can be deployed into service and removed from service (e.g., for maintenance) only at the station $S1$. However, AGV can be parked at the other stations too; assuming only for a shorter period, for loading and unloading, and because of traffic.

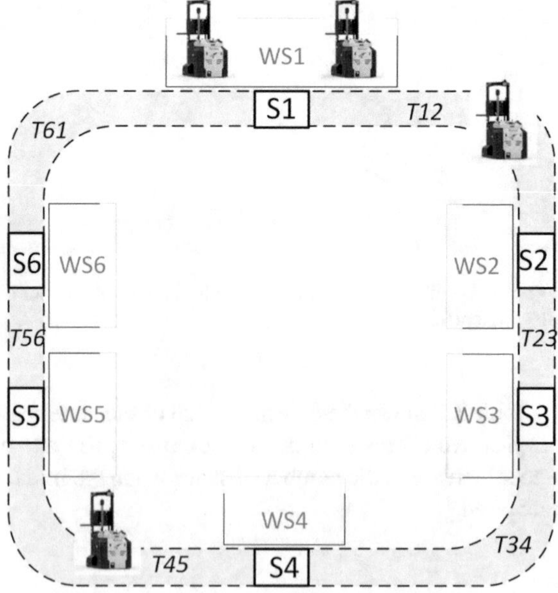

Fig. 3.5 Factory circular transportation System involving AGVs

3.2.1 The Petri Net Model of Circular AVG Transport System

The Petri net model of the circular AGVs is shown in Fig. 3.6. In this model,

- Place $AGVpool$ contains the initial tokens (n number of AGVs). Transition Cin introduces AGVs in the clockwise movement into the network, whereas Ain introduces AGVs in the anti-clockwise movement. Introduction of AGVs into service happens at the station $S1$.

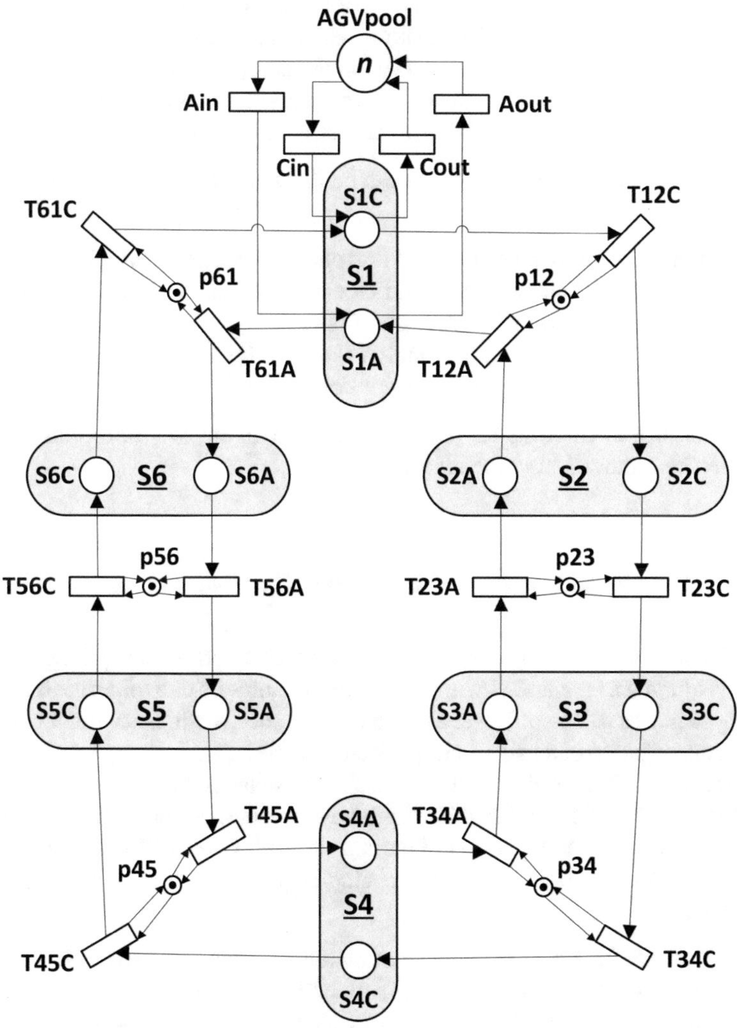

Fig. 3.6 Factory circular transportation system involving AGVs

- Each (physical) station *Si* is represented by two places (logical stations) namely SiC and SiA. For example, *S*1 is represented by $S1C$ and $S1A$. Logical stations SiC and SiA are for the AGVs in the clockwise and anti-clockwise movements, respectively.
- Transitions $TmnC$ and $TmnA$ are for the movement of an AGV between the stations *Sm* and *Sn*; $TmnC$ in the clockwise and $TmnA$ in the anti-clockwise directions. For example, $T34C$ moves an AGV between the stations *S*3 and *S*4 in the clockwise direction, whereas $T34A$ in the anti-clockwise direction.
- Place *pmn* serves as the semaphore for maintaining the track Tmn as a mutual exclusion zone. For example, the only token in $p34$ makes sure that either $T34A$ or $T34C$ fires (moves an AGV), making use of the track $T34$.
- Finally, transition $Cout$ removes AGVs in the clockwise movement from further operations. Whereas, *Aout* removes AGVs in the anti-clockwise movement. AGVs can only be removed from service at the station $S1C$ or $S1A$.

The P/T Petri net shown in Fig. 3.6 can be reduced somewhat by the application of colors:

- Transitions Cin and Ain can be fused into one Tin transition, which can introduce AGVs both in the clockwise and anti-clockwise direction. Similarly, transitions $Cout$ and $Aout$ can be replaced by one $Tout$.
- The places (logical stations) SiA and SiC can be joined to become one Si. This means a station *Si* will be represented by one place *Si* only.

Thus, by the use of coloring, six places (*S*1*A* to *S*6*A*) and two transitions (Ain and $Aout$) can be removed from the model.

3.2.2 Analysis of the Petri Net Model: State Space

Figure 3.7 shows the state space generated from the P/T Petri net model shown in Fig. 3.6. This graph was generated with the initial markings of one token each in all the semaphore places p12 to p61, and a token in AGVpool. With these initial markings, the generated state space had 13 unique states (Table 3.2).

Table 3.2 and Fig. 3.8 show that the number of states in the state space increases *exponentially* with the number of initial tokens in the input buffer AGVpool. This contrasts with the linear expansion of the state space for the FMS example presented in the previous subsection. For the time being, a qualitative reason can be given for this difference:

- In the Petri net for FMS, when an additional token is introduced in pIB1 or pIB2, it goes through the transitions and finally exiting the model at the output buffer pOB. This Petri net for FMS is not *cyclic*, as the token follows a linear path from the input buffer to the output buffer. The token introduced at pIB1 passes through a limited number of places, e.g., pIB1 to pi1AS. Also, tokens from pIB1 and pIB2 are merged into one token by tAS, and they pass through as one token through the

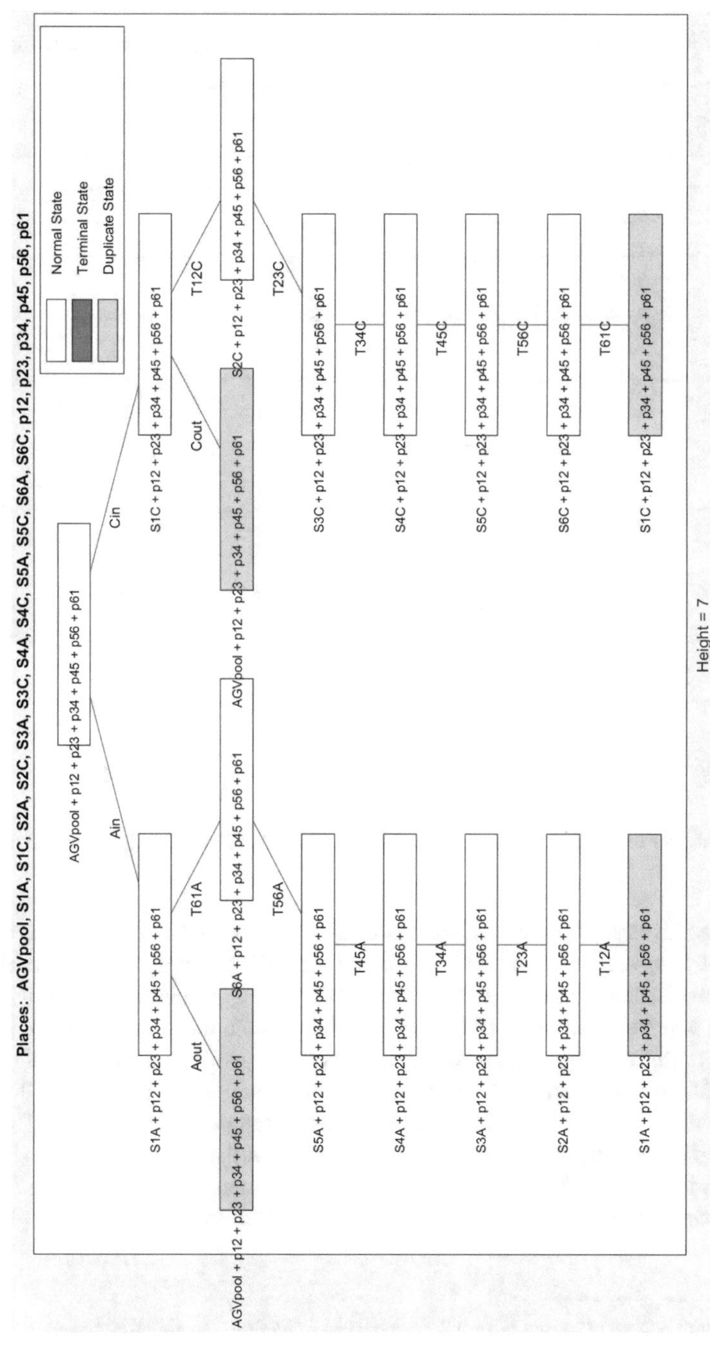

Fig. 3.7 The state space of the circular transportation system

Table 3.2 Number of the unique states in the state space versus number of initial tokens in the input buffer

Number of initial tokens in AGVpool	Number of the unique states in the reachability graph
1	13
2	91
3	455
4	1820
5	6188

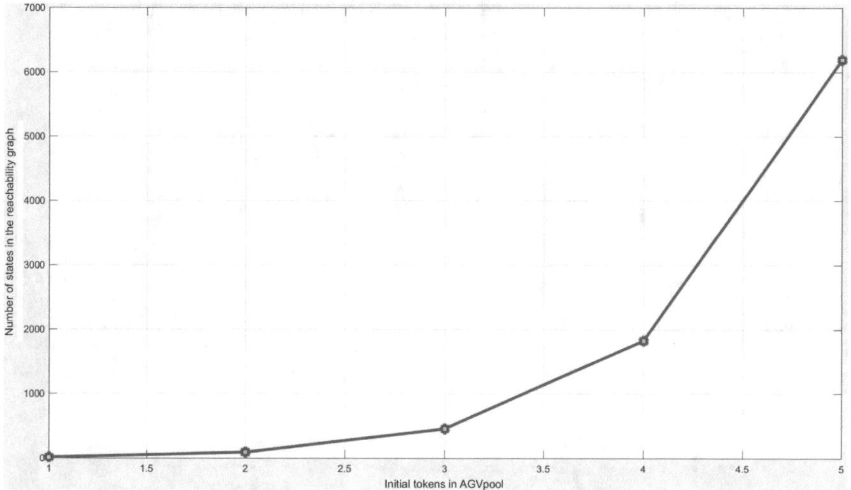

Fig. 3.8 Number of states in the state space versus number of initial tokens in the input buffer

places poAS to pOB. However, the most important reason for the linear expansion of the state space is that the Petri net model for FMS is serially connected blocks, and each block allows only a token to pass through at a time. For example, when a token is introduced into pIB1, it will go through the block for conveyor belt-1, as long as there are no other tokens in it. This is because the conveyor belt-1 block is a "mutual exclusion zone", protected by the *semaphore*[1] token in pC1. After the conveyor belt-1 block, the token will pass through the M1-block. M1-block will also allow only one token to pass through it as the semaphore token in pR1 protects this block. Thus, the serially connected mutual exclusion zones make the state space expansion linear due to the increasing number of tokens in pIB1 or pIB2.

[1] A semaphore is a variable that is used for the control of a critical section for achieving "mutual exclusion". With the semaphore, the critical section is protected so that only one activity at a time is allowed to use the critical section. Semaphore was originally used by Dijkstra in 1962 [6].

- The current example of circular AGVs is a cyclic model. An additional token introduced at AGVpool can go through a complete cycle and thus can be in one of 13 places (AGVpool, S1C to S6C, and S1A to S6A). Thus, if two tokens are introduced at AGVpool as initial tokens, the maximum possible states become $13^2 = 169$. By the same argument, for n number of initial tokens at AGVpool, the state space can have a maximum possible states numbering to 13^n. The cyclic nature of the model adds newer states exponentially to the state space.

3.2.3 Analysis of the Petri Net Model: P-Invariants

The Petri net has several p-invariants. However, the six semaphores (p12 to p61) are standalone p-invariants. For example, p12 is a p-invariant itself; if T12A consumes the token from p12, it will immediately put it back after firing. The seventh p-invariant is a large group of places: AGVpool, S1A, S1C, S2A, S2C, S3A, S3C, S4A, S4C, S5A, S5C, S6A,and S6C, as the total number of AGVs, both in service and out-of-service, will be a constant. The list of p-invariants is given below:
{p12}
{p23}
{p34}
{p45}
{p56}
{p61}
{AGVpool, S1A, S1C, S2A, S2C, S3A, S3C, S4A, S4C, S5A, S5C, S6A, S6C}

3.2.4 Analysis of the Petri Net Model: T-Invariants

There are four t-invariants:

1. Transitions Ain and Aout are a t-invariant. If they fire one after the other, the token that was taken from AGVpool will be placed back into it. Similarly, Cin and Cout are a t-invariant.
2. The combination of the two t-invariants are a t-invariant too.
3. Transitions T12A, T23A, T34A, T45A, T56A, and T61A are a t-invariant. If they fire one after the other, the token will arrive back to the place it was initially taken from. Similarly, transitions T12C, T23C, T34C, T45C, T56C, and T61C are a t-invariant too.

The list of t-invariants is given below:
{Ain,Aout} {Cin,Cout}
{Ain,Aout}{Cin,Cout}{Ain,Aout,Cin,Cout}
{Ain,Aout}{Cin,Cout}{Ain,Aout,Cin,Cout}{T12C,T23C,T34C, ...
↪ T45C,T56C,T61C}
{Ain,Aout}{Cin,Cout}{Ain,Aout,Cin,Cout}{T16A,T21A,T32A, ...
↪ T43A,T54A,T65A}{T12C,T23C,T34C,T45C,T56C,T61C}

3.3 Model-3: Cyclic Processes

The Cyclic Concurrent Processes (cyclic processes, for short) are usually found in production systems. Scheduling and timetabling problems associated with the discrete cyclic processes are also present in multi-tasking operating systems and transportation systems [7–9]. In the production systems, cyclic processes allow the manufacturing of different products on a shared resource (e.g., machining elements) at a high level of resource utilization. The problem is to determine:

- Quantitatively: due time (completion time) of order, given the number of machine elements in one batch is known beforehand.
- Qualitatively: the system is deadlock-free and starvation-free.

The following information is to be found from the simulation of the Petri net model:

1. Dispatching rules.
2. The cycle time (repetitiveness).
3. The number of critical resources.
4. Coefficient of resource utilization $\left(\zeta = \dfrac{\text{usage\_time}}{\text{usage\_time} + \text{idle\_time}}\right)$.

Let us assume that the production system consists of four resources (machining elements) $M_1 - M_4$. The production system is to perform three concurrent processes P_1, P_2, and P_3. (see Fig. 3.9).

It is usual to formulate the production routes and times as the process matrices. The three process matrices shown below represent the production routes and times of the three processes:

$$MP_1 = \begin{bmatrix} 1\ 3\ 4 \\ 4\ 2\ 3 \\ 0\ 0\ 0 \end{bmatrix}, \quad MP_2 = \begin{bmatrix} 4\ 3\ 1\ 2 \\ 5\ 7\ 5\ 4 \\ 0\ 0\ 0\ 0 \end{bmatrix}, \quad MP_3 = \begin{bmatrix} 2\ 1 \\ 4\ 3 \\ 0\ 0. \end{bmatrix} \tag{3.1}$$

Information coded in the process matrices:

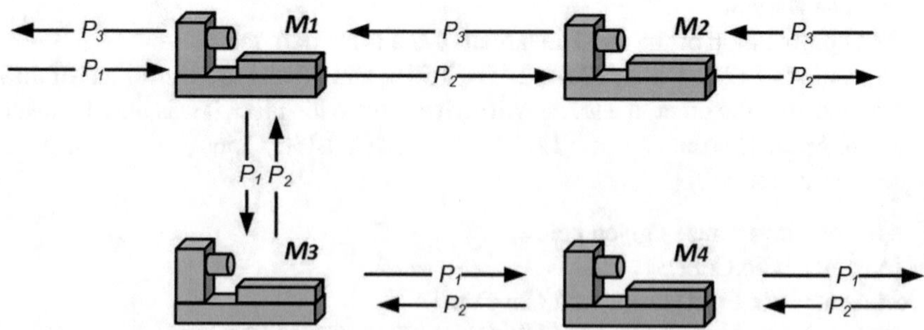

Fig. 3.9 Production of cyclic processes

- The first row of the matrix corresponds to the resources over which the route of the process goes; E.g., Taking MP1 as an example, the first row [1 3 4] depicts that process P1 will be machined by M1 first, and then by M3 and finally by M4.
- The second row is the cycle times on proper resources, meaning the machining time of each operation. E.g., the second row of MP1 [4 2 3] states that machining the first operation of P1 on M1 takes 4 Time Units (TU), the second operation of P1 on M3 takes 2 TU, and finally, the third operation of P1 on M4 takes 3 TU.
- The third row contains setup times. In this example, the setup times are ignored.

3.3.1 Petri Net Model of the Cyclic Processes

In summary, the production involves three processes, having 3, 4, and 2 operations, respectively. Also, the production involves four resources. Figure 3.10 shows the Petri net model. In this model, the operations are represented by transitions (t11, t12, ..., t32) and the resources (machines) by places M_1 to M_4. In this Petri net model, shared places are used to eliminate connections crisscrossing each other. For example, there are three places named as M_1. Only one of them, the one with a token in it, is the place representing the machine M1, and the other two places shown with shaded circle are shared places of M1. For simulations, the initial tokens on the input places p11 to p31 were m = 101, n = 102, and k = 200. These initial tokens represent the number of products to be made.

Figures 3.11 and 3.12 show the simulation results. Figure 3.12 indicates that M1 is the bottleneck, with working cycle time of 15 TU. The results shown in Figs. 3.11 and 3.12 are not generated (and cannot be generated) from the simple P/T Petri net shown in Fig. 3.10. A methodology known as the **Activity-Oriented Petri net (AOPN)** is used to generate these two figures. AOPN is devised by the author of this book [10–15], and it is implemented in the software GPenSIM. AOPN is discussed later in Chap. 10.

3.3.2 Analysis of the Petri Net Model: State Space

Let us assume that m, n, k number of initial tokens ($m, n, k \in \mathbb{N}$) in p11, p21, and p31, respectively. The absolute maximum number of states of the reachability graph would be $4^m \times 5^n \times 3^k$. This is because the three processes involve 4, 5, and 3 places, respectively. However, most of the states out of the maximum possible will be either duplicate states or not-reachable (invalid) states leaving only a fraction as the unique states.

To study the state space of the cyclic processes, the initial tokens (on p11, p21, and p31) have to be drastically reduced (otherwise, a huge state space will result). Let us start with $m = n = k = 1$. With these initial tokens, the state space obtained is shown in Fig. 3.13. It is noteworthy that even for this simple net (with just three processes

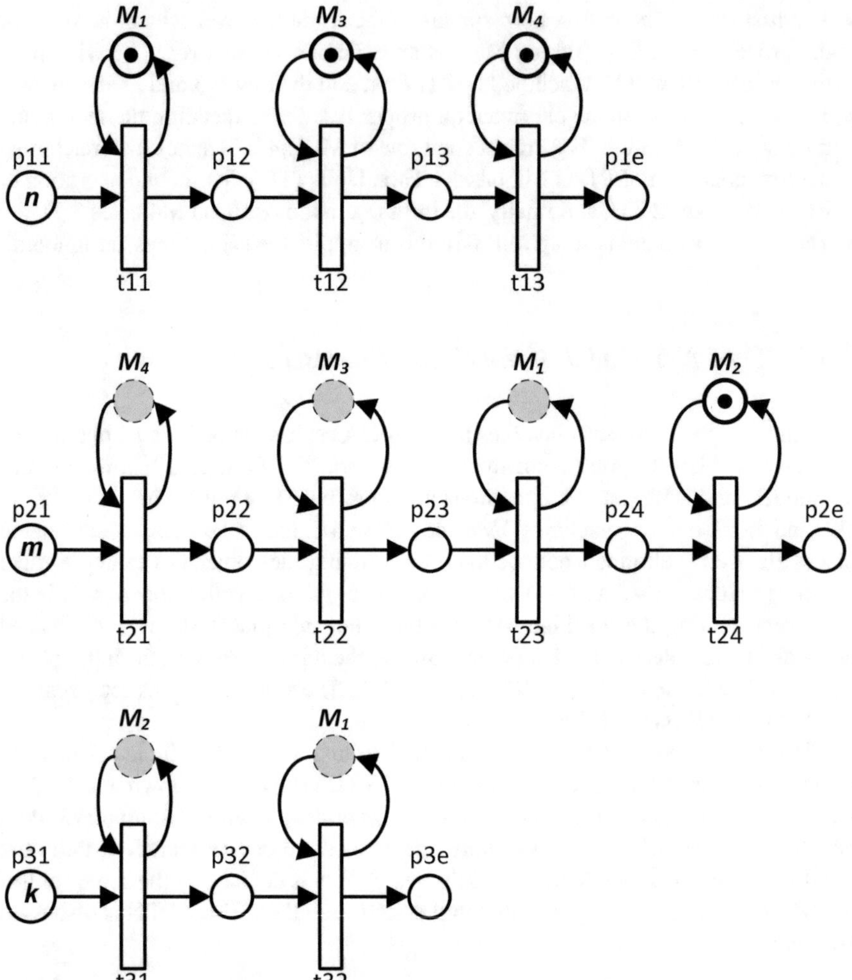

Fig. 3.10 Petri net model of the cyclic processes

with nine activities, and with the minimal initial tokens of one each), the generated state space is already large, consisting of 134 states. Out of these 134 states, only 60 states are unique states, and the rest 74 are duplicate states. This means the unique states shown in Fig. 3.13 is exactly equal to the theoretically maximum possible states $(= 4^1 \times 5^1 \times 3^1)$.

If the initial tokens are increased to $m = n = k = 2$, the resulting state space would have 900 unique states. Further, for $m = n = k = 3$, the number of unique states would become 7000, which is far less than the theoretically maximum possible (including duplicate and invalid states) of 216000 states $(= 4^3 \times 5^3 \times 3^3)$.

```
Final tokens: 101p1e + 102p2e + 200p3e

RESOURCE USAGE SUMMARY:
M1:  Total occasions: 403   Total Time spent: 1514
M2:  Total occasions: 302   Total Time spent: 1208
M3:  Total occasions: 203   Total Time spent: 916
M4:  Total occasions: 203   Total Time spent: 813

*****  LINE EFFICIENCY AND COST CALCULATIONS: *****
  Number of servers:  k = 4
  Total number of server instances:  K = 4
  Completion = 1600
  LT = 6400
  Total time at Stations: 4451
  LE = 69.5469 %
  **
```

Fig. 3.11 Summary of the resource usage

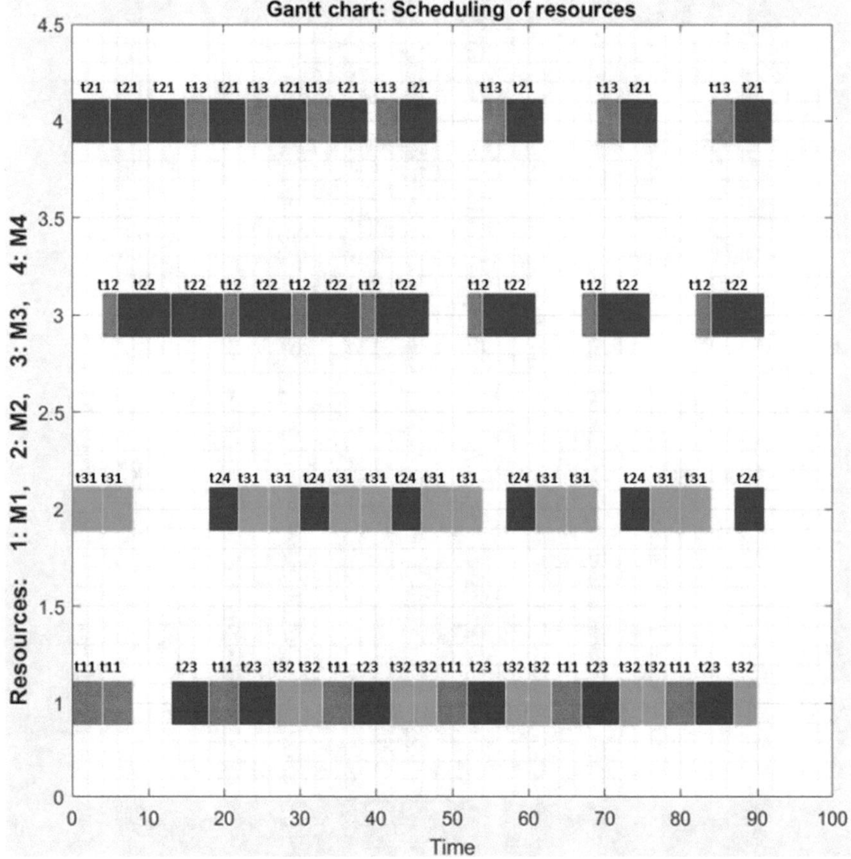

Fig. 3.12 Scheduling of the resources

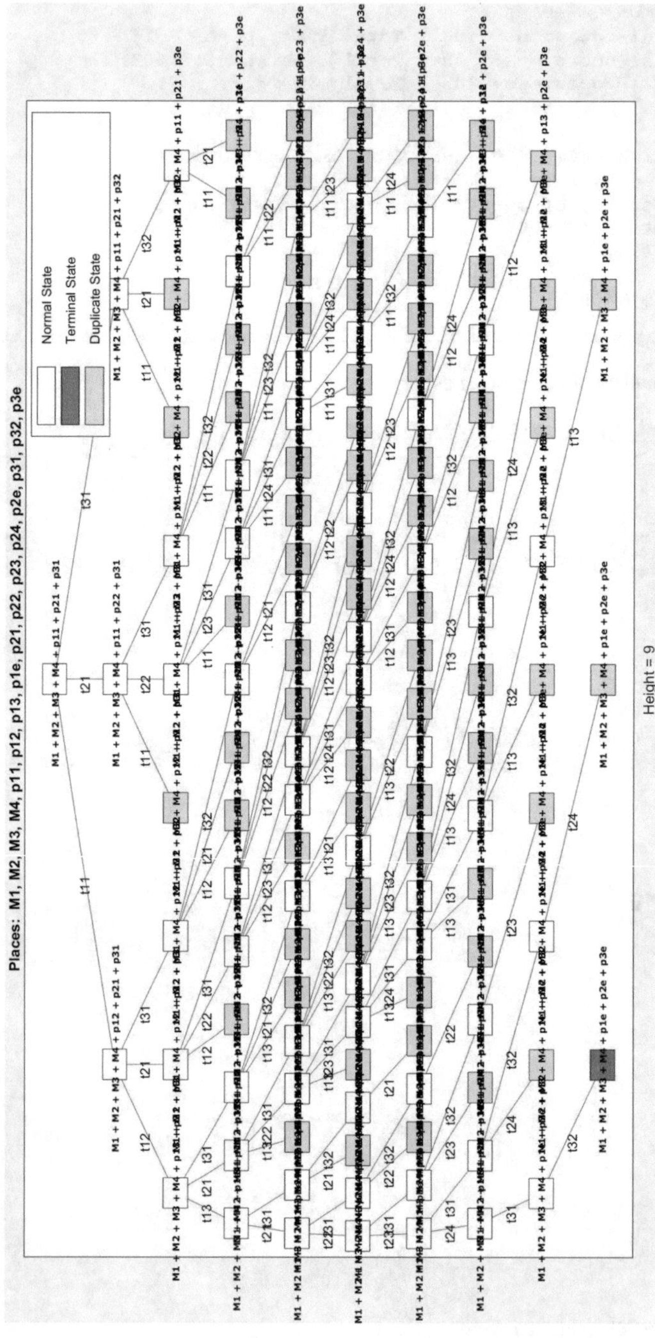

Fig. 3.13 State space of cyclic processes, when $n = m = k = 1$

3.3.3 Analysis of the Petri Net Model: P-Invariants

There are seven p-invariants in this Petri net:

1. Each resource Mi is a p-invariant on its own. For example, M1 looses its token to t11 during the start of the firing. t11 puts the token back into M1 at the completion of firing. Similarly, M2 to M4 are p-invariants on their own.
2. The places involved in the process P_1 such as p11, p12, p13, and p1e are a p-invariant. This is because a token introduced at p11 will pass through all these places, thus summation of the tokens in all these places will be always a constant. By the same argument, the places involved in the other two processes are also p-invariants.

The list of p-invariants is given as follows:
{M1}
{M2}
{M3}
{M4}
{p11, p12, p13, p1e}
{p21, p22, p23, p24, p2e}
{p31, p32, p3e}

3.3.4 Analysis of the Petri Net Model: T-Invariants

Since firings of any single transition or a set of transitions will not bring back to any earlier state, the Petri net is free from t-invariants.

3.4 The Problem with Petri Net Models

The problems associated with modeling real-life discrete event systems with Petri nets are as follows:

- Petri net models of real-life systems are huge: In the previous section, three manufacturing systems, along with their Petri net models, are presented. Though the three examples are simple, the Petri net models of these are not small or compact.
- Slowness in simulation: The simulations take a long time due to the enormous size of Petri nets and due to the way the simulations are done on them (during simulation, the tokens flow through every transition and place on their path, and the transitions have to be checked for their enabledness and the other firing conditions from the environment). As an example, simulation of a stochastic Petri net model of a predator–prey ecological system that can be described as a set of partial

differential equations (the *Lotka–Volterra* equations) within one page needed three hundred thousand iterations and ran for nearly two days [16].

- Difficulty in analyzing the model: Again, due to the huge size of the model, analyzing the model for its structural and behavioral properties become a time-consuming task.
- "State space explosion": One of the most important and useful properties of Petri nets is their explicit stateful information—the state space. The state space is automatically generated, showing every possible state that can be eventually reached from an initial state. However, the state space can become not so useful, as for real-life systems, the state space is huge if not of infinite size. Drawing any conclusions (e.g., model checking) from the huge or infinite state space is often difficult if it is possible at all [17–19]. The literature study provides some slicing algorithms to reduce the size of the Petri net as well as the state space. However, these slicing algorithms though works on small hypothetical example have little or no effect on real-life discrete event systems [20].

3.5 Research Goals of This Book

Petri net modeling problems, such as the slowness in simulation, state explosion, and the resulting difficulties in analyzing, remain unresolved. This book proposes "Petri Modules" and Modular Petri net as the solution for these problems. Literature does not provide clear syntax for modular model building. Further, there isn't any tool for developing Petri modules that support issues such as independent module development and testing and data hiding; see the literature review presented in Chap. 5 for details.

The focus of the book is the following:

1. **Clearly defined syntax for module**: There exist methodologies for some way of improving the modules for independent development and testing (discussed in Sect. 6.1). However, the formal definition of the module and the syntax for creating modules are not presented. This book proposes a new Petri net that supports module composition with clearly defined syntax, while following the accepted practices of modularization (e.g., data hiding).
2. **Decomposing model into modules**: When a new model is built from scratch, it is straightforward to follow the modular model building guidelines. The model can be built in a "bottom-up" fashion, starting with the crude modules, refining these modules step-wise, and finally, connecting these modules to form the overall modular model.

   However, there exist many legacy Petri net models of industrial systems. These Petri nets are valuable as modelers have spent enormous time, money, and energy developing these models. Hence, this book provides automated techniques for decomposing monolithic Petri net models (legacy models) into modules.

3. **Slicing Petri module**: Sometimes, a legacy Petri net model cannot be modularized, as the elements in this model are tightly (or densely) connected. This difficulty in modularizing is especially real when the model uses a large number of resources. As resources are usually connected with various activities, a model with a large number of resources naturally ends up as a tightly connected model that would be difficult to modularize. In this case, this book presents an alternative methodology (known as the Activity-Oriented Petri nets (AOPN)) to modularize otherwise non-modularizable models.
4. **Reducing the simulation time**: Simulation times (model execution times) are large when the modules are run together as a single model. Thus, model-based real-time control is not possible, as the model may fail to capture frequent input signals from the environment (e.g., from the external sensors). Due to the high execution time, it may also not be possible to send high-frequency output signals to the environment (e.g., actuators). Thus, this book proposes that the modules are run in parallel on different computers. The modules' distribution allows every module to be hosted on computers that are physically close to the relevant environment. Placing a module closer to the relevant environment reduces the latency time in the communication between the environment and the module. Therefore, this book explores the possibility of connecting modules in different configurations ("network of modules").
5. **Network Algorithms**: When the modules of a large model are executed on computers that are geographically separated, one or more modules may become unreachable (failed to communicate). The book provides algorithms to check the configuration of the connection between the modules and to propose alternative configurations in case of communication faults.
6. Extending **GPenSIM**: Finally, all the issues mentioned above should be implemented in the software GPenSIM so that GPenSIM can be applied to solve practical problems too.

References

1. Davidrajuh R, Skolud B, Krenczyk D (2018) Gpensim for performance evaluation of event graphs, Advances in Manufacturing, number 201519 in Lecture Notes in Mechanical Engineering. Springer International Publishing, Cham, pp 289–299
2. Davidrajuh R, Skolud B, Krenczyk D (2018) Performance evaluation of discrete event systems with gpensim. Computers 7(1):1–8
3. Davidrajuh R (N.D.) Modeling AGV operations with modular Petri nets. unpublished
4. Krenczyk D, Davidrajuh R, Skolud B (2017) An activity-oriented Petri net simulation approach for optimization of dispatching rules for job shop transient scheduling. In: International joint conference SOCO "17-CISIS" 17-ICEUTE' 17 León. Spain, September 6–8, 2017. Springer, Proceeding, pp 299–309
5. Skolud B, Krenczyk D, Davidrajuh R (2016) Solving repetitive production planning problems. an approach based on activity-oriented Petri nets. In: International joint conference SOCO' 16-CISIS' 16-ICEUTE' 16. Springer, pp 397–407

6. Dijkstra EW (1968) Cooperating sequential processes. Springer, The origin of concurrent programming, pp 65–138
7. Bocewicz G, Wójcik R, Banaszak ZA (2011) Toward cyclic scheduling of concurrent multimodal processes. In: International conference on computational collective intelligence. Springer, pp 448–457
8. Korbaa O, Camus H, Gentina J-C (2002) A new cyclic scheduling algorithm for flexible manufacturing systems. Int J Flexible Manuf Syst 14(2):173–187
9. Skolud B, Krenczyk D, Davidrajuh R (2017) Multi-assortment production flow synchronization. multiscale modelling approach. In: MATEC web of conferences, vol 112. EDP Sciences, p 05003
10. Davidrajuh R (2011) Representing resources in Petri net models: hardwiring or soft-coding? In: Proceedings of 2011 IEEE international conference on service operations, logistics and informatics. IEEE, pp 62–67
11. Davidrajuh R (2011) Scheduling using "activity-based modeling". In: 2011 IEEE international conference on computer applications and industrial electronics (ICCAIE). IEEE, pp 45–49
12. Davidrajuh R (2012) Activity-oriented Petri net for scheduling of resources. In: 2012 IEEE international conference on systems, man, and cybernetics (SMC). IEEE, pp 1201–1206
13. Davidrajuh R (2013) Realizing simple Petri net models for complex and large scheduling problems: an approach based activity-oriented Petri nets. In: 2013 UKSim 15th international conference on computer modelling and simulation. IEEE, pp 419–423
14. Davidrajuh R (2015) A new two-phase approach for Petri net based modeling of scheduling problems. In: Industrial engineering, management science and applications 2015. Springer, pp 125–134
15. Davidrajuh R (2017) A new Petri nets based approach for modeling of discrete manufacturing system. In: International conference on intelligent systems in production engineering and maintenance. Springer, pp 109–120
16. Davidrajuh R (2010) Gpensim: a new Petri net simulator. Petri Nets Applications, IntechOpen
17. Baier C, Katoen J-P (2008) Principles of model checking. MIT press
18. Clarke E, Grumberg O, Jha S, Lu Y, Veith H (2001) Progress on the state explosion problem in model checking. Springer, Informatics, pp 176–194
19. Valmari A (1996) The state explosion problem. Springer, Advanced Course on Petri Nets, pp 429–528
20. Davidrajuh R, Roci A (2018) Performance of static slicing algorithms for Petri nets. Int J Simul–Syst, Sci Technol 20(S1):15.1–15.7

Chapter 4
GPenSIM for Monolithic Petri Nets

This chapter presents GPenSIM for modeling monolithic (non-modular) Petri nets. It is important to understand how GPenSIM supported the development of monolithic (non-modular) Petri nets as this knowledge will help us understand the extensions to support modules later on. This chapter focuses on the processor files (such as specific processor files and the common processor files) and the visibility of transitions in them. Two examples (on model checking and performance evaluation) are also given on the application of GPenSIM for the simulation of monolithic Petri nets.

4.1 Revisiting the Files in GPenSIM

A Petri net model of a discrete event system developed with GPenSIM consists of a number of files. The Main Simulation File (MSF) is the file that will be run directly by the MATLAB command. In addition to the main simulation file, there will be one or more Petri net Definition Files (PDFs); definition of a Petri net graph (static details) is given in the Petri net Definition File. There may be a number of PDFs, if the Petri net model is divided into many modules, and each module is defined in a separate PDF. While the Petri net definition file has the static details, the main simulation file contains the dynamic information (such as initial tokens in places, firing times of transitions) of the Petri net. In addition to these files (main simulation file and Petri net definition files), there can be a number of processor files too.

If there are additional conditions that determine whether an enabled transition can fire or not, then these conditions are coded in the pre-processor files. The additional conditions are called "user-defined condition" in GPenSIM terminology. There can be a separate pre-processor file for each transition in a Petri net model (called specific pre-processors). Also, the "user-defined conditions" for different transitions can be collected and kept in one file called the common pre-processor "COMMON_PRE" .

R. Davidrajuh, *Petri Nets for Modeling of Large Discrete Systems*, Asset Analytics,
https://doi.org/10.1007/978-981-16-5203-5_4

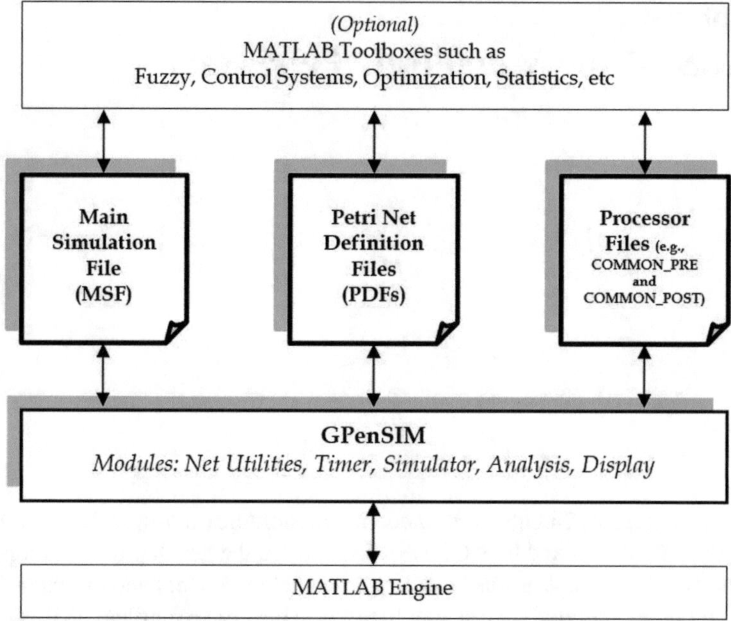

Fig. 4.1 The four GPenSIM files

Similar to the pre-processor files, there exist post-processor files too. When a transition completes firing, there may be some post-firing actions needed to be done. These post-firing actions can be coded in a post-processor file that is specific for the fired transition (called specific post-processors). Also, the post-actions of different transitions can be collected and kept in the common post-processor file called "COMMON_POST".

Usually, specific pre-processors and specific post-processors are need not used. This is because for N number of transitions, there will be N number of specific pre-processor files and an equal of specific post-processor files will clutter the folder. Instead, these $2 \times N$ number of processor files can be replaced by just two common processors namely, the "COMMON_PRE" and the "COMMON_POST". However, for hard real-time systems, it may be necessary to have specific processor files. This is because it is not good for the compiler to process the one large common processor file COMMON_PRE whenever a transition becomes enabled, and the one and large COMMON_POST whenever a transition completes firing.

Ignoring the specific processor files, Fig. 4.1 shows that implementing a Petri net model with GPenSIM usually happens via four MATLAB files (M-files) [1]:

1. Petri net Definition File (PDF) declares the static Petri net graph. The set of places, the set of transitions, and the set of arcs that make up the static Petri net are declared in this file.

2. Main Simulation File (MSF) declares the initial dynamics (e.g., initial tokens in the places, firing times of the transitions, firing costs of the transitions) and runs the simulations. When the simulation is completed, the code for plotting the results are also coded in this file.
3. The common pre-processor file (COMMON_PRE) is for coding the user-defined conditions for the enabled transitions to satisfy before they start firing.
4. The common post-processor file (COMMON_POST) is for coding any post-firing actions to be performed after firing of the transitions.

4.2 Transitions and Their Visibility

There are two key issues behind the design of the processor files in GPenSIM. The two key issues are (1) Activity-orientedness, and (2) Visibility. These two key issues are also discussed in the book on GPenSIM [3]. The key issues are

1. Activity-orientedness: When modeling a discrete event system, transitions are the primary focus.
2. Visibility: Transitions possess different visibility, such as global, modular, and private visibility.

Transitions represent the activities of discrete event systems, whereas places represent the passive elements (e.g., buffers). In a discrete event system, if there is no activity happening now or in future, then the system is dead. Thus, activities are the heartbeat of discrete event systems. The places are just drawn along with the transitions. Hence, the transitions representing activities take the central place in the model building with GPenSIM.

4.3 Visibility in Monolithic Petri Net

In a **monolithic (non-modular) Petri net, all transitions have two types of visibility**: (1) **global visibility**, and (2) **private visibility**.

4.3.1 *Global Visibility*

All the transitions in a monolithic Petri net have global visibility. **A transition that has global visibility is accessible in the *common* processor files COMMON_PRE and COMMON_POST**. Whenever a transition with global visibility becomes enabled, the compiler will automatically check whether there are any pre-conditions in pre-processor file **COMMON_PRE** the transition has to satisfy before starting

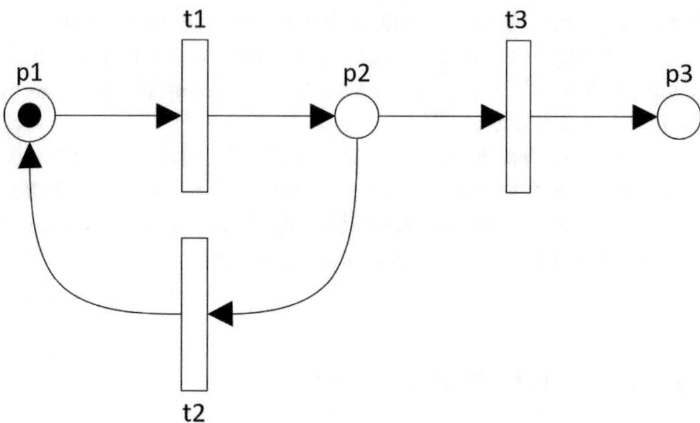

Fig. 4.2 A monolithic P-T Petri net

to fire. If the transition starts firing, when it completes firing, the post-processor **COMMON_POST** will be checked for any post-firing actions to be executed.

4.3.2 Private Visibility

Every transition in a monolithic Petri net has private visibility too. Any transition can have its *own* specific processor files, and in this file the transition is accessible, giving the private visibility.

(Transitions in modular Petri net have one more visibility, known as the modular (or local) visibility, which is discussed later in Sect. 6.2.3.)

Example 4.1 (Global- and Private Visibility) Figure 4.2 shows a simple monolithic Petri net in which all the three transitions t1, t2, and t3 have global visibility and thus are accessible in the common processor files COMMON_PRE and COMMON_POST. If there are exists specific processor files t1_pre and t1_post (for the exclusive use of t1), t2_pre and t2_post (for the exclusive use of t2), and so on, then t1 is accessible in t1_pre and t1_post files too, giving private visibility (resp. t2 in t2_pre and t2_post, and t3 in t3_pre and t3_post).

Example 4.2 (Specific Processors) Figure 4.3 depicts a simple product sorting system in which three robots (tA, tB, and tC) are employed. Let us assume that the common input buffer (pCommonIB) contains some products. The robots pick one product at a time from pCommonIB and place it into their respective output buffer, e.g., tA puts into pA. The only condition is that these three robots fire alternately (not at the same time, to avoid collision), and the preferred firing order is tA first and then tB, and finally tC.

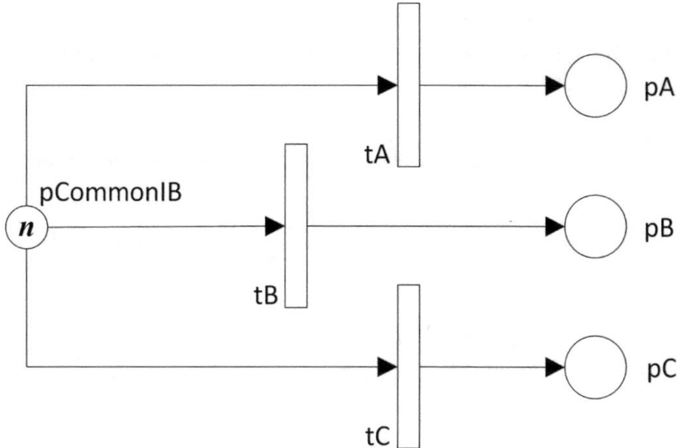

Fig. 4.3 Alternating robots

Figure 4.4 shows the six specific processor files. The alternating firing of tA to tC is achieved through the use of a semaphore; a semaphore is a variable that is used for the control of a critical section for achieving mutual exclusion; see Sect. 3.2.2. The semaphore is set to "tA" in the main simulation file, allowing tA to fire first.

Since pCommonIB has enough enabling tokens, tA, tB, and tC are enabled at the same time. The specific pre-processor for tA (tA_pre) checks whether the semaphore is set to "tA". Since it is, tA starts firing. However, when the specific pre-processor for tB and tC (tB_pre and tC_pre) is checked, false value will be return for "fire" (tB and tC cannot fire), since the semaphore has the value "tA" and not "tB" or "tC". When tA completes firing, the semaphore is set to "tB" in the specific post-processor file of tA (tA_post). By assigning the semaphore the value of "tB" in tA_post, it is assured that tB will be fired next and neither tA nor tC can fire.

The Petri net Definition File (PDF):
Figure 4.5 shows the PDF file. As shown in Fig. 4.5, the PDF is a transformation of the static details shown in the Petri net of Fig. 4.3.

The Main Simulation File (MSF):
The Main Simulation File (MSF) is shown in Fig. 4.6. In the MSF, the PDF is declared first, followed by the declaration of the initial dynamic details (such as firing times "ft" and the initial tokens "m0"). Then, the simulations are invoked by the function "gpensim". When the simulations are complete, the results are plotted with the function "plotp". The results shown in Fig. 4.7 indicate that the output buffers pA, pB, and pC fill up alternatively, proving that tA, tB, and tC fires alternatively.

Example 4.3 (Common Processors) This example is the same as in the previous subsection. However, in this example, rather than the specific processor files, the

Pre-processor for tA ('tA_pre.m'):

```
function [fire, transition] = tA_pre(transition)
global global_info

% can tA start
fire = strcmp(global_info.semafor, transition.name);
```

Post-processor for tA ('tA_post.m'):

```
function [] = tA_post(transition)
global global_info

% when tA completes firing, let tB start
global_info.semafor = 'tB';
```

Pre-processor for tB ('tB_pre.m'):

```
function [fire, transition] = tB_pre(transition)
global global_info

% can tB start
fire = strcmp(global_info.semafor, transition.name);
```

Post-processor for tB ('tB_post.m'):

```
function [] = tB_post(transition)
global global_info

% when tB completes firing, let tC start
global_info.semafor = 'tC';
```

Pre-processor for tC ('tC_pre.m'):

```
function [fire, transition] = tC_pre(transition)
global global_info

% can tC start
fire = strcmp(global_info.semafor, transition.name);
```

Post-processor for tC ('tC_post.m'):

```
function [] = tC_post(transition)
global global_info

% when tC completes firing, let tA start
global_info.semafor = 'tA';
```

Fig. 4.4 The specific processor files

```
% PDF: Alternating firing with semaphore
function [pns] = alternating_pdf()

% name of the module
pns.PN_name = 'Alternatively firing robots';

% set of places
pns.set_of_Ps = {'pCommonIB', 'pA', 'pB', 'pC'};

% set of transitions
pns.set_of_Ts = {'tA', 'tB', 'tC'};

% set of arcs
pns.set_of_As = {...
    'pCommonIB','tA',1, 'tA','pA',1,... % tA
    'pCommonIB','tB',1, 'tB','pB',1,... % tB
    'pCommonIB','tC',1, 'tC','pC',1 ... % tC
                };
```

Fig. 4.5 PDF for alternating robots

```
% Example: Alternating firing with semaphore
global global_info
global_info.semafor = 'tA'; % "tA" fires first
global_info.STOP_AT = 100; % Option: stop simuations after 100 TU

pns = pnstruct('alternating_pdf');    % the PDF file
dynamicpart.m0 = {'pCommonIB', 10};  % initial tokens
dynamicpart.ft = {'tA',5, 'tB',8, 'tC',10}; % firing times

% combine static with initial dynamic details
pni = initialdynamics(pns, dynamicpart);

% run the simulation
sim = gpensim(pni);

% plot the results
plotp(sim, {'pA', 'pB', 'pC'});
```

Fig. 4.6 MSF for alternating robots

common processor files COMMON_PRE and COMMON_POST files are going to be used for manipulating the semaphore.

- PDF: "alternating_pdf.m" is the same as the one given in the previous subsection.
- MSF: "alternating_MSF.m" is also the same as the one given in the previous subsection.

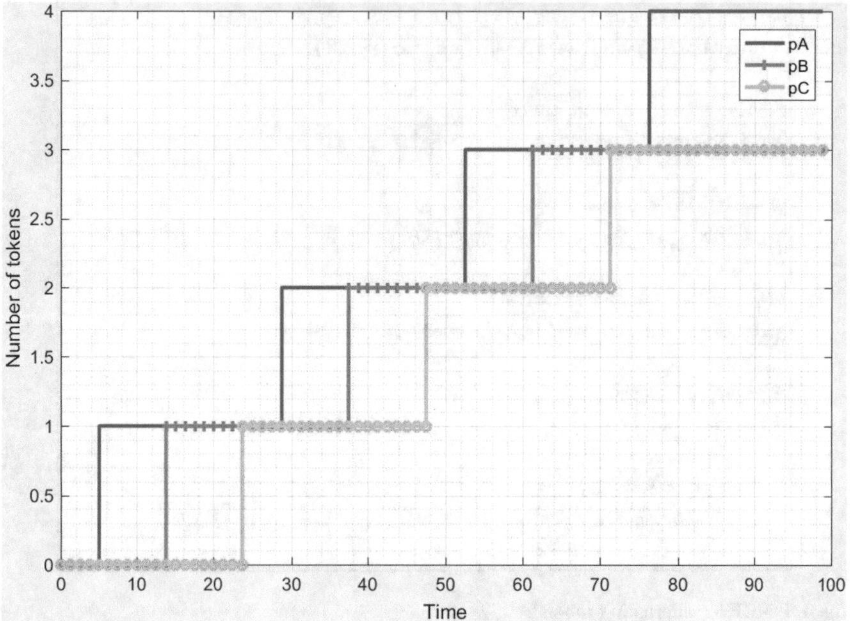

Fig. 4.7 Simulation results

```
function [fire, transition] = COMMON_PRE(transition)
global global_info

% fire only if the enabled transition's name
%  is the same as the value of the semafor
fire = strcmp(global_info.semafor, transition.name);
```

Fig. 4.8 The common pre-processor COMMON_PRE

- Specific pre-files "tA_pre.m", and "tB_pre.m" and "tC_pre.m" are obsolete; these three files are replaced by the common pre-processor "COMMON_PRE.m".
- Specific post-files "tA_post.m", "tB_post.m" and "tC_post.m" are also obsolete; these three files are replaced by the common post-processor "COMMON_POST.m".
- The simulation result is the same as the one shown before in Fig. 4.7.

Figures 4.8 and 4.9 show the common processor files. The compact COMMON_PRE replaces the three specific pre-processors tA_pre to tC_pre. Also, the compact COMMON_POST replaces the three specific post-processors tA_post to tC_post.

```
function [] = COMMON_POST(transition)
global global_info

% after firing:

switch transition.name
    case 'tA' % if the fired transition is tA
        % let tB fire next
        global_info.semafor = 'tB';

    case 'tB' % if the fired transition is tB
        % let tC fire next
        global_info.semafor = 'tC';

    case 'tC' % if the fired transition is tC
        % let tC fire next
        global_info.semafor = 'tA';
end
```

Fig. 4.9 The common post-processor COMMON_POST

4.4 GPenSIM Application-I: Model Checking

This section presents a complete example on model checking of Petri nets. The example is the problem of "soda vending machine". Though the example is simple, the model checking process shown below is applicable to any large Petri nets. However, the problem is purposely chosen to be simple so that the steps involved in the process can be clearly explained. The problem given below is a version of the problem that is presented in some books on model checking (e.g., [1]).

4.4.1 The Soda Vending Machine

The vending machine has the following properties:

- The vending machine dispenses only one type of soft drink, and it can hold a maximum of three drinks after refilling.
- A user can insert only one coin (e.g., a 10 Norwegian Kroner) to get a drink (product).
- After inserting the coin, there will be two options: both the push-button for "Deliver Product" and the push-button for "Money Back" will be highlighted.
- If the user presses the "Deliver Product" button, then the drink will be delivered.

- On the other hand, if the user presses the "Money Back" button, the inserted coin will be returned to the user.
- When the products are emptied, the push-button for requesting a drink will not be highlighted; only the push-button for requesting Money Back will be highlighted.
- When the products are emptied or running low, the process of refilling is not covered in this problem.

4.4.2 *The Petri Net Model*

Figure 4.10 shows the Petri net model of the soda vending machine. Table 4.1 describes the elements (places and transitions) involved in the model. The three initial tokens are put in place "Products", indicating that the system starts with three drinks.

4.4.3 *GPenSIM Implementation*

As described in the introduction, implementing a Petri net model with GPenSIM usually requires the coding of four files, namely PDF, MSF, the pre-processor file,

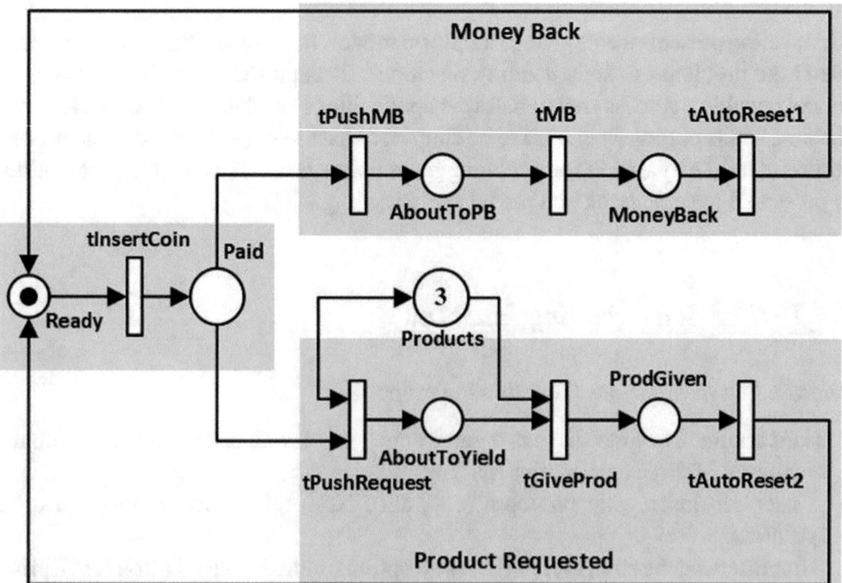

Fig. 4.10 The Petri net model of a simple soda vending machine

Table 4.1 The elements of the Petri net

Set of transitions	Set of places
–	**Ready**: the system is in the ready state
tInsertCoin: the act of inserting the coin	**Paid**: a user has inserted a valid coin
tPushRequest: pressing the button for requesting delivery of a drink	**AboutToYield**: after inserting the coin, the user has pressed the button "Deliver Product"
tPushMB: pressing the button for requesting money back	**AboutToPB**: after inserting the coin, the user has pressed the button "Money Back"
–	**Products**: Number of drinks available for sale (1–3)
tGiveProd: the act of delivering a drink	**ProductGiven**: A drink is already delivered to the user
tMB: the act of returning the coin (Money Back) to the user	**MoneyBack**: The inserted coin is already returned to the user
tAutoReset1 and *tAutoReset2*: the act of resetting back to the ready state after delivery of a product or money back; these activities will be automatically run (internal transitions)	–

and the post-processor file. However, the soda vending machine is so simple that it does not impose any pre-conditions for firing (to be coded in the pre-processor) and post-firing actions (to be coded in the post-processor). Thus, implementing the soda vending machine requires only two files, the PDF and MSF.

PDF: shown in Fig. 4.11.

MSF: shown in Fig. 4.12.

The final statement in the MSF is the creation of the reachability graph. The reachability graph is shown in Fig. 4.13. The reachability graph consists of three blocks: the starter block, the middle block, and the end block.

The reachability graph starts with the starter block on the top. The first state of the reachability graph is the state of three available drinks (in the MSF only three initial tokens as assigned to the place Products) and system readiness. In the middle block, the reachability graph is divided into two columns. The right column shows the process of delivering a drink after the insertion of a coin. The left column shows the process of delivering the money back if the user opts to press the money back button after inserting a coin.

The lower end of the reachability graph shows a group of states when all three products are sold off. In this situation (when the vending machine is empty for products), if a user inserts a coin, he can only press the button for money back (the button for product delivery will not be highlighted), and the money will be paid back eventually.

```
% PDF (Petri Net Definition File): vendingMC2_pdf.m
function [png] = vendingMC2_pdf()
% Assigning a name (label) for the module
png.PN_name = 'Pet Net for soda vending machine-2';

% Declaring the set of places
png.set_of_Ps = {'Ready','Paid', 'AboutToPB',...
'MoneyBack','AboutToYield','ProdGiven','Products'};

% Declaring the set of transitions
png.set_of_Ts = {'tInsertCoin','tPushMB','tMB',...
'tAutoReset1','tPushRequest','tGiveProd','tAutoReset
2'};

% Declaring the set of arcs (connections)
png.set_of_As = {'Ready','tInsertCoin',1,...
    'tInsertCoin','Paid',1, ...
    'Paid','tPushMB',1, 'tPushMB','AboutToPB',1, ...
    'AboutToPB','tMB',1, 'tMB','MoneyBack',1, ...
    'MoneyBack','tAutoReset1',1,
'tAutoReset1','Ready',1, ...
    'Paid','tPushRequest',1,
'Products','tPushRequest',1, ...
    'tPushRequest','AboutToYield',1,
'tPushRequest','Products',1,...
    'AboutToYield','tGiveProd',1,
'Products','tGiveProd',1, ...
    'tGiveProd','ProdGiven',1, ...
    'pProdGiven','tAutoReset2',1,
'tAutoReset2','Ready',1};
```

Fig. 4.11 PDF for the vending machine

```
% MSF (Main Simulation File): vendingMC.m
% Declare the PDF file
pns = pnstruct('vendingMC2_pdf');
% Assign initial tokens
dyn.m0 = {'Ready',1,'Products',3};
% Combine the static and initial dynamics to create
%  the initial Petri Net dynamic structure
pni = initialdynamics(pns, dyn);
% create the reachability graph
cotree(pni, 1, 1);
```

Fig. 4.12 MSF for the vending machine

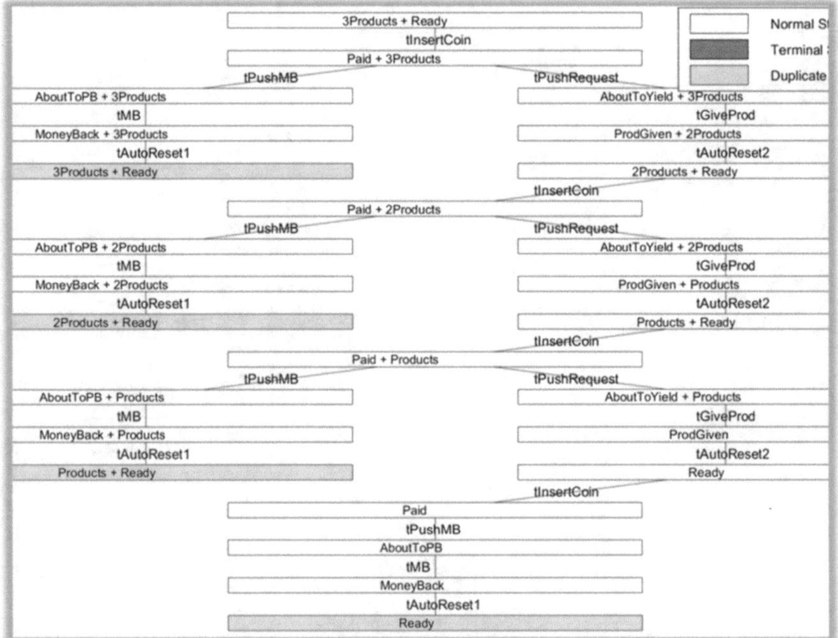

Fig. 4.13 The reachability graph for the vending machine

4.4.4 Model Checking the Petri Net

In this subsection, the Petri net model will be checked for satisfying some basic properties. The basic properties fall into the group of "**fairness**" ("something right or good will eventually happen") and "**liveness**" ("something wrong or bad will never happen") [8].

Model checking for Fairness

Property-A: If the user has inserted a coin and has not pressed the "Request Product", then the user has the possibility to ask for his money back. In Computation Tree Logic (CTL), the property-A can be formulated as follows (in the formulations below, ***A*** ("for all paths") is a path quantifier, and ***N*** ("Next") and ***F*** ("eventually" or "future") are temporal operators):

$$Paid \wedge -(first(tPushRequest)) \longrightarrow \boldsymbol{AF}\ MoneyBack \tag{4.1}$$

Property-B: If the user has inserted a coin and pushed the button for "Request Product", then the user will be given a product in the future. In CTL, the property-B can be formulated as follows:

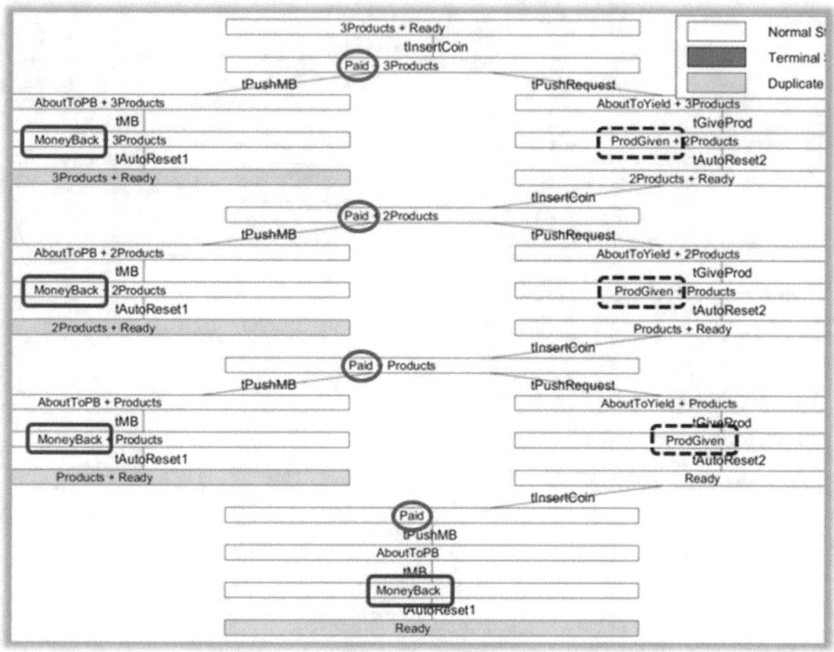

Fig. 4.14 The Petri net model satisfies the properties A and B

$$Paid \wedge first(tPushRequest) \longrightarrow \textbf{\textit{AF}}\ ProductGiven \tag{4.2}$$

Figure 4.14 shows that the property-A is satisfied. In Fig. 4.14, the states that have "Paid" property (marked by red circles), if they are directed by the "PushMB" (press the button for requesting money back) will eventually end up in states that have the "MoneyBack" property (marked by green solid rectangles). Figure 4.14 also shows that the property-B is satisfied too. In Fig. 4.14, the states that have "Paid" property (marked by red circles), if they are directed by the "PushRequest" (press the button for requesting a product) will eventually end up in states that have the "ProductGiven" property (marked by blue dotted rectangles).

Model checking for Liveness

Property-C: If the machine has given a product, then the next state has to be the Ready state. In CTL, the property-C can be formulated as follows:

$$ProductGiven \longrightarrow \textbf{\textit{AN}}\ Ready \tag{4.3}$$

Property-D: If the machine has paid the money back, then the next state has to be the Ready state. In CTL, the property-D can be formulated as follows:

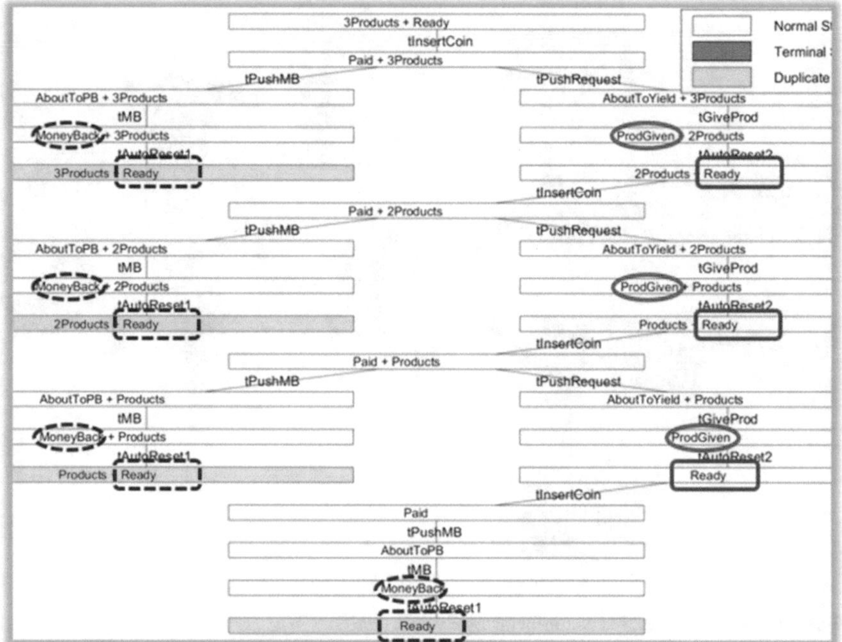

Fig. 4.15 The Petri net model satisfies the properties C and D

$$MoneyBack \longrightarrow AN\ Ready \tag{4.4}$$

Figure 4.15 shows that the property-C is also satisfied. In Fig. 4.15, the states that have "ProductGiven" property (marked by red ovals) are always immediately followed by the states that have the "Ready" property (marked by green solid rectangles). Finally, Fig. 4.15 also shows that the property-D is satisfied too. In Fig. 4.15, the states that have "MoneyBack" property (marked by blue dotted ovals) are always immediately followed by the states that have the "Ready" property (marked by blue dotted rectangles).

4.5 GPenSIM Application-II: Performance Evaluation

The simple Flexible Manufacturing System (FMS) shown in Fig. 4.16 is for making only one type of product. Though the system is simple, it is purposely chosen to show how easily it can be modeled and performance evaluated with GPenSIM.

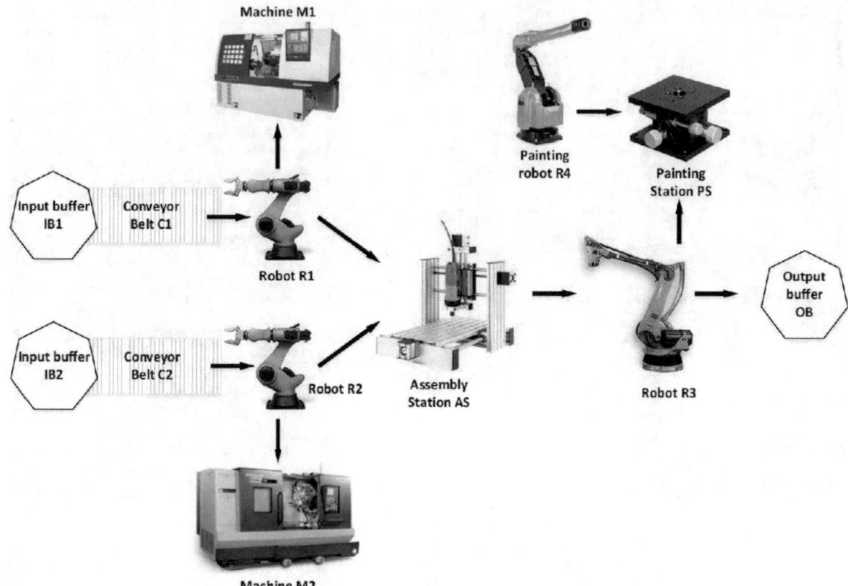

Fig. 4.16 A simple Flexible Manufacturing System (FMS)

4.5.1 Performance Evaluation of an FMS

This problem is already presented in Sect. 3.1 "Model-1: Flexible Manufacturing System". Hence, only the physical configuration of the FMS is reproduced here (Fig. 4.16, which is a copy of Fig. 3.1) for the readers' convenience. The Petri net model is shown in Fig. 4.17, which is a copy of Fig. 3.2. See Sect. 3.1 for the operational specification of the FMS.

The Petri net model of the FMS is shown in Fig. 4.17 is obtained by connecting the operations (listed in the operational specification) one after the other; the times taken by the operations are shown in Fig. 4.17 as the firing times of the transitions. The input buffers IB1 and IB2 (represented by the places pIB1 and pIB2) and the output buffer (place pOB) are for testing purposes only. These three places will be omitted in the final model, in order to make the Petri net a Strongly Connected Event Graph (SCEG). This is because the presence of the three places will destroy the strongly connected property.

4.5.2 GPenSIM Files for Simulation

The following two files are used for the simulation:

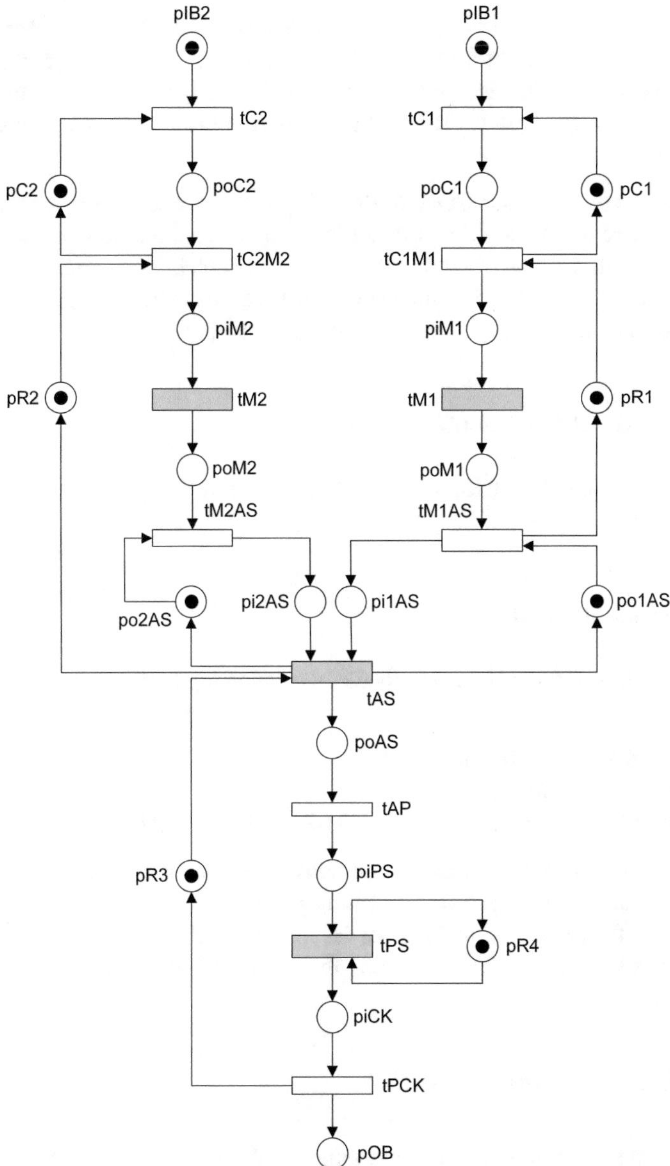

Fig. 4.17 The Petri net model of a Flexible Manufacturing System [4]

1. Petri net Definition File (PDF): This is the coding of the static Petri net (the structure of the Petri net defined by the sets of places, transitions, and arcs).
2. Main Simulation File (MSF): In this file, the initial dynamics (e.g., initial tokens in places pC1, pC2, pR1, pR2, and pR3, and the firing times of transitions) are declared.

The common pre-processor COMMON_PRE is not needed for this example. This is because there are no additional conditions for the enabled transitions to satisfy; the transitions start firing whenever they become enabled. Also, the common post-processor COMMON_POST is not needed, as there are no post-firing actions needed to be performed at the completion of the firing transitions.

4.5.2.1 Petri Net Definition File (PDF)

The PDF is shown in Fig. 4.18, which declares the sets of places, transitions, and the arcs.

4.5.2.2 Main Simulation File (MSF)

The MSF is shown in Fig. 4.19. In this file, the following three evaluations are computed:

- The cycle that creates the deadlock,
- The current flow rate, and
- How can the flow rate be increased to 0.07 tokens per TU?

In the MSF, the three evaluations listed above are computed with the help of the GPenSIM function "mincyctime", meaning minimum cycle time. Function "mincyctime" will further invoke some other GPenSIM functions. A short description to these functions are given after presenting the results in the next subsection.

4.5.3 The Simulation Results

Due to the space restrictions, the simulation result is divided into two portion and shown as Figs. 4.20 and 4.21. Figure 4.20 shows that there are eight elementary circuits ("cycles") in the event graph.

The second part of the simulation result shown in 4.21 indicates that the elementary circuit number-2 is the bottleneck as it has highest cycle time (=21). This means the flow rate of the circuit is 1/21 = 0.0476 tokens per TU. The second highest cycle time (=20) belongs to the circuit number-8, having a flow rate of 1/20 = 0.05.

The final part of the simulation result is the suggestion for performance improvement, suggested by GPenSIM on its own. GPenSIM computes these suggestions for

```
function [png] = fms_pdf()
png.PN_name = 'Event Graph model of FMS';
%%%%%%% set of places

png.set_of_Ps = {'pOC1','pC1','pOC2','pC2',...
                 'piM1','piM2','pR1','pR2',...
                 'poM1','poM2','pR4','piPS',...
                 'po1AS','po2AS','pi1AS','pi2AS', 'pR3',...
                 'poAS','piCK'};
png.set_of_Ts = {'tC1','tC1M1','tC2','tC2M2',...
    'tPCK','tM1','tM2','tPS', 'tM1AS','tM2AS','tAS','tAP'};
png.set_of_As = {'pC1','tC1',1, 'tC1','pOC1',1, ...    %tc1
                 'pR1','tC1M1',1,'pOC1','tC1M1',1, ... %tC1M1
                 'tC1M1','pC1',1,'tC1M1','piM1',1, ... %tC1M1
                 'piM1','tM1',1, 'tM1','poM1',1,...    %tM1
                 'po1AS','tM1AS',1, 'poM1','tM1AS',1, ... %tM1AS
                 'tM1AS','pR1',1, 'tM1AS','pi1AS',1, ...  %tM1AS
                 'pC2','tC2',1, 'tC2','pOC2',1, ...    %tc2
                 'pR2','tC2M2',1,'pOC2','tC2M2',1,...  %tC2M2
                 'tC2M2','pC2',1,'tC2M2','piM2',1,  ...%tC2M2
                 'piM2','tM2',1, 'tM2','poM2',1,...    %tM2
                 'po2AS','tM2AS',1, 'poM2','tM2AS',1,...   %tM2AS
                 'tM2AS','pi2AS',1, ...                    %tM2AS
                 'pi1AS','tAS',1, 'pi2AS','tAS',1, ... %tAS
                 'tAS','po1AS',1, 'tAS','po2AS',1, ... %tAS
                 'tAS','pR2',1, 'tAS','poAS',1, ...    %tAS
                 'pR3','tAS',1,... %tAS input
                 'piPS','tPS',1, 'pR4','tPS',1,...     %tPS
                 'tPS','piCK',1, 'tPS','pR4',1, ...    %tPS
                 'piCK','tPCK',1, 'tPCK','pR3',1,...   %tPCK
                 'poAS','tAP',1, 'tAP','piPS',1 ...    %tAP
                 };
```

Fig. 4.18 The PDF

improvement based on the equations given in the following subsection (Sect. 4.5.4 "GPenSIM for Performance Evaluation"). According to the suggestions, the performance (flow rate) of 0.07 tokens per TU can be achieved by enhancing the bottleneck (circuit number-2). The proposed enhancements are

1. To increase the sum of tokens by one (meaning adding one more robot/machine in parallel), and
2. To decrease the total delay by 6.7 TU (meaning to reduce the firing times of the robot/machine involved in circuit 4 by 6.7 TU).

The result also shows that there are no deadlocks (the Petri net is live) as each elementary circuit has at least one token.

```
global global_info
global_info.STOP_AT = 100; % stop simulation after 100 TU

pns = pnstruct('fms_pdf'); % the PDF

% intial markings
dyn.m0 = {'pC1',1,'pC2',1, 'pR1',1,'pR2',1,'pR4',1,'pR3',1, ...
          'po1AS',1, 'po2AS',1};
% firing times
dyn.ft = {'tC1',10,'tC2',10, 'tM1',5,'tM2',10, 'tAS',7,...
          'tPS',8, 'tPCK',3, 'allothers',2};
% create the initial dynamic Petri net structure
pni = initialdynamics(pns, dyn);

mincyctime(pni, 0.07); % find the minimum cycle
```

Fig. 4.19 The MSF

```
This is a Strongly Connected Petri net.

Cycle-1:    -> pC2 -> tC2 -> pOC2 -> tC2M2
TotalTD = 12    TokenSum = 1     Cycle Time = 12

Cycle-2:    -> tM2AS -> pi2AS -> tAS -> pR2 -> tC2M2 -> piM2 -> tM2 -> poM2
TotalTD = 21    TokenSum = 1     Cycle Time = 21

Cycle-3:    -> pC1 -> tC1 -> pOC1 -> tC1M1
TotalTD = 12    TokenSum = 1     Cycle Time = 12

Cycle-4:    -> pR1 -> tC1M1 -> piM1 -> tM1 -> poM1 -> tM1AS
TotalTD = 9    TokenSum = 1     Cycle Time = 9

Cycle-5:    -> po1AS -> tM1AS -> pi1AS -> tAS
TotalTD = 9    TokenSum = 1     Cycle Time = 9

Cycle-6:    -> pi2AS -> tAS -> po2AS -> tM2AS
TotalTD = 9    TokenSum = 1     Cycle Time = 9

Cycle-7:    -> pR4 -> tPS
TotalTD = 8    TokenSum = 1     Cycle Time = 8

Cycle-8:    -> poAS -> tAP -> piPS -> tPS -> piCK -> tPCK -> pR3 -> tAS
TotalTD = 20    TokenSum = 1     Cycle Time = 20
```

Fig. 4.20 Simulation result identifying the eight elementary cycles

```
Minimum-cycle-time is: 21, in cycle number-2


***  Token Flow Rate:   ***
In steady state, the firing rate of each transition is:
    1/C* = 0.047619
meaning, on average, 0.047619 tokens pass through
any node in the Petri net, per unit period of time.


*** We can increase the current flow rate to 0.05 tokens/TU,
    In the circuit-2 either:
    1. increase the sum of tokens by 1 tokens, or,
    2. decrease the total delay (firing times) by 1 TU.
```

Fig. 4.21 Simulation result showing minimum cycle and token flow rate

Table 4.2 GPenSIM functions for performance evaluation of Strongly Connected Event Graphs (SCEG)

GPenSIM function	Purpose
pnclass	Find out the class of Petri net
stronglyconn	Find out the number of strongly connected components in the Petri net
mincyctime	Finding the performance bottleneck in a SCEG
cycles	Extract the elementary circuits in a Petri net

4.5.4 GPenSIM for Performance Evaluation

In the MSF for the FMS, the function “mincyctime” was used for measuring the performance. However, the function “mincyctime” uses some other functions in return. Table 4.2 lists some of the GPenSIM functions that are exclusively for the performance evaluation of Strongly Connected Event Graphs (SCEG).

Function “pnclass” checks the class of a Petri net and returns a vector of flags representing the following information:

- Flag 1: whether the Petri net is a Binary Petri net or not (0 = not a binary Petri net).
- Flag 2: whether the Petri net is a State Machine or not (0 = not a State Machine).
- Flag 3: whether the Petri net is an Event Graph or not (0 = not an Event Graph).
- Flag 4: whether the Petri net is a Timed Petri net or not (0 = not a Timed Petri net).
- Flag 5: number of Strongly Connected Components in the Petri net.

Function “stronglyconn” returns the number of strongly connected components in a Petri net. If the returned value is a singleton, then the Petri net is strongly connected. There are several algorithms for finding strongly connected components, e.g., a simple two-pass depth-first search algorithm [2] and the recent and more efficient Rader’s method [7]. In GPenSIM, Rader’s method is implemented.

Function “mincyctime” returns the performance bottleneck (critical elementary circuit) of an SCEG. For finding the elementary circuits, this function makes use of the function “cycles”. The function mincyctime also suggests flow rate improvement if the optional input parameter “expected flowrate” is given. Given the current flowrate $r^* = [\sum(M(p_n))/\sum(dt_i)]$ of the critical circuit, the expected flowrate (efr) can be achieved by either:

- Increasing the token count of the critical circuit by $\Delta m0$, where $\Delta m0 = [efr \times \sum(dt_i)] - [\sum(M(p_n))]$; or
- Reducing the delay (total firing times) of the circuit by Δft, where $\Delta ft = [\sum(dt_i)] - -[\sum(M(p_n))/efr]$.

Function “cycles” finds the elementary circuits in a Petri net. There are several algorithms available for finding the elementary circuits, e.g., Tiernan and Tarjan’s method [9] and Johnson’s method [6]. However, the algorithm that is implemented in GPenSIM is a simple variant of the depth-first search technique. Even though this algorithm is not the most efficient, it is chosen because of its ease of implementation.

4.6 Colored Petri Nets with GPenSIM

In P/T Petri net, tokens residing inside a place are homogeneous. **Colored Petri net** is an extended Petri net that allow the distinction between tokens [5]. In colored Petri net, a token can has a data packet attached to it, and this data packet is called the token color. In some Petri net tools like CPN, data packets (color) can be any data type. However, tokens usually contain one data type only, referred to as the “color set” of the place.

GPenSIM allows only one type of “color set”, the set of ASCII text strings. Thus, compared to CPN, GPenSIM offers only a rudimentary facility for coloring tokens. However, this simple coloring mechanism, when combined with the enabling functions and global variables, usually facilitates modeling any complex, large-scale, real-world discrete event systems.

All the research in this book is done on Timed Petri nets. Since there will be some references in this book to colored Petri nets, the formal definition is given for the sake of completion.

Definition 4.1 **Colored Petri nets** is defined a nine-tuple [5]:

$$CPN = (P, T, A, M0, S, C_f, N_f, A_f, G_f, I_f),$$

where:

- $PTN = (P, T, A, M0)$ is a Marked Petri net,
- S is a set of color, containing the colors (c_i) and the operations on the colors.
- C_f is the color function that maps $p_i \in P$ into colors $c_i \in S$.
- N_f is the node function that maps A into $P \times T \cup T \times P$.
- A_f is the arc function that maps each flow (arc) $f \in F$ into the expression e.
- G_f is that guard function that maps each transition $t_i \in T$ to a guard expression g. The output of the guard expression should evaluate to Boolean value: true or false.
- I_f is the initialization function that maps each place $p_i \in P$ into an initialization expression. The initialization expression must evaluate to multiset of tokens with a color corresponding to the color of the place $C(p)$. □

Colored Petri net realization in GPenSIM

In comparison with CPN tool, realization of Colored Petri net in GPenSIM is somewhat simpler and crude. For example,

- In GPenSIM, the set of colors are limited to set of ASCII text strings whereas, in CPN, colors of any datatype can be added to tokens.
- Also in GPenSIM, the functions C_f, N_f, A_f, G_f, and I_f are all fused together and becomes the enabling function that is coded in the pre-processor files.
- In CPN, logical conditions can be imposed on places, transitions, and arcs. In GPenSIM, only transitions can process logical expressions.
- In CPN, the arc weights can dynamically change due to the value of the logic conditions attached to it. However, in GPenSIM, there is a clear separation of static and dynamic details (detailed explanation in given in Chap. 2). Once the static details are coded in the Petri net Definition File (PDF) file, the weights of the arc remain fixed as declared in the PDF.

Even with these simplifications (or perhaps, because of these simplifications), GPenSIM is being used to solve many industrial problems, as described in Sect. 2.6.

References

1. Baier C, Katoen J-P (2008) Principles of model checking. MIT Press
2. Cormen TH, Leiserson CE, Rivest RL, Stein C (2009) Introduction to algorithms, 3rd edn. The MIT Press
3. Davidrajuh R (2018) Modeling discrete-event systems with GPenSIM. Springer International Publishing, Cham
4. Davidrajuh R, Skolud B, Krenczyk D (2018) Performance evaluation of discrete event systems with GPenSIM. Computers 7(1):1–8
5. Jensen K (1993) Coloured Petri nets. In: IEE colloquium on discrete event systems: a new challenge for intelligent control systems. IET, pp 5–1
6. Johnson DB (1975) Finding all the elementary circuits of a directed graph. SIAM J Comput 4(1):77–84

7. Rader CM (2011) Connected components and minimum paths. In: Graph algorithms in the language of linear algebra. SIAM, pp 19–27
8. Sistla AP (1994) Safety, liveness and fairness in temporal logic. Form Asp Comput 6(5):495–511
9. Tiernan JC (1970) An efficient search algorithm to find the elementary circuits of a graph. Commun ACM 13(12):722–726

Part II
Design of Modular Petri Nets

Chapter 5
Literature Review on Modular Petri Nets

P/T Petri nets do not provide any support for modularization. Modular model building with Petri nets has a short history, starting with works in the late 1990s. This chapter presents an extensive literature review on this topic. The conclusions drawn from the literature study is summarized at the end of this chapter. These conclusions are the basis for the new design of Petri net modules presented in this book. The literature study presented in this chapter is a revised version of [11].

5.1 First-Generation Works: Ease of Modeling

References [8, 24] provide, already in the 1990s, a powerful technique for compression of Petri net modules. According to the reduction theorem by [8, 24], if a module is an event graph, and it has transitions as input and output ports, then the module can be compressed to become a much smaller module. References [8, 24] prove that an event graph that possesses only transitions as input and output ports, then it can be represented by a compact module in which the all internal transitions are removed, and also some internal places are removed. Hence, the whole model becomes a set of modules that are compact and connected together by a few buffering places (since the input and output ports are transitions, the connection between the modules must be places). Also, by the reduction theorem, the liveness and boundedness properties of the original modules are preserved.

Reference [13] is one of the early works on modular Petri nets. Reference [13] is concerned about a particular environment, which is the modeling and simulation of interfacing techniques in circuit boards. The paper proposed interfacing at every module level rather than keeping interfacing techniques in one specific module, which was the norm at that time. The paper state that keeping all the interfacing in one module makes communication between the modules unnecessarily complicated. This paper also proposed designing modules with two-level, the lower-level is for

R. Davidrajuh, *Petri Nets for Modeling of Large Discrete Systems*, Asset Analytics,
https://doi.org/10.1007/978-981-16-5203-5_5

Table 5.1 First-generation works on ease of modeling

Work	Topics
Savi and Xie [24] and Claver et al. [8]	Module compression
De and Lin [13]	Clear-cut interfacing
Wang [30] and Wang and Wu [31]	Object-oriented Petri nets
Lee et al. [21]	Decomposing a Petri net into modules based on functionality
Xue et al. [32]	Flexible manufacturing systems as systems with specific subsystems

transmission and synchronization of signals, and the higher-level for communication of messages, resulting in a new communicating Petri net model.

References [30, 31] introduced "Object-oriented Petri nets", to reap the benefits of object-oriented programming also in the modeling of discrete event systems. These works proposed an object-oriented model building approach in which the generic Petri net modules are declared as classes. Then, from the classes, the specific instances of modules are developed for modeling specific problems.

Reference [21] proposed a dual approach for dealing with modular systems. This paper proposed a strategy for identifying specific users and modules that only capture the logic interested to those particular users. In other words, the proposal was for a partition of a large model into separate modules that consist of model logic that will be of interest to those in specific interest areas.

Reference [32] took flexible manufacturing systems as systems with specific subsystems (called subnets). The subnets are identified as transportation of raw material & resources, machining subnets, and finishing subnets.

The contributions of the first-generation works are summarized in Table 5.1.

5.2 Second-Generation Works: Analysis

The first-generation works given in the previous sub-section are on reaping the benefits of the modular model building also with Petri nets. The second-generation works focused on easing the *analysis* of huge and complex Petri nets.

Reference [7] presented a modularization of Petri nets using *fusion places* and *fusion transitions*. Fusion places and fusion transitions are special types of places and transitions, respectively. These places and transitions are only to partition a Petri net model into modules and analyze them individually, due to the firings of the local (members of the module) transitions. For example, the state spaces of the individual modules can be obtained by the firing of the local transitions, starting with the initial markings on the local places. Then, from the individual state spaces, the overall state space of the model can be obtained by putting together the individual state spaces along with the additional state spaces (known as the "synchronization graph").

Synchronization graph connects the individual state spaces by the firing of the fusion transitions. The novelty of ref. [7] is that the authors prove that the modularization preserves the main properties of the model (e.g., the place invariants) while removing the need for generating the overall state space which usually suffers state explosion. Reference [7] also prove that the state space built by the modular approach is much smaller than the state space obtained from the holistic model.

Though fusion places and fusion transitions seem very useful for modular model building, they are against the fundamental concept behind modularization, namely "data hiding"; see the discussion in Chap. 6.

Reference [28] focused on reusable generic modules. This work believes that manufacturing systems consist of specific building blocks such as production line, assembly, disassembly, and parallel machining elements. Once these blocks are developed as generic modules, then by customizing these blocks to suit any specific needs, a model of the system could be built and analyzed. Thus, Ref. [28] reinforces the classical benefits of modularization such as speed and easiness of modeling, and easy adjustment to suit specific needs, as well as analysis. The author's earlier works such as Ref. [29] also focused on customizing generic modules with fuzzy logic to confront uncertainty in the modeling process.

Reference [19] proposed "reconfigurable modules" to tackle uncertainties associated with models. This work states that reconfigurable modules support model development, design variations, and cooperative model development. By reconfiguration, this work classifies the uncertainties into two groups such as variations and ambiguity. Variation in a process means, for example, an operation may take two to three minutes. Ambiguity in a process means, for example, the operation may happen or not depending on certain conditions. Reference [19] used stochastic modules for tackling variations and fuzzy logic for ambiguity, resulting in a new type of Petri net called a Fuzzy Colored Petri net with Stochastic time delay (FCPN-std).

Reference [18] discusses the managerial implications of modularization. This work discusses some issues in modularization, such as the use of "blocks" (modules) for easing the design process and the possibility of reusing the blocks. Also discussed is the issue of redesigning the model by trying out different combinations of modular blocks.

The contributions of the second-generation works are summarized in Table 5.2.

Table 5.2 Second-generation works on analysis of modular Petri nets

Work	Topics
Christensen and Petrucci (2000) [7]	State space analysis
Tsinarakis et al. (2005) [28]; Tsourveloudis et al. (2000) [29]	Reusable module for ease of analysis
Lee and Banerjee (2009) [19]	Reconfigurable modules to tackle uncertainties associated with models
Latorre-Biel et al. (2017) [18]	Managerial implications of modularization

5.3 Third-Generation Works: Applications and Tools

Reference [4] presents a tool known as "Exhost-PIPE", for modular timed and colored Petri nets. With the tool, the work shows how a multi-agent environment (e.g., a swarm robot or an aircraft crew) can be modeled and simulated. Reference [3] presents a modular Petri net model for modeling and simulation of molecular networks. In this work, proteins are represented as Petri net modules. Each module has an interface to access publicly available information about the intra-molecular changes; thus, the modules can update themselves independently. This work presents the design of the interface, the formalized language for modular communication, and the Petri net model of the molecular network.

A modular Petri net model of the "Spanish National Health System" is described in [22, 23]. References [22, 23] show the largeness and complexity of the Spanish Health System. These works show that without a modular approach, it would not be able to model and analyze such a large and complex system. In the modular model, each module is independently modeled, keeping the state-machine Petri net as the backbone for modeling the medical protocols. The modules can load the medical resources themselves. Reference [14] presents a modular p-timed (timing associated with places) Petri net model for analyzing traffic signal control of a network of intersections. This work also shows a light-weight approach for model checking with Linear Time Logic (LTL)-based specifications.

Reference [26] tries to model Non-Linear Process Planning (NLPP) in manufacturing systems with a modular Petri net known as Object Observable Petri Net (OOPN). The approach presented in this paper uses three steps. In the first step, the system resources are grouped into two groups: (1) processing resources (e.g., machine tools), and (2) part-flow resources (e.g., conveyor belts and buffers). It is an assumption in the approach that any machining activity uses at least one system resources. In the second step, the model is divided into modules, each module composed of resources with limited capacity. In the final step, each module is converted into a resource operation template (a Petri net module) adhering to the resource constraints. Reference [26] uses transitions as the input and output ports for communication between the modules; thus, the communication of a module with the outside world is streamlined through the input and output ports. Though the approach presented in this work is straightforward, and the resulting modules are simple and elegant, the overall model becomes huge. It is also not clear whether a tool (software) is available that can automatically perform the steps involved, or even development of such as a tool is feasible. Without a software tool, it will be impossible to model, even the simplest manufacturing system, with the approach proposed in this paper.

Reference [10] shows a modular Petri net-based approach for detection and elimination of redundancy in virtual enterprises. In the modular Petri net, each module represents one participating enterprise. The participating enterprises on the upstream are raw-material suppliers, part-suppliers, and transporting agents. On the downstream, distributors and sales agents are the participating enterprises. It is noteworthy that all these Petri net modules are event graphs. An event graph is a P/T Petri net in which each place has precisely one input transition and one output transition. Also, the interfaces of the modules are input and output ports that are transitions.

The approach by [10] is elegant as it introduces a clear-cut input and output ports that are transitions. The approach also proposes the use of colored Petri nets. Otherwise, it will be impossible to route a token from a buffering place to the correct module should more than one module is output to that buffering place. Also, forcing all the modules to be devised as event graphs can put a lot of strain on the modeler. This is because "the choice" cannot be modeled in an event graph, and a place gathering tokens from different transitions is also not possible.

Reference [15] presents a framework for performance evaluation of the intermodal transportation chain in Freight Transport Terminals. The framework is based on a modular timed Petri nets. In this timed Petri net, places represent resources, capacities, and conditions, whereas transitions represent activities such as inputs and flows into the terminal. Finally, tokens represent intermodal transport units. This work uses Generalized Mutual Exclusion Constraints (GMECs, [17]) for realizing the control elements, and the software HYPEN [25] for simulation. Reference [16] models and analyzes Web service composition. The reason for the analysis is to guarantee the timely completion of the web service. Hence, temporal constraints are emphasized in this work. The problem of state-space explosion is also addressed in this work, albeit not in a transparent manner. This work claims that the model is modular by showing some modules. However, the issue of modularity is not discussed in detail.

The contributions of the third-generation works are summarized in Table 5.3.

Table 5.3 Third-generation works on tools and application of modular Petri nets

Work	Topics
Bonnet-Torres et al. (2006) [4]	Tool: Exhost-PIPE Application: Modeling Multi-Agent environment
Blatke et al. (2011) [3]	Tool: Formal language for modular communication Application: Modeling Molecular Networks
Mahulea et al. (2012) [22]; Mahulea et al. (2018) [23]	Application: Modeling Spanish National Health System
Du et al. (2013) [16]	Application: Web Service Composition
Dotoli et al. (2016) [15]	Application: Evaluation of Intermodal Freight Transport Terminals
Dos and Vrancken (2012) [14]	Tool: Modular Place-Timed Petri net Application: Traffic signal control of network of intersections
Slota et al. (2016) [26]	Tool: Object Observable Petri net Application: Modeling non-linear process planning in manufacturing systems
Davidrajuh (2013) [10]	Tool: GPenSIM (earlier version)—modules with clear-cut input and output ports Application: Elimination of redundancy in virtual enterprises

5.4 Fourth-Generation Works: Independent Modules for Modeling Smart Manufacturing

In the era of **Smart manufacturing** and **Industry 4.0**, manufacturing systems are composed of interoperable intelligent systems. These intelligent systems are independent and exchange a great amount of data in real time with their counterparts that are located in geographically separated areas. Finally, smart manufacturing happens via the events that are triggered by networked sensors [5, 12, 20].

Reference [1] is a recent work that develops a modular Petri net for modeling "the availability of risks of IT threats" in Smart Factory Networks (SFN). First, the model is divided into two blocks, one for the information and control network (IN block), and the other for production network (PN block).

The IN block is hierarchical, consisting of three layers. A server is placed on the top layer, which is connected to many IT-service nodes in the middle layer. Each of the IT-service nodes is connected with several machine-control nodes in the bottom layer. These machine-control nodes are the ones that directly interact with the nodes in the PM block. The IN block is hierarchical in a sense each node is connected with several nodes in the lower layer (1:n connection). Whereas a node is connected with only one node in the layer above, forming a tree-like structure. All the nodes in the IN layer (called information component—IC) are the same, simple, and generic Petri net modules.

The PN block consists of nodes (called production machine components—PM) that are connected in a way to represent the logical production and flow of manufactured items. The PM components are also simple and generic Petri net modules. This means the whole model can be developed with just two simple Petri net modules: one IC module for the nodes in the IN block, and PM module for nodes in the PN block.

Perhaps the approach may solve the prescribed problem (namely, "modeling the availability of risks of IT threats in Smart Factory Networks"). However, the resulting model will be huge. This is because two types of simple generic Petri net modules are repeatedly used to compose any eventual functionality. Besides, the approach uses many Petri net extensions such as inhibitor arcs, reset arcs, and testing arcs. Though the use of these arcs paves a compact module, it prohibits the use of the readily available techniques and algorithms (e.g., for reachability graph). Unique algorithms have to be developed for the analysis of models developed by this approach. However, the availability of such special algorithms and the need for it is not discussed in [1]. The usefulness of this paper is the following; this paper introduces a separate hierarchical block (the IN block) that function as the inter-modular connector of the modules in the PM block.

5.5 Research Gap: Conclusions of Literature Study

The following conclusions can be drawn from the literature study on the works on modular Petri nets. These conclusions are treated as the research gap. The research gap, along with the research goals identified in Sect. 3.5 "Research Goals of this book", will be used in the latter sections on the design of a new modular Petri net.

- Advantages of modularizing: Literature study reveals that modularization is to reap the benefits such as flexibility (ability to add or change functionality), comprehensibility (readability of the models), reduction in the development time, and robustness (less prone to error).
- On the modularity of systems: Petri net models of real-life discrete event systems are large and complex. However, these large and complex systems can be modeled as modular models.
- On the scope of a module: A module can trap a specific type of model logic for particular users.
- On interfacing the modules: Old fashioned monolithic pathways (based on master or supervisor) interfacing is not appropriate for inter-modular communication. Interfacing must be at every module level, making the module independently react with the rest of the system and the environment.
- On the design of modules: Timed P/T Petri net can serve as the skeleton of the module. Colored Petri nets are for embedding more detailed data on tokens.
- Hard-wiring versus soft coding: Some of the model logic can be taken away from Petri net and programmed as logical conditions in software (e.g., as logic conditions in processor files). Moving the details from hard-wiring (Petri net) to soft coding (processor files) will make the Petri net less complicated. However, it will also make Petri net less expressive as well [9].
- On the synchronization of modules [2, 6, 7, 26, 27]:

- Fusion places: The fusion places are for modeling convenience as they are aliases for a place; the fusion places are to eliminate arcs crisscrossing the model. If the fusion places are put in different modules, since they represent the same place, these will be used to synchronize the modules.
- Substitution transition: A substitution transition is for information hiding; a substitution transition represents a complete Petri net module consisting of many places and transitions. Thereby, a substitution transition hides the lower-level details of a module on a higher-level (overall) model.
- Fusion Transitions: A fusion transition (some times referred to as "shared transition") is to allow synchronization of Petri net modules. The shared transitions reside in different modules, but they represent the same transition. Thus, the shared transitions synchronize the modules.
- Modular communication: Communication of a module with the outside world must be streamlined through input and output ports; transitions can be used as ports.

References

1. Berger S, Bogenreuther M, Häckel B, Niesel O (2019) Modeling availability risks of IT threats in smart factory networks-a modular Petri net approach, Twenty-Seventh European Conference on Information Systems (ECIS2019). Stockholm-Uppsala, Sweden, Association for Information Systems, AIS Electronic Library (AISeL), pp 1–17
2. Billington J, Christensen S, Van Hee K, Kindler E, Kummer O, Petrucci L, Post R, Stehno C, Weber M (2003) The Petri net markup language: concepts, technology, pp 483–505
3. Blätke MA, Meyer S, Marwan W (2011) Pain signaling-a case study of the modular Petri net modeling concept with prospect to a protein-oriented modeling platform. In: Proceedings of the 2nd international workshop on biological processes and petri nets (BioPPN 2011). Newcastle upon Tyne, United Kingdom, pp 1–19
4. Bonnet-Torrès O, Domenech P, Lesire C, Tessier C (2006) E xhost-pipe: pipe extended for two classes of monitoring Petri nets, pp 391–400
5. Brettel M, Friederichsen N, Keller M, Rosenberg M (2014) How virtualization, decentralization and network building change the manufacturing landscape: An industry 4.0 perspective. Int J Mech Ind Sci Eng 8(1):37–44
6. Bucci G, Vicario E (1995) Compositional validation of time-critical systems using communicating time Petri nets. IEEE Trans Softw Eng 21(12):969–992
7. Christensen S, Petrucci L (2000) Modular analysis of Petri nets. Comput J 43(3):224–242
8. Claver J, Harhalakis G, Proth J, Savi V, Xie X (1991) A step-wise specification of a manufacturing system using Petri nets. In: IEEE International Conference on systems, man, and cybernetics Conference proceedings 1991, IEEE, pp 373–378
9. Davidrajuh R (2011) Representing resources in Petri net models: Hardwiring or soft-coding? In: Proceedings of 2011 IEEE international conference on service operations. Logistics and Informatics, IEEE, pp 62–67
10. Davidrajuh R (2013) Distributed workflow based approach for eliminating redundancy in virtual enterprising. J Supercomput 63(1):107–125
11. Davidrajuh R (2019) A new modular Petri net for modeling large discrete-event systems: a proposal based on the literature study. Computers 8(4):83
12. Davis J, Edgar T, Porter J, Bernaden J, Sarli M (2012) Smart manufacturing, manufacturing intelligence and demand-dynamic performance. Comput Chem Eng 47:145–156
13. De Jong GG, Lin B (1994) A communicating Petri net model for the design of concurrent asynchronous modules. In: IEEE 31st design automation conference. IEEE, pp. 49–55
14. dos Santos Soares M, Vrancken J (2012) A modular Petri net to modeling and scenario analysis of a network of road traffic signals. Control Eng Pract 20(11):1183–1194
15. Dotoli M, Epicoco N, Falagario M, Cavone G (2015) A timed Petri nets model for performance evaluation of intermodal freight transport terminals. IEEE Trans Autom Sci Eng 13(2):842–857
16. Du Y, Tan W, Zhou M (2013) Timed compatibility analysis of web service composition: a modular approach based on Petri nets. IEEE Trans Autom Sci Eng 11(2):594–606
17. Giua A, DiCesare F, Silva M (1993) Petri net supervisors for generalized mutual exclusion constraints. IFAC Proc 26(2):379–382
18. Latorre-Biel JI, Jiménez-Macías E, García-Alcaraz JL, Muro JCS-D, Blanco-Fernandez J, Parte MPDL (2017) Modular construction of compact Petri net models. Int J Simul Process Model 12(6):515–524
19. Lee H, Banerjee A (2009) A modular Petri net based architecture to model manufacturing systems exhibiting resource and timing uncertainties, pp 525–530
20. Lee J, Bagheri B, Kao HA (2015) A cyber-physical systems architecture for industry 4.0-based manufacturing systems. Manufact Lett 3:18–23
21. Lee WJ, Cha SD, Kwon YR (1998) Integration and analysis of use cases using modular Petri nets in requirements engineering. IEEE Trans Software Eng 24(12):1115–1130
22. Mahulea C, García-Soriano JM, Colom JM (2012) Modular Petri net modeling of the spanish health system. In: Proceedings of 2012 IEEE 17th international conference on emerging technologies and factory automation (ETFA 2012), IEEE, pp 1–8

23. Mahulea C, Mahulea L, Soriano JMG, Colom JM (2018) Modular Petri net modeling of healthcare systems. Flex Serv Manuf J 30(1–2):329–357
24. Savi VM, Xie X (1992) Liveness and boundedness analysis for Petri nets with event graph modules, pp 328–347
25. Sessego F, Giua A, Seatzu C (2008) Hypens: a matlab tool for timed discrete, continuous and hybrid Petri nets, pp 419–428
26. Slota A, Zajkac J, Uthayakumar M (2016) Synthesis of Petri net based model of a discrete event manufacturing system for nonlinear process plan. Manage Prod Eng Rev 7(2):62–72
27. Song YJ, Lee JK (2000) Analysis of Petri net models using transitive matrix. In: 2000 IEEE International conference on systems, man and cybernetics. SMC 2000 Conference Proceedings cybernetics evolving to systems, humans, organizations, and their complex interactions (cat. no. 0, vol. 4, IEEE, pp. 3122–3127)
28. Tsinarakis GJ, Tsourveloudis N, Valavanis KP (2005) Modular Petri net based modeling, analysis, synthesis and performance evaluation of random topology dedicated production systems. J Intell Manuf 16(1):67–92
29. Tsourveloudis N, Dretoulakis E, Ioannidis S (2000) Fuzzy work-in-process inventory control of unreliable manufacturing systems. Inf Sci 127(1–2):69–83
30. Wang LC (1996) Object-oriented Petri nets for modelling and analysis of automated manufacturing systems. Comput Integr Manuf Syst 9(2):111–125
31. Wang LC, Wu SY (1998) Modeling with colored timed object-oriented Petri nets for automated manufacturing systems. Comput Ind Eng 34(2):463–480
32. Xue Y, Kieckhafer R, Choobineh F (1998) Automated construction of gspn models for flexible manufacturing systems. Comput Ind 37(1):17–25

Chapter 6
Toward Developing a New Modular Petri Net

With the conclusion from the literature study done in the previous chapter (Sect. 5.5 "Research Gap: Conclusions of Literature Study") and the research goals identified in Sect. 3.5 "Research Goals of this book", this chapter takes the first attempt to design a modular Petri net. This chapter introduces the main elements of a modular Petri net, such as Petri modules and Intern-Modular Components (IMC). Also, the input and out ports (IO ports) of a module are introduced. The material presented in this chapter is an extended version of [3].

Table 6.1 summarizes the history of research and development on modular Petri nets. It started with ease of modeling with modules and then advanced to the analysis of large Petri nets with modular nets. Then, the tools were made available, and some applications began to appear. Finally, the modular approach is tried for reducing the complexities in cyber-physical systems in Industry 4.0.

This book is to design a modular Petri net belonging to the fourth generation that is capable of

- Independent development of modules and analysis (to reduce the complexity of development and analysis of the overall model).
- The modules must be capable of running independently, presumably on different processors (CPU, to reduce the computation time).

6.1 Toward Independent Development of Modules

Let us study the modular approach realized with fusion places and fusion transitions in [1]. To understand how the methodology works, let us consider the example of a Resource Allocation System (RAS) given in [1] and also shown in Fig. 6.1.

As the example of fusion places-based modular model building, the RAS is remodeled into a two-modules-based modular system shown Fig. 6.2.

In the modular RAS shown in Fig. 6.2, the two modules A and B are synchronized by the fusion places R_X and R_Y. By the definition of fusion places, the places R_X in the different modules is the same. If any changes happen to a place R_X in one

R. Davidrajuh, *Petri Nets for Modeling of Large Discrete Systems*, Asset Analytics,
https://doi.org/10.1007/978-981-16-5203-5_6

Table 6.1 Literature on Modular Petri nets

Generation	Topics
First generation	**Ease** of modeling
Second generation	**Analysis** of large Petri nets
Third generation	**Tools** for modeling modular Petri nets, and **applications**
Fourth generation	**Modules**: Modeling large discrete event systems with modules

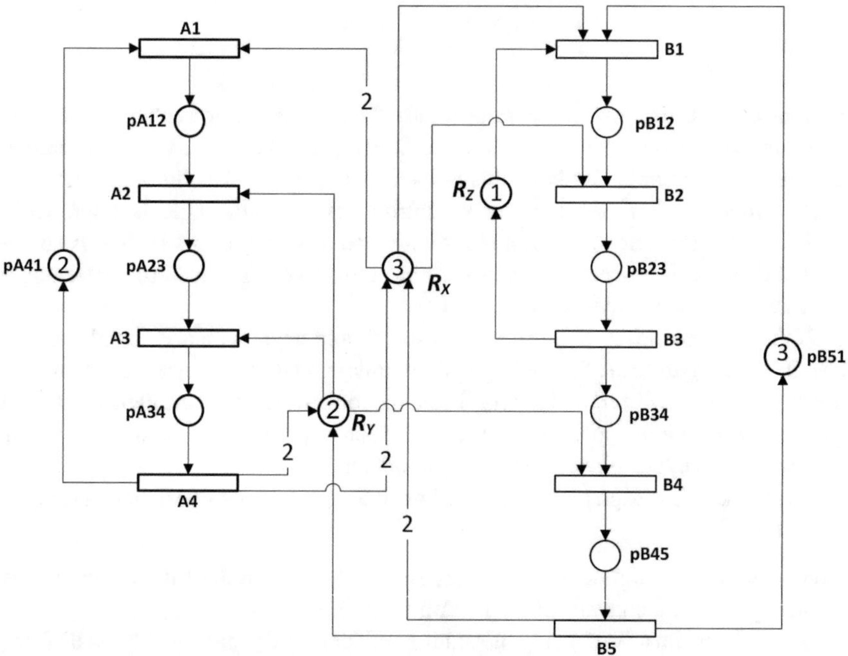

Fig. 6.1 Resource allocation system [1]

module, the other R_X in the other module will also be affected. This kind of sharing of local members of modules between the modules hampers independent module development.

Let us assume that independent groups develop these two modules. However, due to the sharing R_X and R_Y, the developers of module-A should always be aware of R_X and R_Y in module-B, making the development less independent. The exposure of internal details to the outside world is also against the concept of "data hiding", which is an important concept in modularity.

Modular model development using fusion transition works very similar to fusion places, and the only difference is that the (fusion) transitions are shared rather than

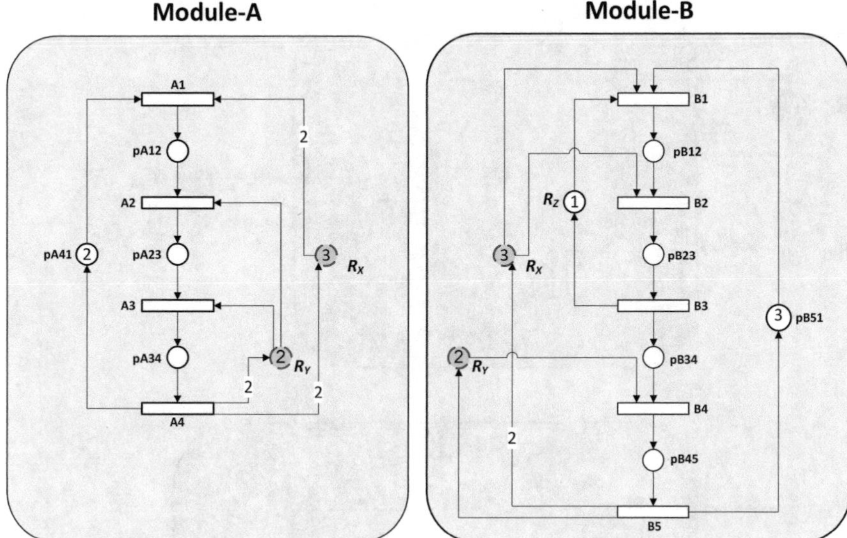

Fig. 6.2 Modularization using fusion places [1]

the places. Hence, here too, the modular model building is prone to internal data exposure, hindering data hiding and independent model development.

Can the modules that are shown in Fig. 6.2 be improved to become more "modular", following the better practices of module making?

The subsequent sections present the complete design details of a new modular Petri net. As a quick introduction, Fig. 6.3 shows a modular version; in this modular model, RAS is composed of two modules, module-A and module-B, and the **Inter-Modular Connector (IMC)** that consists of just the three places representing the resources R_X, R_Y, and R_Z. The modular model supports data hiding, clear-cut interfacing, and suited for parallel execution:

- Interface to the module: Module-A possesses input ports (A1, tD1, and tD2) and output ports (A4) that function as the input and output interface of the module. The input and out ports have global visibility and can be accessed like global variables.
- Data hiding: Module-A also possesses local members (transitions A2 and A3, and places pA12, pA23, pA34, pD1, and pD2) that have local (modular) visibility, thus can not be seen or accessed outside the module.
- Independent module development: As seen in Fig. 6.3, module-A can be independently developed, with two drivers replacing the places R_X and R_Y, and two stubs[1] also replacing the places R_X and R_Y.

[1] Drivers and Stubs: during testing, a module can be fed or input from a driver (source). Also, output of a module can be collected by a stub (or sink).

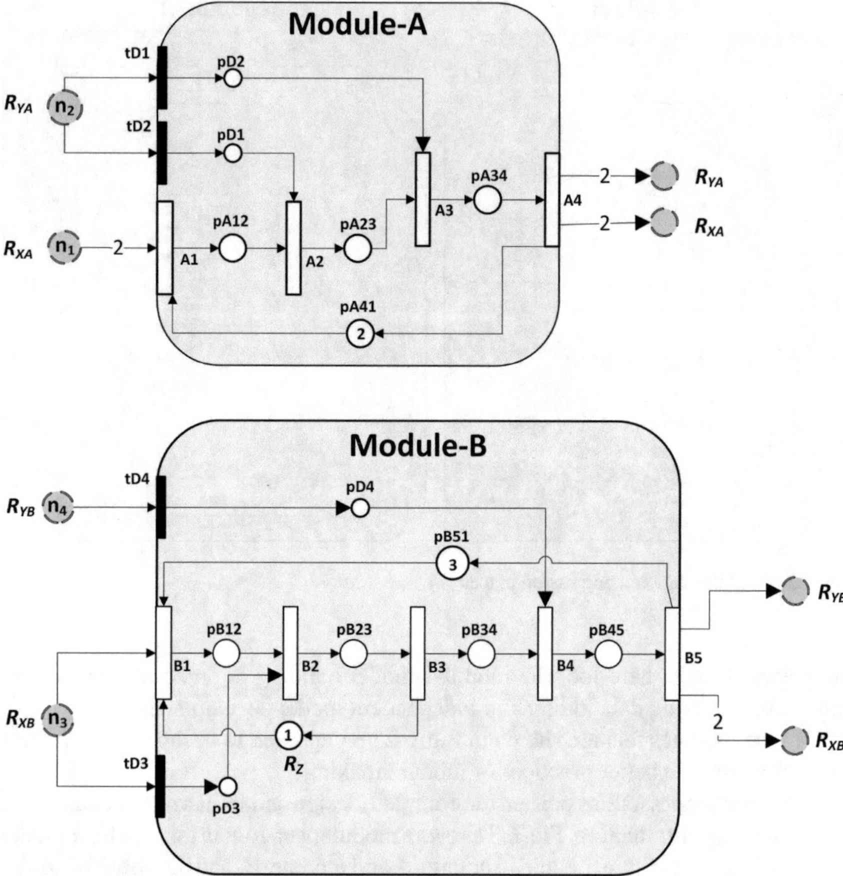

Fig. 6.3 Modular Petri net model of RAS: a proposal

6.2 Design of Modular Petri Nets

The previous section presented some conclusions drawn from the literature study. Partly based on these conclusions, and with the addition of new (modern) ideas, this section presents the unique design of a new Modular Petri net. At this juncture, it must be emphasized that the approach for modular Petri net given in this and the following sections are specially designed for GPenSIM implementation. The theory that is given in this book and its implementation in the software GPenSIM grew together. Hence, the use of GPenSIM terminology (see [2]) in this book is unavoidable.

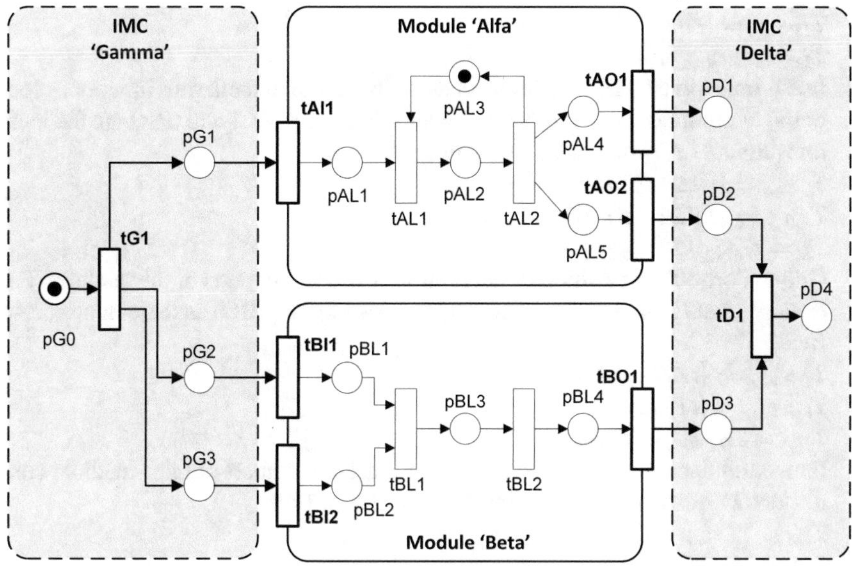

Fig. 6.4 A modular Petri net with two modules and two IMCs

6.2.1 *Composition of Modular Petri Nets*

A modular Petri net consists of one or more **Petri Modules**. The symbol Φ represents a Petri module. Zero or more **Inter-Modular Connectors** connects these Petri modules. The symbol Ψ represents an inter-modular connector.

Figure 6.4 shows a modular Petri net with two Petri modules "Alfa" and "Beta", and two Inter-Modular Connectors (IMCs) "Gamma" and "Delta".

What are IMCs? When a modular model is developed, it happens that there exist one or more elements that cannot be included in any of the modules. The reason can be that the model logic of the modules excludes the inclusion, or simply, the element is an inter-module connector. For simplicity, these "leftover" elements can be grouped into a segment (or segments) and be called an IMC (IMCs).

6.2.2 *Transitions in Modular Petri Nets*

There are four types of transitions in modular Petri nets (see Fig. 6.4):

1. Input Ports: The transitions that function as the input ports of the modules. For example, tAI1 is the input port of Alfa. tBI1 and tBI2 are the input ports of Beta. Thus,
   $T_{IP\Phi_{\text{Alfa}}} = \{tAI1\}$

$T_{IP\Phi_{\text{Beta}}} = \{tBI1, tBI2\}$
$T_{IP} = T_{IP\Phi_{\text{Alfa}}} \cup T_{IP\Phi_{\text{Beta}}}$

2. Local transitions: The transitions that are internal members (not input or output ports) of modules. For example, tAL1 and tAL2, and tBL1 and tBL2 are the local transitions of Alfa and Beta, respectively.
   $T_{L\Phi_{\text{Alfa}}} = \{tAL1, tAL2\}$
   $T_{L\Phi_{\text{Beta}}} = \{tBL1, tBL2\}$
   $T_L = T_{L\Phi_{\text{Alfa}}} \cup T_{L\Phi_{\text{Beta}}}$
3. Output Ports: The transitions that function as the output ports of the modules. For example, tAO1 and tAO2 are the output ports of Alfa. tBO1 is the output port of Beta.
   $T_{OP\Phi_{\text{Alfa}}} = \{tAO1, tAO2\}$
   $T_{OP\Phi_{\text{Beta}}} = \{tBO1\}$
   $T_{OP} = T_{OP\Phi_{\text{Alfa}}} \cup T_{OP\Phi_{\text{Beta}}}$
4. Inter-Modular transitions: The transitions that are members of Inter-modular connectors. For example, tG1 in Gamma, and tD1 in Delta.
   $T_{IM\Psi_{\text{Gamma}}} = \{tG1\}$
   $T_{IM\Psi_{\text{Delta}}} = \{tD1\}$
   $T_{IM} = T_{IM\Psi_{\text{Gamma}}} \cup T_{IM\Psi_{\text{Detla}}}$

$T_{\Phi_{\text{Alfa}}} = T_{IP\Phi_{\text{Alfa}}} \cup T_{L\Phi_{\text{Alfa}}} \cup T_{OP\Phi_{\text{Alfa}}}$ (all the transitions of Alfa)
$T_{\Phi_{\text{Beta}}} = T_{IP\Phi_{\text{Beta}}} \cup T_{L\Phi_{\text{Beta}}} \cup T_{OP\Phi_{\text{Beta}}}$ (all the transitions of Beta)
$T = T_{IP} \cup T_L \cup T_{OP} \cup T_{IM}$ (the set of all transitions in the Petri net)
Also, $T = T_{\Phi_{\text{Alfa}}} \cup T_{\Phi_{\text{Beta}}} \cup T_{IM}$ (the set of all transitions in the Petri net)

There are two types of places in modular Petri nets (see Fig. 6.4):

1. Local places: The places that are local to modules. For example, pAL1 to pAL5 in Alfa, and pBL1 to pBL4 in Beta.
   $P_{L\Phi_{\text{Alfa}}} = \{pAL1, \ldots, pAL5\}$ (local places of Alfa)
   $P_{L\Phi_{\text{Beta}}} = \{pBL1, \ldots, pBL4\}$ (local places of Beta)
   $P_L = P_{L\Phi_{\text{Alfa}}} \cup P_{L\Phi_{\text{Beta}}}$ (local places of all the modules)
2. Inter-Modular places (P_{IM}): The places that are members of IMCs. For example, pG1 to pG3 in Gamma, and pD1 to pD4 in Delta.
   $P_{IM\Psi_{\text{Gamma}}} = \{pG1, \ldots, pG3\}$ (IM places of Gamma)
   $P_{IM\Psi_{\text{Delta}}} = \{pD1, \ldots, pD4\}$ (IM places of Delta)
   $P_{IM} = P_{IM\Psi_{\text{Gamma}}} \cup P_{IM\Psi_{\text{Detla}}}$ (IM places of all IMCs)

   $P = P_L \cup P_{IM}$ (set of all the places in the Petri net)

6.2.3 Visibility of Transitions in a Modular Petri Net

Transitions in modular Petri nets have three different visibility, such as **global visibility**, **local** (or **modular**) **visibility**, and **private visibility**:

1. Inter-modular transitions have global visibility: All the transitions of the inter-modular connectors ($\forall t \in T_{IM}$) have global visibility, and thus are accessible in COMMON_PRE and COMMON_POST.
2. Input and output ports have global visibility: All the transitions that are input or output ports of modules ($\forall t \in (T_{IP} \cup T_{OP})$) also have global visibility, and thus are accessible in COMMON_PRE and COMMON_POST.
3. Local transitions have modular visibility: Transitions that are local members of modules ($\forall t \in T_L$) have local visibility as they are accessible only in their modular processors **MOD_PRE** & **MOD_POST**. For example, transitions tAL1 and tAL2 (tBL1 and tBL2) are local members of the modules **Alfa** (resp. **Beta**), and hence are accessible only in their modular processors MOD_**Alfa**_PRE, MOD_**Alfa**_POST (resp. MOD_**Beta**_PRE, MOD_**Beta**_POST).
However, these local transitions are not accessible in COMMON_PRE and COMMON_POST, as these transitions do not possess global visibility.
4. Input and output ports have modular visibility too: Transitions that are input or output ports of modules ($\forall t \in (T_{IP} \cup T_{OP})$) are also members of their respective modules. Hence, they are accessible in their respective MOD_PRE and MOD_POST files too. For example, input port tAI1 is accessible in COMMON_PRE and COMMON_POST (global visibility). As the input port of Alfa, tAI1 is accessible in MOD_Alfa_PRE and MOD_Alfa_POST too (modular visibility).
5. Every transition in a modular Petri net ($\forall t \in T$) has its private visibility. Any transition, be a local member, input or output port of a module, or a member of an inter-modular connector, can have its own processor files. For example, tG1, tAI1, tBO1, tBL2 are accessible in their own processor files, such as tG1_pre & tG1_post, tAI1_pre & tAI1_post, tBO1_pre & tOB2_post, and tBL2_pre & tBL2_post, respectively, if these files exist.

References

1. Christensen S, Petrucci L (2000) Modular analysis of Petri nets. The Comput J 43(3):224–242
2. Davidrajuh R (2018) Modeling discrete-event systems with GPenSIM. Springer International Publishing, Cham
3. Davidrajuh R (2019) A new modular Petri net for modeling large discrete-event systems: a proposal based on the literature study. Computers 8(4):83

Chapter 7
Design of a New Modular Petri Nets

This chapter presents complete details about modular Petri nets, providing the formal definitions to all the elements (such as Petri Module, Inter-Modular Connector, and the modular Petri net). An application example on modular Petri net is also given in Sect. 7.4. Some technical issues like hosting the different modules on different computers are discussed in the final section.

The important goals of the new design [3]:

- Data hiding: Data hiding inside modules is to abstract away the internal details at higher levels.
- Independent modules: The modules are independent of each other, and have the potential to become autonomous.
- Synchronization of modules: Synchronization ensures that modules must be able to run on different processors. For example, modules are wrapped as agents and run in parallel in a swarm environment.

Because of these goals (data hiding, independence, parallel execution), *fusion places* and *fusion transitions* are not supported in the new design. Fusion places cannot be allowed, as fusion places allow places in different modules to share internal information. Fusion transitions are not needed either, as in the new design, synchronization is realized at the input or output ports of modules or inside the inter-modular connectors (outside the modules).

7.1 Petri Module

In the new design, as shown in Fig. 6.4, **modular Petri net model** in GPenSIM consists of one or more **Petri Modules**. The Petri modules are self-contained and can be developed in isolation and independently tested. The inter-modular connector (IMC, for short) is to connect the modules together.

R. Davidrajuh, *Petri Nets for Modeling of Large Discrete Systems*, Asset Analytics,
https://doi.org/10.1007/978-981-16-5203-5_7

A Petri module has four distinct sets of elements:

1. **Input ports** T_{IP}: Input port transitions function as the input gates of a module. **Only through these transitions (input ports), tokens can be directed into the module**. These input port transitions have global visibility (accessible in COMMON_PRE and COMMON_POST). Also, due to the belonging to a module, these transitions have local visibility too (accessible in their own modular MOD_PRE and MOD_POST).
2. **Output ports** T_{OP}: Output port transitions function as the output gates of a module. **Only through these transitions (output ports), tokens can be directed away from the module**. Just like the input port transitions, these output port transitions also have global visibility (can be accessed in COMMON_PRE and COMMON_POST), and local visibility too (accessible in the modular MOD_PRE and MOD_POST).
3. **Local transitions** T_L: As the local member (internal element) of a module, a local transition consumes tokens from local input places and deposits tokens into local output places. A local transition cannot have any direct connection with the external places (places outside the modules).
   The local transitions of a module have limited visibility (only modular visibility) as these can be accessed only in the modular MOD_PRE and MOD_POST. The local transitions are not accessible in the global COMMON_PRE and COMMON_POST processors.
4. **Local places** P_L: As the local member of a module, a local place feeds tokens to either local transitions or input and output ports of the module. A local place gets tokens from either local transitions or input and output ports of the module. A local place cannot have any direct connection with the external transitions.

7.2 Inter-Modular Connectors

In the new design, as shown in Fig. 6.4, a modular Petri net model in GPenSIM consists of zero or more **Inter-Modular Connectors** (IMC, for short). The IMCs are not modules thus don't possess the input and output ports. They possess **Inter-Modular transitions** (IM transitions, for short) and **Inter-Modular places** (IM places, for short):

- **IM transitions** T_{IM}: IM transitions have global visibility and are accessible in the COMMON_PRE and COMMON_POST processors. Since IMCs are not modules, these transitions don't have the modular processors MOD_PRE and MOD_POST.
- **IM places** P_{IM}: just like the local places inside the modules, the IM places are passive too.

7.3 Formal Definitions for the New Entities

This section presents the formal definitions for the newly designed entities. Let a marked Petri net **PTN** be defined as a four-tuple: $PTN = (P, T, A, M_0)$.

7.3.1 Formal Definition of Petri Module

Definition 7.1 A **Petri Module** is defined as a six-tuple:

$$\Phi = (P_{L\Phi}, T_{IP\Phi}, T_{L\Phi}, T_{OP\Phi}, A_\Phi, M_{\Phi 0}),$$

where,

- $T_{IP\Phi} \subseteq T$: $T_{IP\Phi}$ is known as the input ports of the module.
- $T_{L\Phi} \subseteq T$: $T_{L\Phi}$ is known as the local transitions of the module.
- $T_{OP\Phi} \subseteq T$: $T_{OP\Phi}$ is known as the output ports of the module.
- $T_{IP\Phi}$, $T_{L\Phi}$, and $T_{OP\Phi}$, are all mutually exclusive: $T_{IP\Phi} \cap T_{L\Phi} = T_{L\Phi} \cap T_{OP\Phi} = T_{OP\Phi} \cap T_{IP\Phi} = \emptyset$.
- $T_\Phi = T_{IP\Phi} \cup T_{L\Phi} \cup T_{OP\Phi}$ (the transitions of the module).
- $P_{L\Phi} \subseteq P$ is known as the set of local places of the module. Since a module has only local places, $P_\Phi \equiv P_{L\Phi}$.
- $\forall p \in P_{L\Phi}$,
  - $\bullet p \in (T_\Phi \cup \emptyset)$. Input transitions of local places are either the transitions of the module or none (none means a local place can be a source, without any input transition).
  - $p\bullet \in (T_\Phi \cup \emptyset)$. Output transitions of local places are either the transitions of the module or none (none means a local place can be a sink, without any output transition). This means, local places cannot have direct connections with external transitions.
- $\forall t \in T_{L\Phi}$,
  - $\bullet t \in (P_{L\Phi} \cup \emptyset)$. Input places of local transitions are either the local places or none (none here means that a local transition can be a cold start (a source), without any input places).
  - $t\bullet \in (P_{L\Phi} \cup \emptyset)$. Output places of local transitions either the local places or none (none means the local transition is a sink, without any output places).
- $\forall t \in T_{IP\Phi}$,
  - $\bullet t \in (P_{L\Phi} \cup P_{IM} \cup \emptyset)$ (input places of input ports can be local places or places in inter-modular connectors or can be even an empty set).
  - $t\bullet \in (P_{L\Phi} \cup \emptyset)$ (output places of input ports can only be local places, or empty set).

- $\forall t \in T_{OP\Phi}$,
  - $\bullet t \in (P_{L\Phi} \cup \emptyset)$ (input places of output ports can be local places or an empty set).
  - $t\bullet \in (P_{L\Phi} \cup P_{IM} \cup \emptyset)$ (output places of output ports can be local places or places in inter-modular connectors or empty set).
- $A_\Phi \subseteq (P_L \times T_\Phi) \cup (T_\Phi \times P_L)$: where $a_{ij} \in A_\Phi$ is known as the internal arcs of the module.
- $M_{\Phi 0} = [M(p_L)]$ is the initial markings in the local places. □

7.3.2 *Formal Definition of Inter-Modular Connector*

Definition 7.2 An **Inter-modular Connector (IMC)** is defined as a four-tuple:

$$\Psi = (P_\Psi, T_\Psi, A_\Psi, M_{\Psi 0})$$

where

- $P_\Psi \subseteq P$: P_Ψ is the set of places in the IMC (known as the IM places). $\forall p \in P_\Psi$,
  - $\bullet p \in (T_{OP} \cup T_\Psi \cup \emptyset)$ (input transitions of IM places are either the output ports of modules, IM transitions of this IMC, or none).
  - $p\bullet \in (T_{IP} \cup T_\Psi \cup \emptyset)$ (output transitions of IM places are either the input ports of modules, IM transitions of this IMC, or none). This means, IM places cannot have direct connections with local transitions, or IM transitions of other IMCs.
- $\forall p \in P_\Psi$, $\forall i\ p \notin P_{\Phi_i}$ (an IM place cannot be a local place of any Petri module).
- $T_\Psi \subseteq T$: T_Ψ is the transitions of the IMC (known as the IM transitions). $\forall t \in T_\Phi$,
  - $\bullet t \in (P_\Psi \cup \emptyset)$ (input places of IM transitions are either the IM places of this IMC, or none (cold start)).
  - $t\bullet \in (P_\Psi \cup \emptyset)$ (output places of IM transitions either the IM places of this IMC, or none (sink)).
- $\forall t \in T_\Psi$, $\forall i\ t \notin T_{\Phi_i}$ (an IM transition cannot be a transition of any Petri module).
- $A_\Psi \subseteq (P_\Psi \times (T_\Psi \cup T_{IP})) \cup ((T_\Psi \cup T_{OP}) \times P_\Psi)$: where $a_{ij} \in A_\Psi$ is known as the IMC arcs.
- $M_{\Psi 0} = [M(p_\Psi)]$ is the initial markings in the IM places. □

7.3.3 *Formal Definition of Modular Petri Net*

Definition 7.3 A **Modular Petri net** is defined as a two-tuple:

$$MPN = (\mathbb{M}, C)$$

where

- $\mathbb{M} = \sum_{i=1}^{m} \Phi_i$ (one or more Petri Modules).
- $\mathcal{C} = \sum_{j=0}^{n} \Psi_j$ (zero or more Inter-Modular Connectors). □

7.4 Application Example: A Modular Petri Net

In this application example, a modular Petri net model is developed for a system involved in computing a quadratic function (e.g., $f = ax^2 + bx + c$). This example is an extended version of the problem stated in [2].

7.4.1 The Problem: Computing a Quadratic Function

The system possesses three communicating agents such as the *client*, and the two workers such as the *multiplier* and the *adder*.

1. The client provides the job to compute, providing the values of the parameters involved (such as a, b, and c).
2. The multiplier performs multiplications. For example, for an input (a, x, x), multiplier returns $(a \cdot x^2)$. Similarly, if (b, x) is input, multiplier returns $(b \cdot x)$.
3. The adder computes the arithmetic sums. For example, for an input (x, y, z), adder returns the sum $(x + y + z)$.

Figure 7.1 shows the sequence diagram describing the sequences of messages and acknowledgements between the three agents that are involved in performing the job collaboratively.

7.4.2 Petri Module of a Communicating Agent

Three main functional entities are usually part of a communicating agent [2]:

1. Observation.
2. Process the inputs and make decisions.
3. Actions.

Thus, the three main functional entities are also represented by some transitions in the Petri module (Fig. 7.2):

- Transition *tCreatMsg* is for creating a message, and *tDispMsg* dispatches the messages. A copy of the transmitted message is kept in the place *pDispdMsg* until the acknowledgement for the message is received.

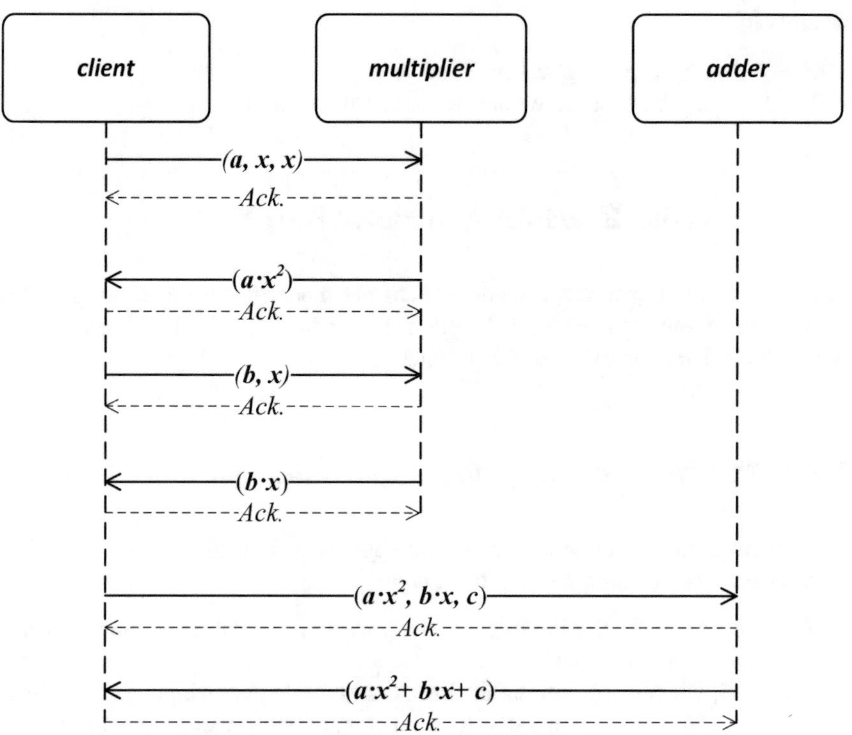

Fig. 7.1 The messages and interactions between the agents

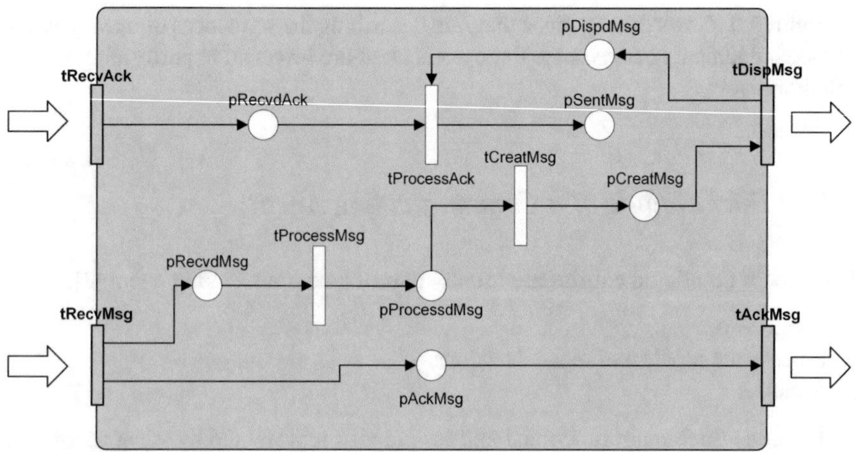

Fig. 7.2 Generic Petri module of a communicating agent

Table 7.1 Elements of the generic Petri module for communicating agent

Element	Purpose
tRecvAck	Receives acknowledgements
pRecvdAck	Buffer for received acknowledgements
tProcessAck	Processes received acknowledgements
pSentMsg	Buffer for storing sent messages
tCreatMsg	Creates new messages
pCreatedMsg	Buffer for newly created messages
tDispMsg	Dispatches messages
pDispdMsg	Dispatched messages are kept until Ack. are received
tRecvMsg	Receives messages
pRecvdMsg	Buffer for newly received messages
tProcessMsg	Processes received messages
tProcessdMsg	Buffer for storing processed messages
pAckMsg	Buffer for keeping Ack. before dispatch
tAckMsg	Sends acknowledgement for the received messages

- Transition *tRecvMsg* receives the messages. Acknowledgement for the received messages is sent by *tAckMsg*. *tProcessMsg* is for processing the arrived message.
- Transition *tRecvAck* is for receiving an acknowledgement for the message that was sent earlier. When an acknowledgement is received then the corresponding message (copy of the message) is removed from the buffer *pDispdMsg*.

Table 7.1 explains the functions of the elements of the Petri module for communicating agent.

7.4.3 Modular Petri Net Model

The modular Petri net model is shown in Fig. 7.3. Figure 7.3 shows that the three agents are represented by Petri modules that are connected via an IMC. All the messages and acknowledgments are passed between the agents in the form of tokens. The data (the values of the parameters in the quadratic function a, b, c, and x), the computed values, and the acknowledgements are attached to the tokens as colors. Thus, a Colored Petri net is the backbone of the model.

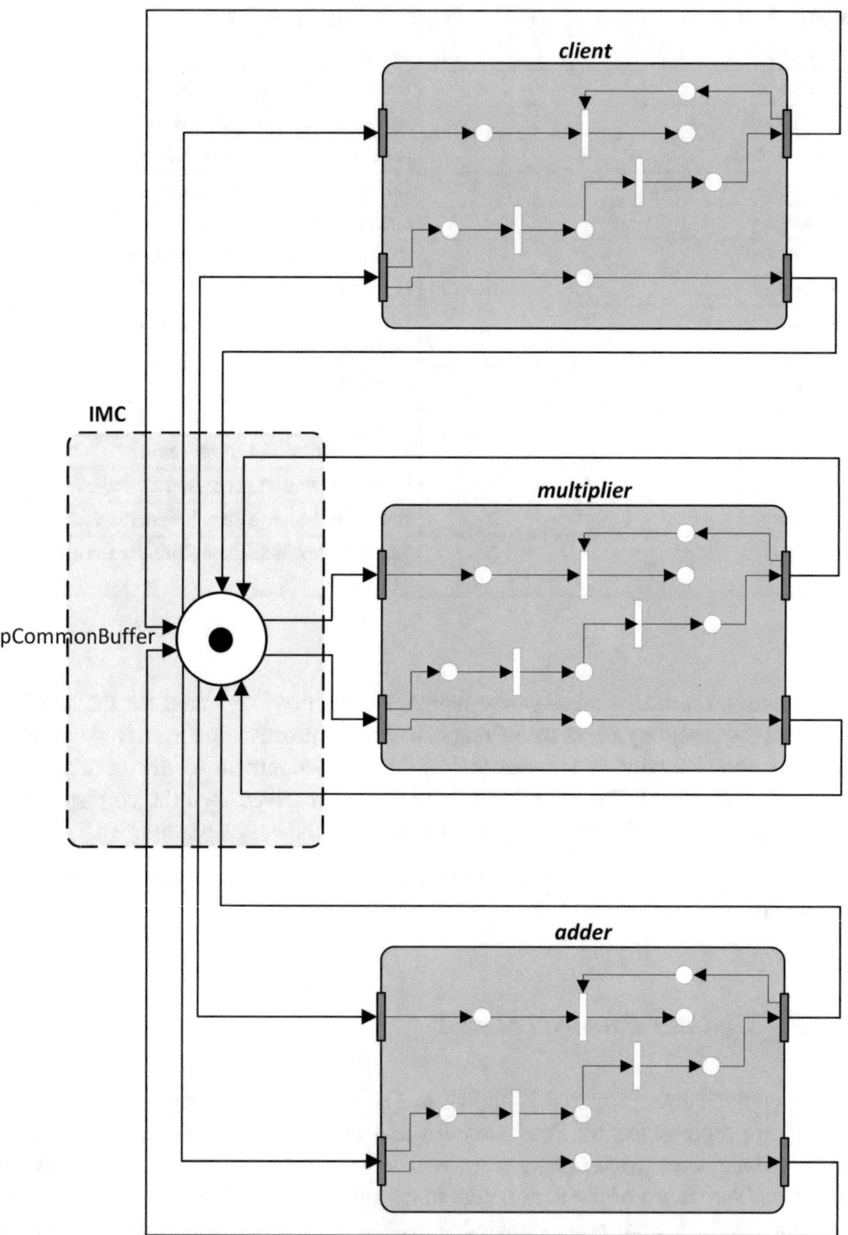

Fig. 7.3 The modular Petri model

7.5 Chapter Summary

This chapter presents a new modular Petri net that is designed especially for modeling discrete event systems that result in large Petri net models. With this modular Petri net, a large model can be decomposed into modules, and these modules can be developed, analyzed, and run independently.

The design approach presented in this chapter advocates the use of transitions as the input and output ports of modules. The use of transitions as input and output ports provides the following benefits:

- Active push/pull: Transitions functioning as the input ports can actively pull the tokens from the outside buffers. Hence, these tokens need not be inserted into the modules, by some other external (residing outside the module) transitions. If external transitions inject tokens into a module, it can be considered as a violation of data hiding. Also, input ports of a module actively pulling the tokens (e.g., messages) into the modules from the common buffers (which are outside the module) is a vital mechanism without which developing intelligent agents with Petri nets will be impossible. Intelligent agents are supposed to act autonomously. In other words, transitions as input and output ports of modules enable the development of independent agents in a peer-to-peer topology.
  In a similar line, transitions functioning as the output ports can flush the output tokens out of the modules into the output buffers. Also, no external transitions can grab the tokens from inside the module. This property is also important for modeling independent and autonomous modules (e.g., intelligent agents).
- Compression of model: As discussed in the section on literature study, Savi and Xie [6] presents a powerful technique for module compression, only if the module possesses transitions as input and out ports. However, this technique also demands that the module is modeled as an event-graph.

Also, simulation time will be large when the modules are run together as one monolithic model on one host (computer or CPU). If the modules are run in parallel on different computers, then the execution time of the modules will drop drastically. Figure 7.4 shows the three modules in Fig. 7.3 running on three different computers, reducing the overall execution time. Figure 7.4 shows that the modules (client, multiplier, and adder) can send and receive tokens as messages through the TCP/IP socket.

Figure 7.4 also shows that hosting the IMC place **pCommonBuffer** on a separate computer needs some adaption. A place (e.g., pCommonBuffer) cannot pull or flush tokens by itself. Some transitions must be introduced as IO ports to get (push) messages from (resp. to) the TCP/IP socket. Note: the operating system, networking, and hardware details are abstracted away in Fig. 7.4, focusing only on the exchange of tokens as messages over the TCP/IP-based communication channel.

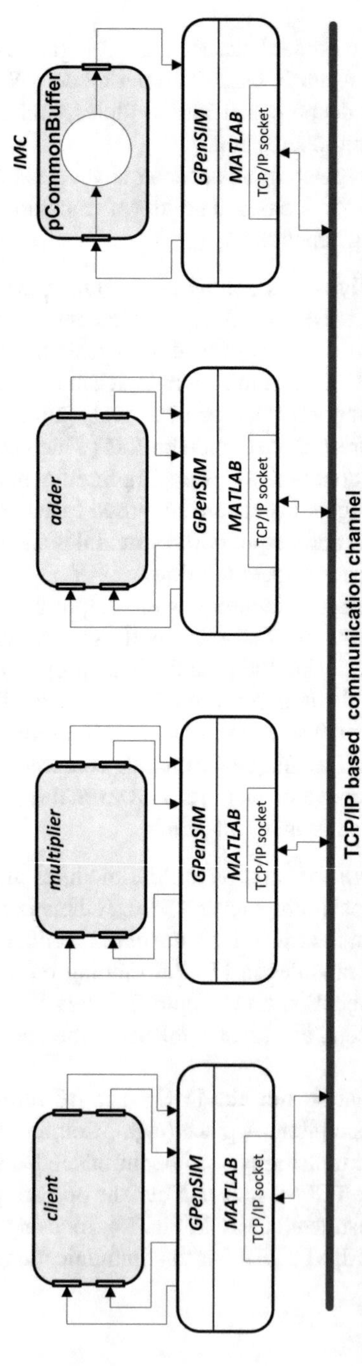

Fig. 7.4 Parallel execution of modules

7.5.1 Technical Notes on TCP/IP Based Communication

The inter-modular communication shown in Fig. 7.4 is based on TCP/IP-based client-server architecture [1, 7]. MathWorks [5] describes TCP/IP communication in the MATLAB environment. Any module that wants to send a token creates a server socket on its side and waits for clients to contact. After the initial connection is established, the server module can start sending the tokens to its clients.

In this network configuration, the IO ports of the modules play a decisive role. It is the input ports of a module that continuously watches the channel and pull any tokens that may have arrived through the channel. The input port fetches the tokens (messages) and places into the local buffer inside the module, which will be processed by the local transitions of the module.

Similarly, any outgoing tokens of a module will be placed into the input buffer of an output port. It is the function of the output port to transfer the token into the buffer of the TCP/IP socket so that it will be eventually transmitted.

This type of client-server-based architecture necessitates a central server. This central server can receiver tokens from different modules and then re-direct it to the relevant modules, effectively functions as a transceiver. In Fig. 7.4, the IMC functions as the centralized server. Though this centralized server configuration is simple and effective, it has some disadvantages such as non-fault tolerant [4]. However, fault-tolerance is out-of-scope of this book.

References

1. Bertocco M, Ferraris F, Offelli C, Parvis M (1998) A client-server architecture for distributed measurement systems. IEEE Trans Instrum Meas 47(5):1143–1148
2. Davidrajuh R (2017) Modular Petri net models of communicating agents. In: Proceeding of the international joint conference SOCO'17-CISIS'17-ICEUTE'17 León, Spain, September 6–8, 2017. Springer, pp 328–337
3. Davidrajuh R (2019) A new modular Petri net for modeling large discrete-event systems: a proposal based on the literature study. Computers 8(4):83
4. El-Desoky AE, Ali HA, Azab AA (2007) A pure peer-to-peer desktop grid framework with efficient fault tolerance. In: 2007 International conference on computer engineering and systems. IEEE, pp 346–352
5. MathWorks I (2019) Instrument control toolbox: user's guide. The MathWorks Inc.
6. Savi VM, Xie X (1992) Liveness and boundedness analysis for Petri nets with event graph modules. In: International conference on application and theory of Petri nets. Springer, pp 328–347
7. Seth S, Venkatesulu MA (2009) TCP/IP architecture, design, and implementation in Linux, vol 68. Wiley

Chapter 8
GPenSIM Support for Petri Modules

This chapter presents the extension to GPenSIM to support developing modular Petri nets. This chapter discusses the programming constructs provided by GPenSIM for the development of modular Petri net models. As discussed in Chap. 4 "GPenSIM for Monolithic Petri nets", GPenSIM did not support modularization before. GPenSIM was extended to support modularization. The newer version of GPenSIM (version 10) allows modularization so that flexibility (ability to add or change functionality) and comprehensibility (readability) of the models can be improved. Modularization reduces the development time of large Petri net models too, as modelers can separately develop different modules at the same time. Also, modularization increases the robustness (less prone to error) of the models. Also, modules can run faster as they can be executed in parallel on different computers.

8.1 Modular Model Building

In the modular model building, there are two new fundamental issues:

- **IO ports**: For a module, transitions function as the input and output ports (IO ports).
- **Modular processor files**: in addition to specific processor files and COMMON processor files, there are modular processor files too.

R. Davidrajuh, *Petri Nets for Modeling of Large Discrete Systems*, Asset Analytics,
https://doi.org/10.1007/978-981-16-5203-5_8

8.1.1 Declaring Modules with the IO Ports

Figure 8.1 shows a Petri net model with three **Petri modules** namely, **Adder**, **Multiplier**, and **Client**. For this model, three PDFs can be defined, one for each module. Also, in each of these PDFs, **there must be a declaration about the IO ports of these modules**. For example, the PDF for the module Adder is shown in Fig. 8.2.

In Fig. 8.2, the final statement states that there are two transitions (tAI and tAO) that function as the IO ports of the module. It is this statement that declares Adder as a module.

Figure 8.3 shows the PDF for the module Multiplier. Here again, the final statement of the PDF states that there are two transitions (tMI and tMO) that function as the IO ports. Because of this statement, the PDF represents the module Multiplier. Finally, Fig. 8.4 shows the PDF for the module Client.

In the PDF for module Client, the final statement declares transitions tCI and tCO as the IO ports. Since transitions takes central place in model development with GPenSIM, **only transitions can be IO ports**.

8.2 Modular Processor Files

This section introduces two more processor files—the modular processor files. So far, the following four processor files are used:

- Specific pre-processor file: specific pre-processor file is for coding pre-conditions for firing a specific transition. This means, for a Petri net with n transitions, there can be up to n specific pre-processor files, where each pre-processor file coding the pre-conditions of a specific transition.
- COMMON_PRE file: This file declares the pre-conditions for all the enabled transition. COMMON_PRE has the universal scope, as all the enabled transitions are visible here.
- Specific post-processor file: specific post-processor file is for coding post-actions when a specific transition completes firing. This means, for a Petri net with n transitions, there can be up to n specific post-processor files, each post-processor file coding the post-actions of a specific transition.
- COMMON_POST file: This file declares the activities that are to be done after transitions complete firing. COMMON_POST has the universal scope, as all the transitions that complete firing is visible here.

In addition to the four types of processor files mentioned above, when modules are in use, two more modular processor files per module can be used:

- The modular pre-processor file MOD_*_PRE, and
- The modular post-processor file MOD_*_POST,

where the asterisk (*) represents the name of the module.

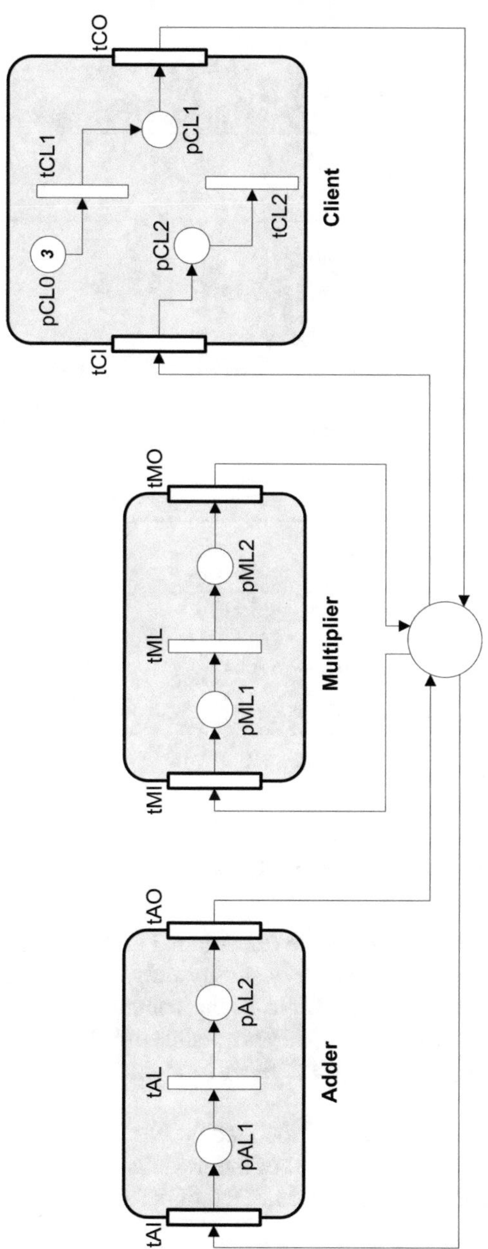

Fig. 8.1 A Petri net model with three Petri modules

```
% PDF for module Adder:
function [png] = Adder_pdf()
png.PN_name = 'Adder'; % name of the module
png.set_of_Ps = {'pAL1','pAL2'};
png.set_of_Ts = {'tAI','tAL','tAO'};
png.set_of_As = {'tAI','pAL1',1, 'pAL1','tAL',1,...
    'tAL','pAL2',1, 'pAL2','tAO',1};
png.set_of_Ports = {'tAI','tAO'}; % IO ports of this module
```

Fig. 8.2 **PDF** for the module **Adder**

```
% PDF for module Multiplier:
function [png] = Multiplier_pdf()
png.PN_name = 'Multiplier'; % name of the module
png.set_of_Ps = {'pML1','pML2'};
png.set_of_Ts = {'tMI','tML','tMO'};
png.set_of_As = {'tMI','pML1',1, 'pML1','tML',1,...
    'tML','pML2',1, 'pML2','tMO',1};
png.set_of_Ports = {'tMI','tMO'}; % IO ports of this module
```

Fig. 8.3 **PDF** for the module **Multiplier**

```
% PDF for module Client:
function [png] = Client_pdf()
png.PN_name = 'Client'; % name of the module
png.set_of_Ps = {'pCL0','pCL1','pCL2'};
png.set_of_Ts = {'tCI','tCL1','tCL2','tCO'};
png.set_of_As = {'tCI','pCL2',1, 'pCL2','tCL2',1,...
    'pCL0','tCL1',1, 'tCL1','pCL1',1, 'pCL1','tCO',1};
png.set_of_Ports = {'tCI','tCO'}; % IO ports of this module
```

Fig. 8.4 **PDF** for the module **Client**

8.3 Modular Visibility of Transitions

The transitions residing inside a module (the internal or local transitions of a module) possess limited visibility (module visibility only, and not global visibility); thus, the local transitions are not visible in the common processor files (COMMON_PRE and COMMON_POST). They are visible only in the modular processor files (MOD_*_PRE and MOST_*_POST files), in addition to their specific processor files.

The input and output transitions of the module (the IO ports) are visible in the modular processor files, as they are part of the module. Also, the IO ports are also visible in the COMMON_PRE and COMMON_POST files.

- Each module can have their own modular pre-processor file (MOD_*_PRE file) and modular post-processor file (MOD_*_POST file).

- Modular pre-processor file (MOD_*_PRE file): This file defines the pre-conditions for all the transitions of a module (the local transitions of the module as well as the IO ports of the module).
- Modular post-processor file (MOD_*_POST file): This file defines the post-firing actions for all the transitions of a module (the local transitions of the module as well as the IO ports of the module).
- The local transitions are visible only in the modular processors. They are not visible in the common processors.
- IO ports are visible in the modular processors as well as in the common processors.

8.3.1 Modular Visibility: An Example

Taking the model shown in Fig. 8.1 as an example:

- Module Adder:
  - IO ports: tAI and tAO.
  - local transitions: tAL1.
- Module Multiplier:
  - IO ports: tMI and tMO.
  - local transitions: tML.
- Module Client:
  - IO ports: tCI and tCO.
  - local transitions: tCL1 and tCL2.
- Inter-Module Connectors (IMC): though transitions are allowed as IMCs, no transition function as IMC in this example, only place pCommon functions as an IMC.

The processor files for the model shown in Fig. 8.1:

- Up to two common processor files: COMMON_PRE and COMMON_POST.
- Up to six modular processor files:
  - For Adder module: pre-processor MOD_Adder_PRE and post-processor MOD_Adder_POST.
  - For Multiplier module: pre-processor MOD_Multiplier_PRE and post-processor MOD_Multiplier_POST.
  - For Client module: pre-processor MOD_Client_PRE and post-processor MOD_Client_POST.
- Up to twenty specific processor files: there are ten transitions in the model. Each transition can have their own specific pre-processor and post-processor.

8.3.2 Modular Visibility: Summary

Figures 8.5, 8.6 and 8.7 summarize the visibility of the different transitions of the modular Petri net model shown in Fig. 8.1.

There are no IMC transitions in Fig. 8.1. If there are, then each of these transitions is visible in their own specific processor files (private visibility) as well as in the common processor files (public visibility). Since IMC transitions have no module belonging, they are not visible in any modular processors.

Visibility	**IO ports: tAI and tAO**	**Local transitions: tAL**
Private visibility	**Yes**, in their specific pre- and post-processor files.	
Modular visibility	**Yes**, as ***all*** the transitions of module Adder are visible in their modular processor files **MOD_Adder_PRE** and **MOD_Adder_POST**.	
Public visibility	**Yes.** IO ports are visible in the common processor files COMMON_PRE and COMMON_POST.	**No**. Local transitions are not visible in the common processor files.

Fig. 8.5 Transitions of the module **Adder** and their visibility

Visibility	**IO ports: tMI and tMO**	**Local transitions: tML**
Private visibility	**Yes**, in their specific pre- and post-processor files.	
Modular visibility	**Yes**, as ***all*** the transitions of module Adder are visible in their modular processor files **MOD_Multiplier_PRE** and **MOD_ Multiplier _POST**.	
Public visibility	**Yes.** IO ports are visible in the common processor files COMMON_PRE and COMMON_POST.	**No**. Local transitions are not visible in the common processor files.

Fig. 8.6 Transitions of the module **Multiplier** and their visibility

Visibility	**IO ports: tCI and tCO**	**Local transitions: tCL1 and tCL2**
Private visibility	**Yes**, in their specific pre- and post-processor files.	
Modular visibility	**Yes**, as ***all*** the transitions of module Adder are visible in their modular processor files **MOD_Client_PRE** and **MOD_ Client _POST**.	
Public visibility	**Yes.** IO ports are visible in the common processor files COMMON_PRE and COMMON_POST.	**No**. Local transitions are not visible in the common processor files.

Fig. 8.7 Transitions of the module **Client** and their visibility

Note that, for simplicity, all the three modules possess only one input port and one output port. However, **a module can have any number of input ports and output ports**.

8.4 Developing Modules with GPenSIM

This section presents a complete example of the application of GPenSIM to develop a modular Petri net. The example is the same example on solving quadratic equations using three communicating agents (client, adder, and multiplier) that was introduced in Sect. 7.4.1; and also in [1, 2]. Section 7.4.1 proposes the use of generic modules for the three agents so that the three agents looks similar. However, in this section, the generic modules are not used; much simpler modules are used for convenience.

Figure 8.1 shows the overall model, showing the three modules and the inter-modular connection between them.

The following subsections explore the modules one-by-one. The modules and the corresponding modular pre-processor files are discussed. Since there is no need for post-firing actions, post-processors are not used.

8.4.1 The Adder Module

Figure 8.8 shows the adder module. Transitions tAI and tAO function as the input and output port of the module. tAL is the local transition. The two places pAL1 and pAL2 are the local places.

tAI takes the token that is intended for addition from the common buffer pCommon. tAI places this token into pAL1. tAL works on this token, performing three simple tasks:

1. Open the token and get the two numbers.
2. Add the numbers together.
3. Put the results of the addition as a new color on the output token that will be deposited into pAL2.

The output port tAO takes the token from pAL2 and flushes it into the common buffer pCommon so that the client will take it.

Figure 8.9 shows the MOD_Adder_PRE file. All the three transitions tAI, tAL, and tAO are visible in MOD_Adder_PRE. However, the code in this file addresses only tAL, as the other two transitions are dealt with in the common pre-processor file. The code in this file simply states that whenever token arrives at the place pAL1, tAL has to perform three simple tasks mentioned above.

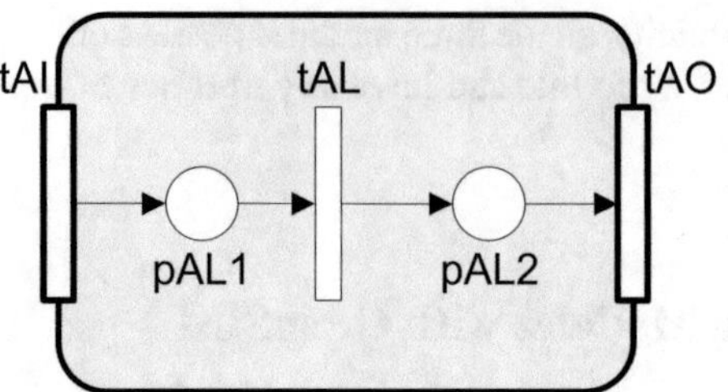

Fig. 8.8 Three communicating agents: the Adder module

```
function [fire, transition] = MOD_Adder_PRE (transition)

switch transition.name
    case {'tAI', 'tAO'}
        % no additional conditions,
        % other than in COMMON_PRE
        fire = 1;

    case 'tAL'
        Sigma = 0;
        tokID1 = tokenAny('pAL1',1);
        colors = get_color('pAL1', tokID1);
        for i = 1:numel(colors)
            colorI = colors{i};
            numI = str2num(colorI); %#ok<ST2NM>
            if not(isempty(numI))
                Sigma = sum(numI);
            end
        end
        transition.override = 1;
        transition.new_color = {num2str(Sigma)};
        fire = 1;

end
```

Fig. 8.9 The MOD_Adder_PRE file

8.4.2 The Multiplier Module

Figure 8.10 shows the multiplier module, which is identical to the adder module. Transitions tMI and tMO function as the input and output port of the module. tML is the local transition. The two places pML1 and pML2 are the local places.

Figure 8.11 shows the MOD_Multipler_PRE file, which is also very similar to MOD_Adder_PRE file. The only difference is that the logic of addition is replaced by multiplication. Although all the three transitions tMI, tML, and tMO are visible in MOD_Multiplier_PRE, the code in this file addresses only tML, as the other two

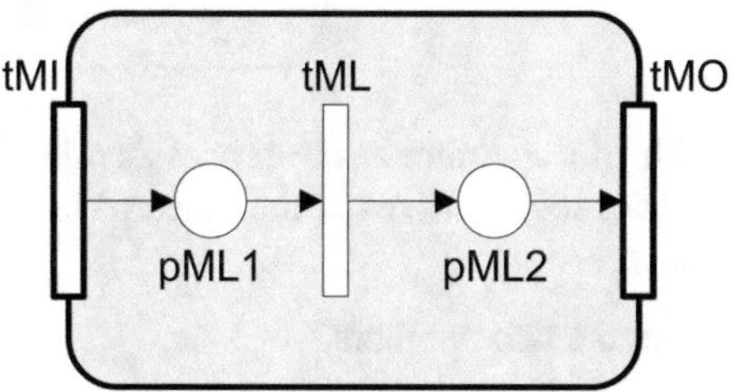

Fig. 8.10 Three communicating agents: the Multiplier module

```
function [fire, transition] = MOD_Multiplier_PRE (transition)

switch transition.name
    case {'tMI', 'tMO'}
        % no additional conditions,
        % other than in COMMON_PRE
        fire = 1;

    case 'tML'
        multX = 1;
        tokID1 = tokenAny('pML1',1);
        colors = get_color('pML1', tokID1);
        for i = 1:numel(colors)
            colorI = colors{i};
            numI = str2num(colorI);
            if not(isempty(numI))
                multX = prod(numI);
            end
        end
        transition.override = 1;
        transition.new_color = {num2str(multX)};
        fire = 1;
end
```

Fig. 8.11 The MOD_Multiplier_PRE file

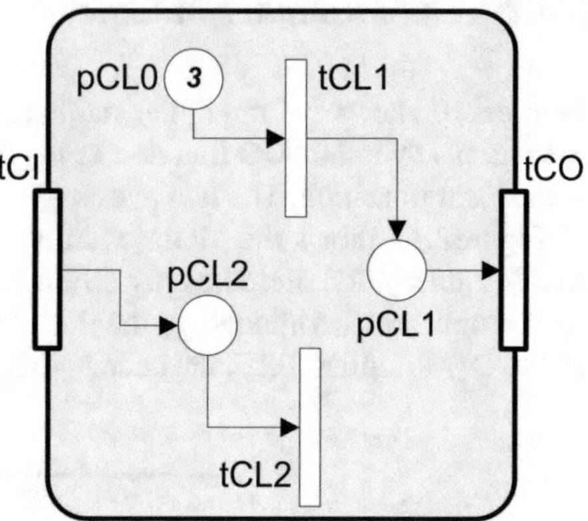

Fig. 8.12 Three communicating agents: the Client module

transitions are dealt with in the common pre-processor file. The code in this file simply states that whenever token arrives at the place pML1, tML has to perform three simple operations:

1. Open the token and get the two numbers.
2. Multiply the numbers together.
3. Put the results of the multiplication as a new color on the output token that will be deposited into pML2.

8.4.3 The Client Module

Figure 8.12 shows the client module, which is different from the other two modules. In addition to the transitions tCI and tCO which function as the input and output port of the module, there are two more transitions tCL1 and tCL2 which are the local transitions. There are also two places pCL1 and pCL2 that are the local places.

The three initial tokens in pCL0 indicate that there are three tasks carried out by the client:

1. Send (a, x, x) to the Multiplier to multiply (Multiplier will return x^2).
2. Send $(b, x, 1)$ to the Multiplier to multiply (Multiplier will return $b \cdot x$).
3. Send (x^2, bx, c) to the Adder (Adder will return $(x^2 + bx + c)$).

8.4.4 Putting All Together

Figure 8.13 shows the common pre-processor "COMMON_PRE". All the input and output ports are visible in this file (in this example, there are no IMC transitions). This file simply instructs the input ports to take only the relevant token from the common buffer. For example, tAI can take only tokens marked with color "Adder".

```
function [fire, transition] = COMMON_PRE (transition)

switch transition.name
    case 'tAI'
        tokID1 = tokenAnyColor('pCommon',1, {'ADD'});
        transition.selected_tokens = tokID1;
        fire = tokID1;

    case 'tAO'
        transition.new_color = {'CLIENT'};
        fire = 1;

    case 'tMI'
        tokID1 = tokenAnyColor('pCommon',1, {'MULT'});
        transition.selected_tokens = tokID1;
        fire = tokID1;

    case 'tMO'
        transition.new_color = {'CLIENT'};
        fire = 1;

    case 'tCI'
        tokID1 = tokenAnyColor('pCommon',1, {'CLIENT'});
        transition.selected_tokens = tokID1;
        fire = tokID1;

    case 'tCO'
        fire = 1;
end
```

Fig. 8.13 The COMMON_PRE file

Also, COMMON_PRE instructs the output ports tAO and tMO to add the color “Client” so that the outputs of the modules Adder and Multiplier should be taken only by the Client module.

8.4.5 Technical Note on Independent Module Development

It is repeatedly stated in this book that by modularization, the modules can be developed and tested independently. Let us assume that the module Adder is going to be developed and tested independently. The following steps help this process:

Step-1: Creating the "Global contract" (Common processor files):
At the start, developers agree on the overall interface: how the individual modules are going to interface the common buffer pCommon. When a module deposits a token into the buffer, what are the colors the module should add to the token, so that the correct recipient can take this token and also identify the sender? For example, if the module "Client" is to send a job (token) to the "Adder", what are the colors the token should have (e.g., two colors, like "From: Client" and "To: Adder"). Once these interfacing details are agreed, these details will be coded in the common pre-processor file COMMON_PRE. Hence, COMMON_PRE functions as the common contract for the different set of developers that are developing modules separately (if COMMON_POST is available, it will be too; however, in this example, there is no COMMON_POST).

Step-2: Creating the "Local contract" (Modular processor files):
The team developing the module "Adder" will also have the description of the behavior of the local members in the form of MOD_Adder_PRE (also, MOD_Adder_POST too, if it is available). However, the team that is developing the module "Adder" is free to change the coding (representing the behavior of the local members) of the modular processor files, as these are for local use only. The other teams that are developing the other modules are not interested in what the local members of "Adder" are doing. Hence, the other teams will no have access to the modular processor files of Adder.

Using the global contract that is static (do not change) and a local contract that can vary, is a universal practice is software engineering [6].

Figure 8.14 shows that the common processor files act as a global contract between the different development teams, and the modular processor files working as a local contract.

Step-3: Testing of Individual modules, independently:
During the development of a module, the common processor files clearly show how to interface the module with the "outside world" (rest of the modules). Figure 8.15 shows how the module "Adder" can be independently tested. A **testing driver** tDriver can produce a token and deposit into pDriver; pDriver functions as a substitute for pCommon. When tDriver creates a token, it adds the colors as these would be added by the module "Client". When the module "Adder" consumes this token, and the results will be output in the form of a token in the **testing stub** pStub. By inspecting

Developer:	**Developer – A**	**Developer – C**	**Developer – M**
In-charge of module:	**"Adder"**	**"Client"**	**"Multipler"**
Global contract (static)	**COMMON_PRE COMMON_POST**		
Local contract	**MOD_Adder_PRE MOD_Adder_POST**	**MOD_Client_PRE MOD_Client_POST**	**MOD_Multiplier_PRE MOD_ Multiplier _POST**

Fig. 8.14 The Global contract and the local contracts

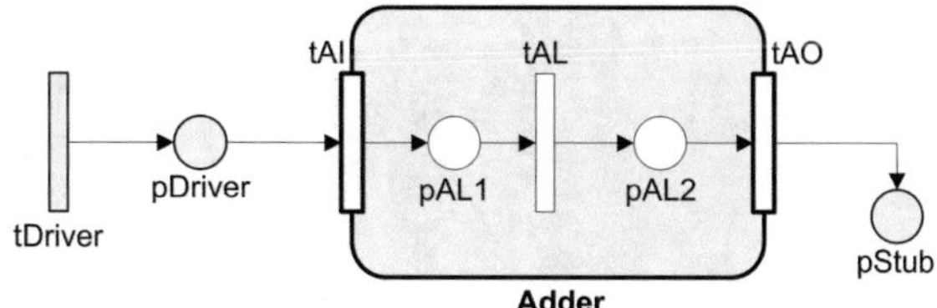

Fig. 8.15 Independent testing of a module

the colors of the token in pStub, it can be made sure the module "Adder" is functioning properly.

Using the testing drivers and stubs is also universal practice in testing software modules [6], (also, [3–5]).

References

1. Davidrajuh R (2017) Modular Petri net models of communicating agents. In: Proceeding of the international joint conference SOCO'17-CISIS'17-ICEUTE'17 León, Spain, September 6–8, 2017. Springer, pp 328–337
2. Davidrajuh R (2019) A new modular Petri net for modeling large discrete-event systems: a proposal based on the literature study. Computers 8(4):83
3. Gao J (1999) Testing component-based software. In: Proceedings of STARWest, San Jose, USA
4. Gao J (2000) Component testability and component testing challenges. In: Proceedings of the 3rd ICSE workshop on component-based software engineering
5. Renzelmann MJ, Kadav A, Swift MM (2012) Symdrive: testing drivers without devices. In: Presented as part of the 10th USENIX symposium on operating systems design and implementation (OSDI'12), pp 279–292
6. Sommerville I (2011) Software engineering, 9th ed. ISBN-10137035152

Part III
Legacy Petri Nets

Chapter 9
Module Extraction

Modularization of a monolithic model starts with identifying segments (groups of elements) of the model that can become the modules; the modules are supposed to decompose the model into a set of connected independent modules. Literature provides some techniques for identifying segments of a model that can become modules (e.g., [4–6]).

Once the segments are identified, how can the segments be carved out as modules so that these modules individually adhere to the formal definition of modules? This chapter proposes a new algorithm for transforming the segments into modules. The algorithm uses some fixes during the transformation. This chapter presents an analysis of these fixes too. The analysis proves that by modularization, the fixes do not destroy the model's original structural properties. This chapter is an extended version of [3].

9.1 Rules of Interfacing

Section 6.2 "Design of Modular Petri nets" introduced the composition of a modular Petri net (Petri modules and IMCs). Also, Sect. 7.3 "Formal Definitions for the New Entities" gave complete information about the modules and IMCs. From the information given in these two sections, let us focus on the module interface (the borders or input and output ports). For extracting a module from a large Petri net, the border rules can be summarized as follows:

- Inputs to a module: all the inputs to a module can only pass through the input ports of the module. An external element (outsider of a module) is not allowed to input directly to a local member of a module or an output port.
- Outputs from a module: all the outputs from a module can only pass through the output ports of the module. It is not allowed for a local member or an input port to directly output to an external element.
- Internal arcs (connections) of a module: As members of a module, a module consists of three types of transitions (input port, local transition, and output port),

R. Davidrajuh, *Petri Nets for Modeling of Large Discrete Systems*, Asset Analytics,
https://doi.org/10.1007/978-981-16-5203-5_9

and local places. It is allowed that a transition that is a member of a module can be input and out to any local places, and vice versa.

With the rules given above, an algorithm is given below for extracting the modules.

9.2 Algorithm: Module Extraction

Algorithm 1: Algorithm for extracting a module from a large Petri net

```
input : Petri net PN = (P, T, A)
output: [set of modules], [set of IMCs]
% find set of segments by peer-pressure algo
[set_of_segments C_i] = FindSegments(PN)

% for all segments; n_1: number of segments
for i = 1 to n_1 do
    % discard small segments with <= 3 elements;
    % hand-pick the IO ports
    C_i = ProcessSegments(C_i)

% PASS - 1:
% loop for all the processed segments;
% n_2: number of processed segments
for i = 1 to n_2 do
    % pass-1 is to check & fix the output members
    M_i = ProcessModule(C_i, PN)

% PASS - 2:
% transpose Petri net, the input & output ports
TrPN = transpose(PN)
M_i'.input_ports = M.output_ports
M_i'.output_ports = M.input_ports

% for all the rudimentary modules (n_2)
for i = 1 to n_2 do
    % pass-2 is to check & fix the input members
    M_i' = ProcessModule(M_i', TrPN)

% extraction is complete
% transpose back Petri net
PN = transpose(TrPN)
```

Algorithm 1 is a two-pass algorithm. In Pass-1: a rudimentary module is formed, by checking and fixing the outputs of all the members of the module. In Pass-2: all the inputs of the members of the module are checked and fixed. For this purpose, the transpose of the Petri net is used.

In detail, the algorithm consists of the following steps:

- Line 02: Using the extended peer-pressure algorithm [4–6], all the segments of the Petri net are identified by the function "FindSegments". These segments are to be refined as modules in the following steps.
- (Lines 05–08) **Finding and processing the segments**: Some of the segments found by "FindSegments" may possess elements numbering less than or equal to three. Usually, due to their smaller size, these segments are not suitable for functioning as a module. Thus, the elements in these segments can become IMCs, or become part of other segments. Function "ProcessSegments" process each segment to check whether they are suitable to become a module; if a segment is eligible to become a module, then both the input ports and the output ports are also determined.
  After processing, the segments become rudimentary modules, possessing the input ports, the output ports, and the internal elements (local transitions and local places). However, the input connections and output connections of the members of the module may violate the rules of interfacing discussed above. These violations are fixed in the two passes.
- (Lines 13–15) **Pass-1**: the function "ProcessModules" uses an modified "Depth-first-search" traversal. The traversal starts with the input ports, one at a time. While traversing, from an input port or from a local member, if there is an output to an outside node, then this is considered as a violation, and it is fixed. The function terminates after checking and fixing all the outputs of all the members of the module (the input ports, output ports, and the internal elements such as local transitions and local places).
- (Lines 19–27) **Pass-2**: In Pass-1, all the outputs of the members of the module are checked and fixed. Pass-2 is for checking and fixing the inputs of the members, using the same function "ProcessModules". However, to check the inputs, the Petri net is transposed, and the transposed Petri net is input to the function. Also, the input ports and the output ports are exchanged. This means the output ports are fed into the function "ProcessModules" as input ports, and similarly input ports as output ports.
  After pass-2, all the members of the module is thoroughly checked, verifying whether their input and output connections obey the rules of interfacing.
- (Line 30) Completion: Once the Petri net is transposed back to its normal form, there will be a number of modules, clearly identified and encapsulated by the input and output ports. All the transitions and places that reside outside of these modules will become the IMC.

During the two passes, the algorithm uses fixes for correcting the connections (arcs) that violate the rules of interfacing. The process of fixing is explained in the following two subsections, Sects. 9.2.1 and 9.2.2.

Running time of the algorithm:
As shown in Algorithm 1, the algorithm mainly consists of three functions:

- FindSegment: This function takes $\mathcal{O}(r \cdot V^3)$ time, where r is the number of iterations and V is the number of elements (places and transitions) in the Petri net.
- ProcessSegments: This function cannot be executed automatically, as this function needs the experience and insight of the modeler. The steps described in this function are to be followed by a modeler, e.g., hand-picking input and output ports, moving elements in and out of segments.
- ProcessModules (in Pass-1 and Pass-2): ProcessModules is a modified depth-first-search (DFS) algorithm (the running time of DFS is $\mathcal{O}(V + E)$, where V and E are the numbers of vertices and edges, respectively). The DFS will be repeated two times for each source node (input port, output port, and any other source node). Assuming the total number of input and output ports $|T_I + T_O| \ll V$, the running time of the function ProcessModules becomes $\mathcal{O}(V + E)$. Since Petri nets are generally sparsely connected [9], $V \approx E$, it be can be concluded that the running time of the function ProcessModules in terms of V is $\mathcal{O}(V)$.

Hence, neglecting the function "ProcessSegments", the running time of the algorithm for extraction of modules becomes $\mathcal{O}(r \cdot V^3) + \mathcal{O}(V) = \mathcal{O}(r \cdot V^3)$.

9.2.1 *Fixing Violations in Pass-1*

In Pass-1, if an **output arc** from an input port or a local member hits a node that is outside the module, it is considered as a violation. Figure 9.1a shows such a situation. When the traversal is started with an input port, there may be an arc from the input port to an outside node. This is not acceptable, as input ports (and local transitions) are only supposed to feed tokens to local places inside a module. In this case, this violation can be fixed by introducing a "dummy" place–transition pair, as shown in Fig. 9.1b. The dummy transition tD now acts as an output port too.

A similar situation is described in Fig. 9.2a. In this case, a local transition tL has an output arc to an outside place. This can also be corrected with a dummy place–transition pair, as shown in Fig. 9.2b. Also, there could be another possibility as shown in Fig. 9.2c; in this case, the local transition tL can be "promoted" to become an output port tO, eliminating the necessity of injecting a dummy place–transition pair.

Figure 9.3a looks into the problem of a local place having an output to a transition that is residing outside the module. In this case, the solution is to inject a dummy transition–place pair; the dummy transition tD becomes an output port, whereas the dummy place pD is placed outside the module meaning it becomes a part of an IMC.

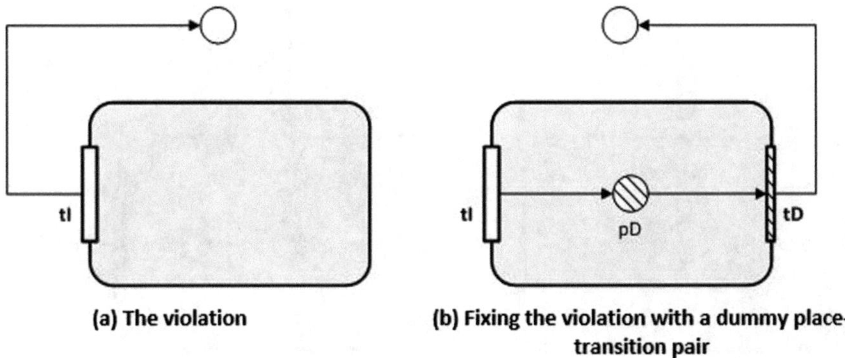

Fig. 9.1 Violations in the output connections from an input port

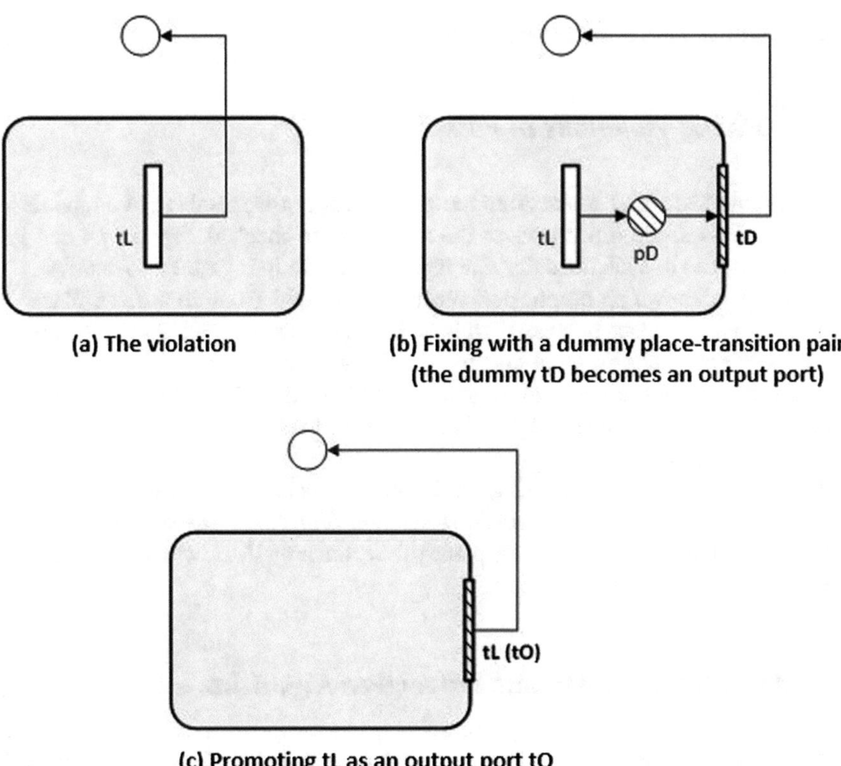

Fig. 9.2 Violations in the output connections from a local transition

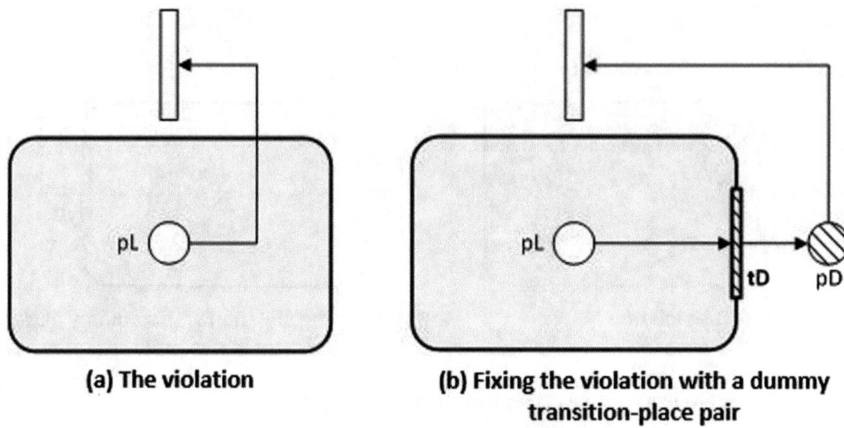

Fig. 9.3 Violations in the input connections from a local place

9.2.2 Fixing Violations in Pass-2

The previous Sect. 9.2.1 looked into the output arcs of the members of a module in Pass-1. In Pass-2, the **input arcs** of the members are checked. Figures 9.4 and 9.5 show three types of violations that can happen, and the fixings are also shown.

Figure 9.4a shows an output port receiving an input from an outside place. A dummy transition–place pair can fix this violation as shown in Fig. 9.4b; the dummy transition tD becomes an input port too. In Fig. 9.4c, a local transition receives an input from an outside place, and the solution with a dummy transition–place pair is shown in Fig. 9.4d. Another solution is to make the local transition as an input port, as shown in Fig. 9.4e.

Figure 9.5 shows the final fixing. In this case, a local place violates the rules by receiving direct inputs from an outside transition (Fig. 9.5a). The solution is shown in Fig. 9.5b. Here again, the dummy place pD becomes an IMC, whereas the dummy transition tD becomes an input port.

9.3 Application of Module Extraction Algorithm

In this section, modularization is done using the extraction algorithm. Five modules will be created this time, and an explanation is given on how the extraction algorithm is used in this process. Table 9.1 shows the segments that are chosen for modularization and the hand-picked input and output ports of the modules.

The inter-modular components are the elements that do not fall into any of the six modules. The IM places are pC1, pC2, poC1, poC2, pR2, pi1AS, pi2AS, po1AS, po2AS, pR3, and poAS. tAS is the only IM transition.

Let us go through these five modules in the following subsections.

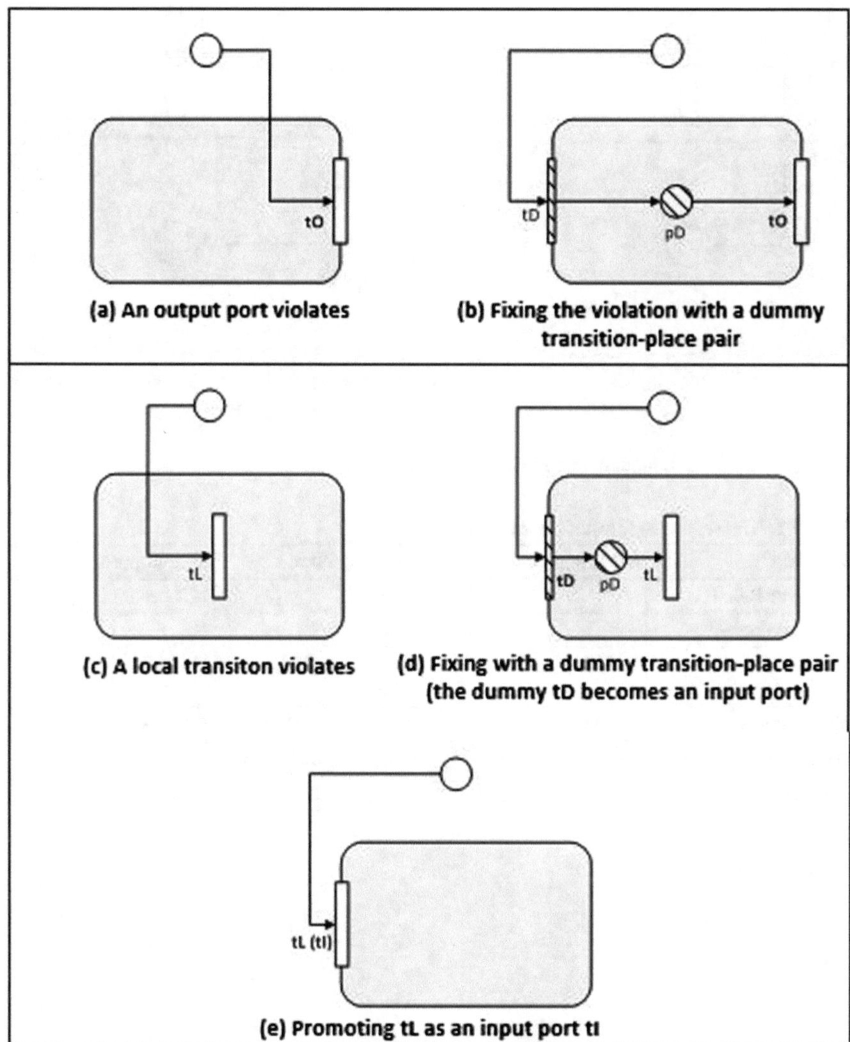

Fig. 9.4 Violations in the input connections of members of a module

9.3.1 *Input Modules*

Two input modules deal with the arrival of input (raw) material into the production line and transporting the material on the conveyor belts. The two input modules are "Conveyor Belt-1" and "Conveyor Belt-2". Since these two modules are similar, let us focus on "Conveyor Belt-1".

Figure 9.6 shows the segment of Petri net that represents the arrival of input material-1. Figure 9.7 shows the modular version. In the segment, pC1 and pIB1 are the two inputs to tC1. In the module, since tC1 functions as an output port, it cannot

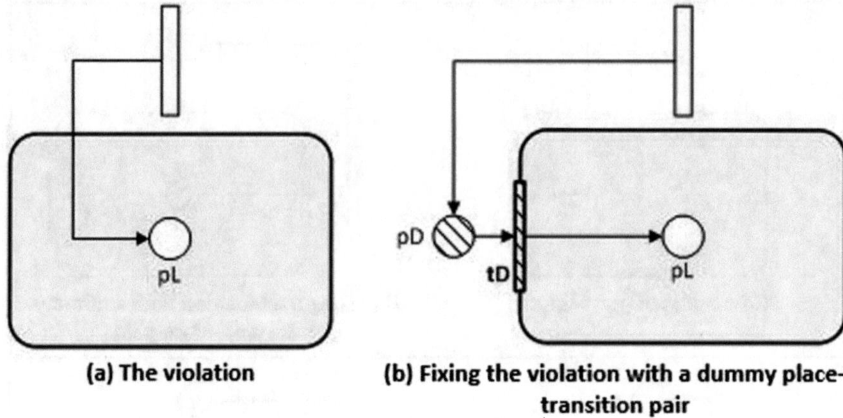

Fig. 9.5 Violations in input connections of local place

Table 9.1 The segments for modularization

Module	Input ports	Local members	Output ports
Conveyor Belt-1	–	pIB1	**tC1**
Conveyor Belt-2	–	pIB2	**tC2**
Machining-1	**tC1M1**	piM1, pR1, tM1, poM1	**tM1AS**
Machining-2	**tC2M2**	piM2, tM2, poM2	**tM2AS**
Product finishing	**tAP**	piPS, tPS, pR4, piCK, pOB	**tPCK**

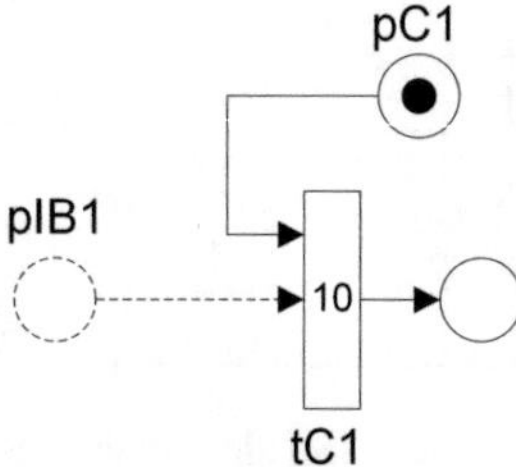

Fig. 9.6 Conveyor Belt-1: the segment

receive any input from the external places. Thus, in Pass-2, a dummy transition–place pairs (tD1IP1 and pD1IP1) are introduced so that pC1 can still input tokens into tC1 via tD1IP1.

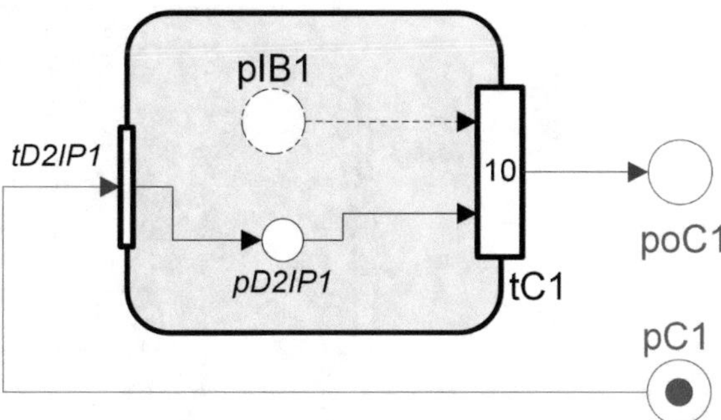

Fig. 9.7 Conveyor Belt-1: the module

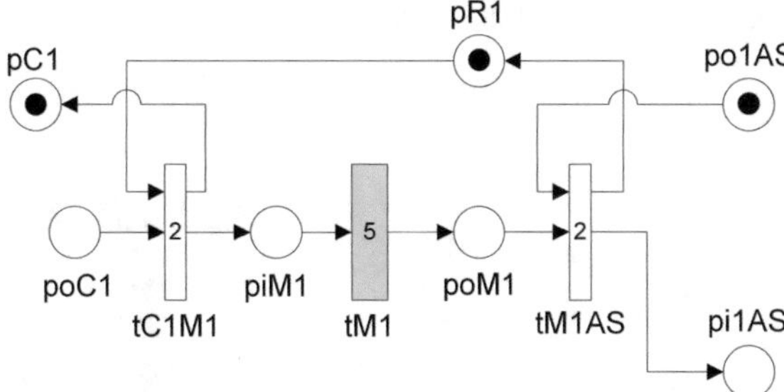

Fig. 9.8 Machining-1: the segment

9.3.2 *Machining Modules*

There are two machining modules, "Machining-1" and "Machining-2". Since these two modules are similar too, let us focus on the module "Machining-1" only.

Figure 9.8 shows the input port tC1M1 outputs to an outside element pC1. During the Pass-1, this violation is fixed with a dummy place–transition pair pD2M1–tD2M1. Also, the output port tM1AS receives tokens from the outside place po1AS, which will be fixed in Pass-2. Figure 9.9 shows the resulting module.

9.3.3 *Finishing and Output Module*

Figure 9.10 shows the final segment. The connections of the input port **tAP**, the local members piPS, tPS, pR4, and piPCK, and the output port **tPCK** do not cause any violation. Thus, during the two passes, there was no need to fix any connections. Figure 9.11 shows the resulting module.

9.3.4 *Inter-Modular Connector*

All those elements that are not a member of any modules become IMC. The following IM places that function as buffers between the modules: pC1, pC2, poC1, poC2, pR2,

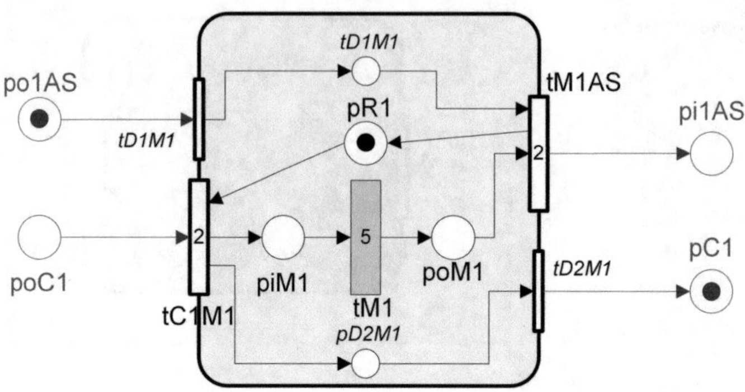

Fig. 9.9 Machining-1: the module

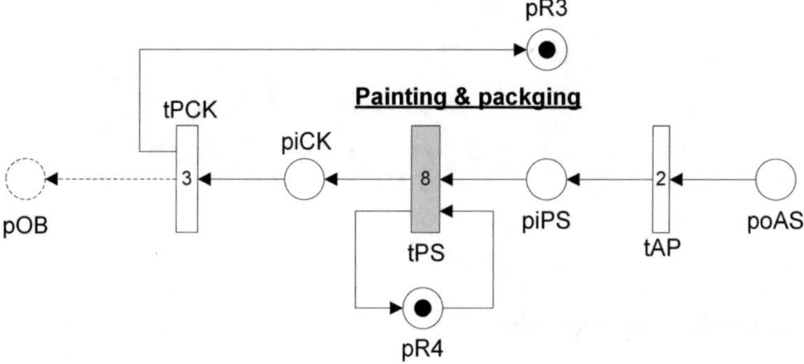

Fig. 9.10 Finishing: the segment

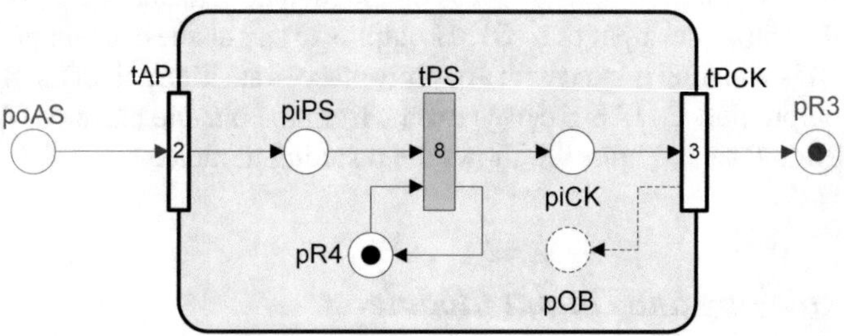

Fig. 9.11 Finishing: the module

pi1AS, pi2AS, po1AS, po2AS, pR3, and poAS. Note that pIB1, pIB2, and pOB in a way special IMCs, as these are the sources and the sink of the model. Also, tAS is the only transition of the IMC.

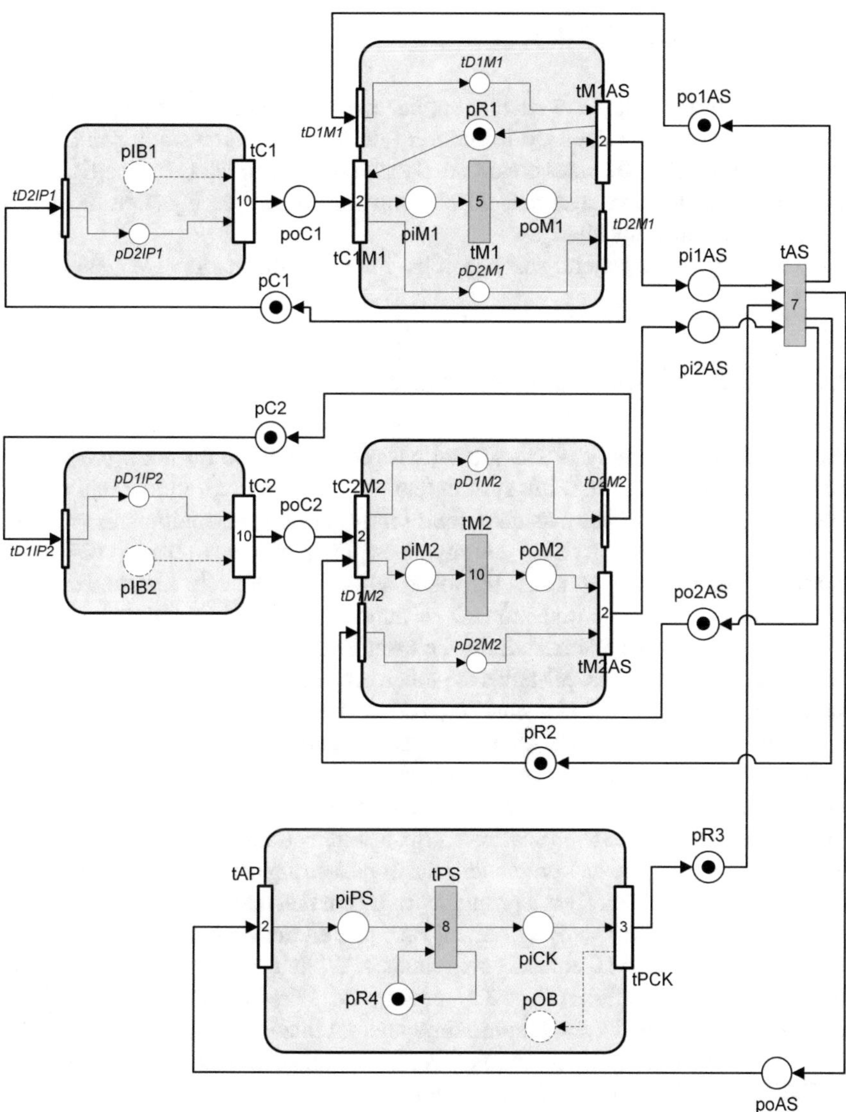

Fig. 9.12 Modular Petri net model of FMS

9.3.5 The Complete Modular Petri Net

Figure 9.12 shows the modular Petri net that is composed of the five modules.

9.4 Analyzing the Fixes

The algorithm for module extraction applies fixes in the formation of modules; in Pass-1 and Pass-2, the fixes are injection of dummy place–transition pairs. In this section, the impact of the fixes is studied. By studying the structural properties place-invariant and transition-invariant, this section shows that the injection of dummy places do not cause any changes.

Let us start with a general analysis of the impact of the dummy elements.

9.4.1 General Analysis of the Fixes

Dummy places: Dummy places are virtual places as these do not represent any passive elements in the real-life system (e.g., pD does not represent a real buffer). Thus, because of the virtual existence, the dummy places do not malfunction anytime.

In a fix, [real transition tX → dummy place pD → dummy transition tD], whenever pD receive a token from tX, the token will be immediately snatched away by tD. Similarly, in [dummy transition tD → dummy place pD → real transition tX], whenever pD receive a token from tD, the token will be immediately snatched away by tX. Thus, in both cases, pD holds the token only momentarily. Therefore, in both cases, it can be assumed that always, $m(pD) = 0$.

Dummy transitions: Like dummy places, dummy transitions are also virtual as these do not represent any active elements in the real-life system (e.g., tD does not represent a real machine). Thus, because of the virtual existence, the dummy transitions do not malfunction anytime. Also, a dummy transition tD fire immediately as it cannot be assigned any pre-conditions or post-firing actions.

For untimed Petri net, tD is a primitive transition that do not possess a firing time (in other words, $ft(tD) = 0$). For timed Petri net, all transition must have non-zero firing time (at least, in GPenSIM environment). While $t_i \in T$ takes non-zero firing time, the dummy transitions $tD_i \in TD$ are suppose to fire immediately. Hence, firing time of tD_i is assigned the minimum time interval that is possible, $ft(tD) = \Delta T$. ΔT is the absolute minimum time in GPenSIM realization that is not zero (known as "DELTA_TIME" in GPenSIM reference manual [2]. Since the firing time of tD is negligible when the activities in real-systems are considered, even for timed systems, it can be safely assumed that $ft(tD) = 0$.

Figures 9.1, 9.2, 9.3, 9.4 and 9.5 show six cases of fixes. All these fixes can be grouped into three types:

1. Input or output connection of a local place is fixed, as shown in Fig. 9.13. By the proof shown in [7] ("fusion of series places"), [original place pL → dummy transition tD → dummy place pD] (Fig. 9.13a) is equivalent to the original place pL. Similarly, [dummy place pD → dummy transition tD → original place pL] (Fig. 9.13b) is equivalent to the original place pL.

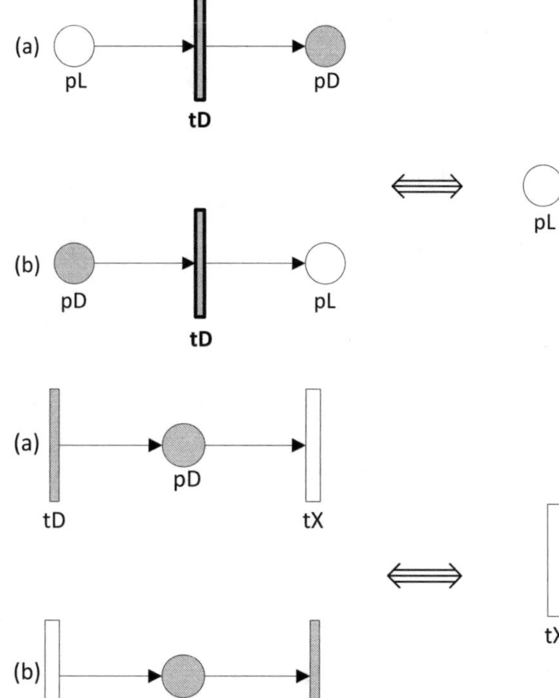

Fig. 9.13 Fix-1: Original place pL and a dummy transition–place pair

Fig. 9.14 Fix-2: Original transition tX and a dummy place–transition pair

2. Input or output connection of a transition is fixed, as shown in Fig. 9.14. Again, by the proof shown in [7] ("fusion of series transitions"), [dummy transition tD + dummy place pD + original transition tX] (Fig. 9.14a) is equivalent to the original transition tX; tX can be a local transition tL or an output port tO.
   Similarly, [original transition tX → dummy place pD → dummy transition tD] (Fig. 9.14b) is equivalent to the original transition tX; in this case, tX can be a local transition tL or an input port tI.
3. A local transition is promoted to either an input port or an output port. In this case, there is no change in structural or behavioral properties.

9.4.2 *P-Invariants*

Consider the RAS problem shown in Fig. 6.1, which is reproduced as Fig. 9.15 for easy access. The RAS has the following p-invariants:

1. PI_{pA41} is for preserving the initial tokens in pA41.

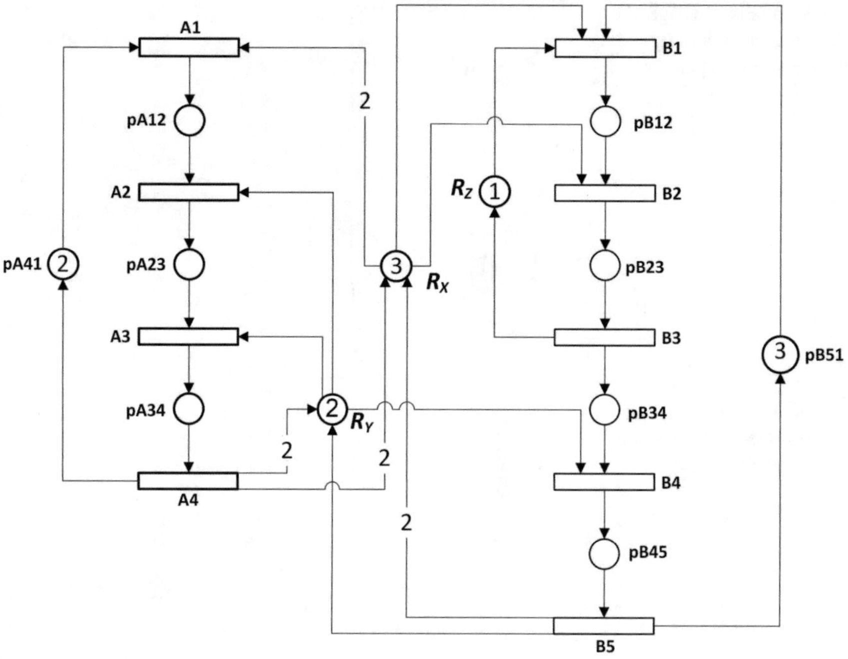

Fig. 9.15 Resource allocation system [1]

2. PI_{pB51} is for preserving the initial tokens in pB51.
3. PI_{R_X} is for preserving the initial tokens in R_X.
4. PI_{R_Y} is for preserving the initial tokens in R_Y.
5. PI_{R_Z} is for preserving the initial tokens in R_Z.

The invariants of RAS model:

PI_{pA41}: $m(pA12) + m(pA23) + m(pA34) + m(pA41) = 2$.
PI_{pB51}: $m(pB12) + m(pB23) + m(pB34) + m(pB45) + m(pB51) = 3$.
PI_{R_X}: $m(pR_X) + m(pB12) + 2 \times (m(pA12) + m(pA23) + m(pA34) + m(pB23) + m(pB34) + m(pB45)) = 3$.
PI_{R_Y}: $m(pR_Y) + m(pA23) + m(pB45) + 2 \times m(pA34) = 2$.
PI_{R_Z}: $m(pR_Z) + m(pB12) + m(pB23) = 1$.

The remodeled RAS problem (discussed in Sect. 6.1) as a modular Petri net is shown in Fig. 6.3, which is reproduced as Fig. 9.16, again for easy access.

Let us study the p-invariants of the two modules A and B. While performing the invariant analysis, the complete instances of the resources (in other words, the initial tokens) should be included in the drivers as shown in Fig. 9.16. The invariants of the module-A:

PI_{pA41}: $m(pA12) + m(pA23) + m(pA34) + m(pA41) = 2$.

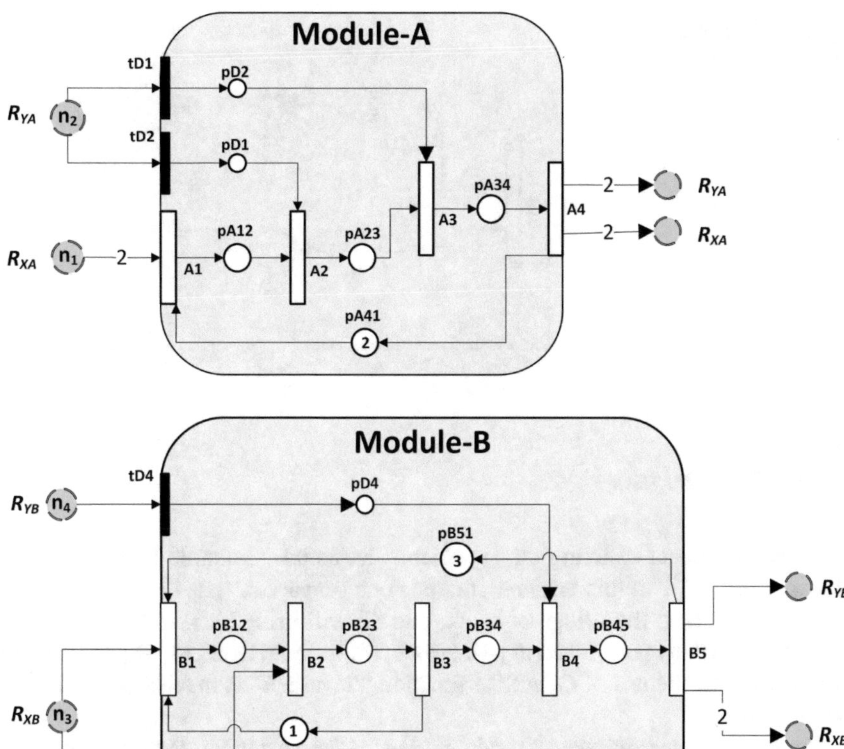

Fig. 9.16 Modular Petri net model of RAS

$PI_{R_{XA}}$: $m(pR_{XA}) + 2 \times (m(pA12) + m(pA23) + m(pA34)) = n_1$.
$PI_{R_{YA}}$: $m(pR_{YA}) + m(pD1) + m(pA23) + m(pD2) + 2 \times m(pA34) = n_2$.

The invariants of the module-B:

PI_{pB51}: $m(pB12) + m(pB23) + m(pB34) + m(pB45) + m(pB51) = 3$.
$PI_{R_{XB}}$: $m(pR_{XB}) + m(pD3) + m(pB12) + 2 \times (m(pB23) + m(pB34) + m(pB45)) = n_3$.
$PI_{R_{YB}}$: $m(pR_{YB}) + m(pD4) + m(pB45) = n_4$.
PI_{R_Z}: $m(pR_Z) + m(pB12) + m(pB23) = 1$.

By setting all $m(pDn) = 0$, it can be seen that

- $PI_{R_X} = PI_{R_{XA}} + PI_{R_{XB}}$, as $n_1 + n_3 = 3$ (the initial tokens in R_X).
- $PI_{R_Y} = PI_{R_{YA}} + PI_{R_{YB}}$, as $n_2 + n_4 = 2$ (the initial tokens in R_Y).

Thus, the presence of the dummy places do not disturb the p-invariants.

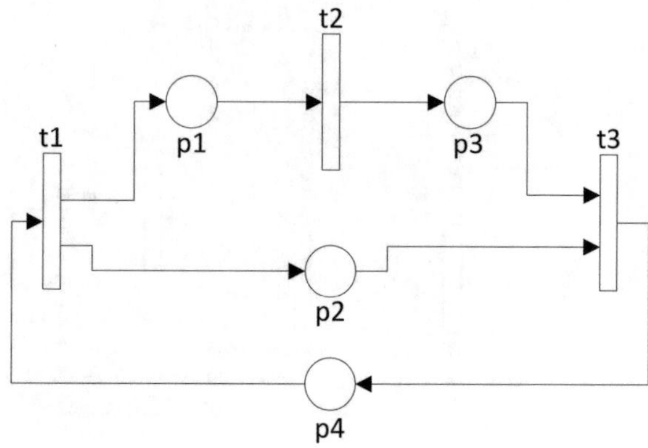

Fig. 9.17 T-invariants of a Petri net

9.4.3 T-Invariants

To study the impact of fixing on t-invariants, let us take a simple Petri net that is shown in Fig. 9.17. In this Petri net, there is one t-invariant: {t1, t2, t3}. If a token is put into p4, then the firings of t1, t2, and t3, will bring back to the same state where started (that is one token in p4). Hence, t-invariant {t1, t2, t3} is justified. For large Petri nets, the use of GPenSIM function "tinvariant" is inevitable for finding the t-invariants.

Figure 9.18 shows one way of modularizing the Petri net in Fig. 9.17. In the modular Petri net, transitions t1 and t3, and places p2 and p4 become members of module-A. Module-A is free from any fixing as all the connections of its members (t1, t3, p2, p4) do not violate the rules of interfacing.

The rest of the places in Fig. 9.17, p1 and p3, and the transition t2 become the members of module-B. Since p1 cannot have direct input from outside transition, and p3 output to outside transition, these two connections are fixed. The fixing makes use of the dummy transitions tD1 and tD2 as the input and output port of module-B. Also, due to the fixing, dummy places pD1 and pD2 become IMCs.

Studying the modular Petri net reveals that the modular model posses a t-invariant too, which is {t1, t2, t3, tD1, tD2} (running the GPenSIM function "pinvariant" will give the same result). For example, if one token is put in p4, and let the transitions t1, tD1, t2, tD2, and t3 to fire in that order, the system goes back to the original state of one token in p4. Since it is already shown in Sect. 9.4.1 "General analysis of the Fixes" that tDi can be neglected in comparison with the real transitions, the t-invariant of the modular Petri net becomes the same as its monolithic version.

A note on the process of rearranging segments:
In the example shown above, the monolithic Petri net posses a t-invariant consisting of the transitions t1, t2, and t3. The t-invariant could be a cycle that might frequently occur. In the modular version, the cycle is broken into two groups of transitions, and one group (t1 and t3) become members of one module (module-A) and the other group (t2) a member of the other module (module-B). Technically seen, these two

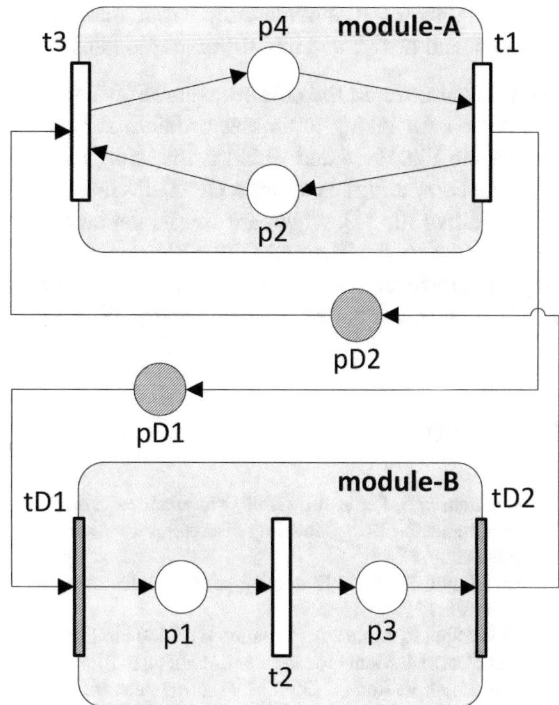

Fig. 9.18 T-invariants of a modular Petri net

versions, monolithic and modular, are the same and provide the results (e.g., same t-invariants as shown above). However, there is a big difference between these two versions:

- If the t-invariant (consisting of the transitions t1, t2, and t3) represents a *frequently occurring cycle of a real system*, then splitting the cycle into two or more modules is a bad idea. This is because of the cycle that span several modules will pass tokens from module to module that may incur additional communication delays, assuming that the modules are hosted on different computers.

As described earlier in Sect. 9.2 "Algorithm: Module Extraction", function "ProcessSegment" is not an automated process as it has to be done by a modeler. It is easy to make a costly mistake during this process. For example, an active cycle (where a cycle involving a number of elements are repeatedly executed) can be broken into several modules during the modularization, due to the inexperience or oversight of the modeler. Decomposing an active cycle into different modules can cause unnecessarily high inter-modular communication, and high simulation time. Hence, the modeler is supposed to analyze and understand the cycles in a monolithic Petri net, before starting to decompose it. In other words, it could be a good idea to perform a top-down approach; starting with crude monolithic Petri net, analyze it for the cycles, and then start modularizing, while making sure that the active cycles are not dissected and distributed into different modules.

A technical note on the computation of T-invariants:
The reason for taking a simpler problem shown in Fig. 9.17 for t-invariants (not the ones in Figs. 9.15 and 9.16) is that computation of t-invariants takes a load of time. For computing t-invariants, GPenSIM uses code that implements the algorithms proposed by [10, 11], which are simple yet takes time as the algorithm is based on numerical analysis. The code GPenSIM uses is implemented by the University of Cagliari. However, there exist newer and faster algorithms (e.g., [8]) for computation of t-invariants, but not yet implemented in GPenSIM.

References

1. Christensen S, Petrucci L (2000) Modular analysis of Petri nets. Comput J 43(3):224–242
2. Davidrajuh R (2018) Modeling discrete-event systems with GPenSIM. Springer International Publishing, Cham
3. Davidrajuh R (2020) Extracting petri modules from large and legacy petri net models. IEEE Access 8:156539–156556
4. Davidrajuh R, Krenczyk D, Skolud B (2019) Finding Clusters in Petri Nets. An approach based on GPenSIM. Model Identif Control 40(1):1–10
5. Davidrajuh R, Rong C (2018) Measuring network centrality in Petri nets, pp 320–323
6. Davidrajuh R, Rong C (2019) Finding the pivotal elements for modularization of Petri nets, pp 92–97
7. DiCesare F, Harhalakis G, Proth J-M, Silva M, Vernadat F (1993) Practice of Petri nets in manufacturing. Springer
8. Ge Q-W, Fukunaga T, Nakata M (2005) On generating elementary t-invariants of Petri nets by linear programming. In: 2005 IEEE international symposium on circuits and systems. IEEE, pp 168–171
9. Jensen J, Kendall WS (1993) Networks and chaos-statistical and probabilistic aspects, vol 50. CRC Press
10. Krückeberg F, Jaxy M (1986) Mathematical methods for calculating invariants in Petri nets. In: European workshop on applications and theory in Petri nets. Springer, pp 104–131
11. Martínez J, Silva M (1982) A simple and fast algorithm to obtain all invariants of a generalised Petri net. In: Application and theory of Petri nets. Springer, pp 301–310

Chapter 10
Activity-Oriented Petri Nets (AOPN)

Sometimes, it may not be possible to modularize a legacy Petri net model due to its crisscrossing internal connections between the elements inside it. For example, a system may have a topology of connections that is close to a complete graph. A complete graph is a graph in which every node is directly connected with all other nodes. A complete graph will be hard to decompose into modules. In this case, "Activity-Oriented Petri nets (AOPN)" could be a remedy.

AOPN is an approach that can be used to simplify Petri modules and Petri net models, especially ones with a large number of system resources. In addition to the Petri net simulator functions, GPenSIM also realizes AOPN on the MATLAB platform. Thus, AOPN has become an integral part of GPenSIM. This chapter also presents a simple application example of AOPN for reducing the size of a Petri net model of a flexible manufacturing system.

10.1 The Background of AOPN

Preliminary work on AOPN was introduced as "Petri net Interpreted for Scheduling (PNS)" in earlier works of this author, e.g., [1, 2]. AOPN is only useful when there are many resources involved in a system, and these resources need not be shown in the Petri net model. Resources always make a Petri net model huge. Let us consider a system with m resources that are shared by n activities. In the Petri net model, there will be m places representing the resources and n transitions for activities. In addition, there will be $(m \times n)$ input arcs from places to transitions, and an equal number of output arcs from the transitions to places. The addition of m places, n transitions, and $(2 \times n \times m)$ arcs will simply overwhelm the Petri net model [3].

R. Davidrajuh, *Petri Nets for Modeling of Large Discrete Systems*, Asset Analytics,
https://doi.org/10.1007/978-981-16-5203-5_10

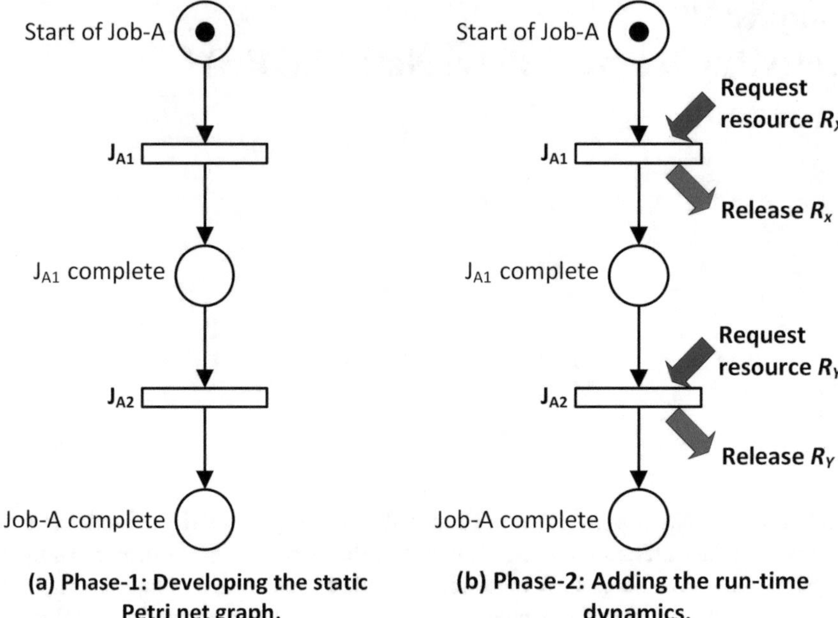

Fig. 10.1 Developing an AOPN model in two phases

10.1.1 Formal Definition of AOPN

Definition 10.1 An **Activity-Oriented Petri net (AOPN)** is defined by the quintuple [3, 4]: $AOPN = (PN, \zeta, IR)$ Where,

- PN is the P/T Petri net given by the Definition 1.1, consisting of a set of places, a set of transitions, a set of bipartite arcs with arc weights, and a set of initial markings.
- $\zeta : T \rightarrow IR$ is a one-to-one function that maps the transition set T onto a set of logical assertions containing logical variables, predicates, events, and the empty symbol; the logical assertions include requests for resources as pre-condition (enabling condition) to start firing.
- IR is a set of resources. □

10.2 Two Phases of the AOPN Approach

The model building with AOPN is performed in two phases, as shown in Fig. 10.1.

In the first phase, the static Petri net graph is developed, with the focus is on the activities. The resources are grouped into two groups such as focal resources and utility resources. Focal resources may also be added to the static Petri net graph, represented by places. Also, utility resources are not considered. The first phase yields a compact static Petri net graph (the "skeleton"), since only the activities (represented by transitions) are put in the Petri net, together with the connections to the focal resources. However, the utility resources are not completely given up, as they will be considered in the second phase. Using the tool GPenSIM, coding the static Petri net in Phase-1 will result in the Petri net definition file (PDF).

The second phase is about the development of the run-time model. In Phase-2, the following run-time issues that are relevant for resource management are considered:

- Transitions (activities) request utility resources to start firing.
- If the requested utility resources are available and allocated to the transition, then the transition starts firing (provided that the other enabling conditions are also satisfied)
- After firing, the transition releases any resources that were allocated to it.

Using the tool GPenSIM, the run-time details in Phase-2 will result in the common processor files COMMON_PRE and COMMON_POST.

During the run-time, the resource management (transitions requesting resources, resource allocation, and transitions releasing resources after use) are abstracted away from the Petri net model and be handled by the underlying infrastructure. The underlying infrastructure also logs the resources usage (e.g., how many times the individual resources are used, by which activities, and for how long; how many times the resource requests were denied; if costs are attached to the resources, then the usage costs of individual resources, posted to which activities).

Finally, the resource management infrastructure is implemented as a part of the software GPenSIM. Hence, the tool GPenSIM can be used for modeling, simulation, and analysis of real-life discrete event systems that involve a large number of resources.

10.3 Application Example on AOPN

Let us take the same Flexible Manufacturing System (FMS) that was introduced in Sect. 3.1 "Model-1: Flexible Manufacturing System" and analyzed in Sect. 4.5 "GPenSIM Application-II: Performance Evaluation". The Petri net model of FMS is reproduced in Fig. 10.2 given below, for the convenience of the readers. In this section, the FMS example is remodeled using the AOPN approach so that the Petri net model becomes much simpler.

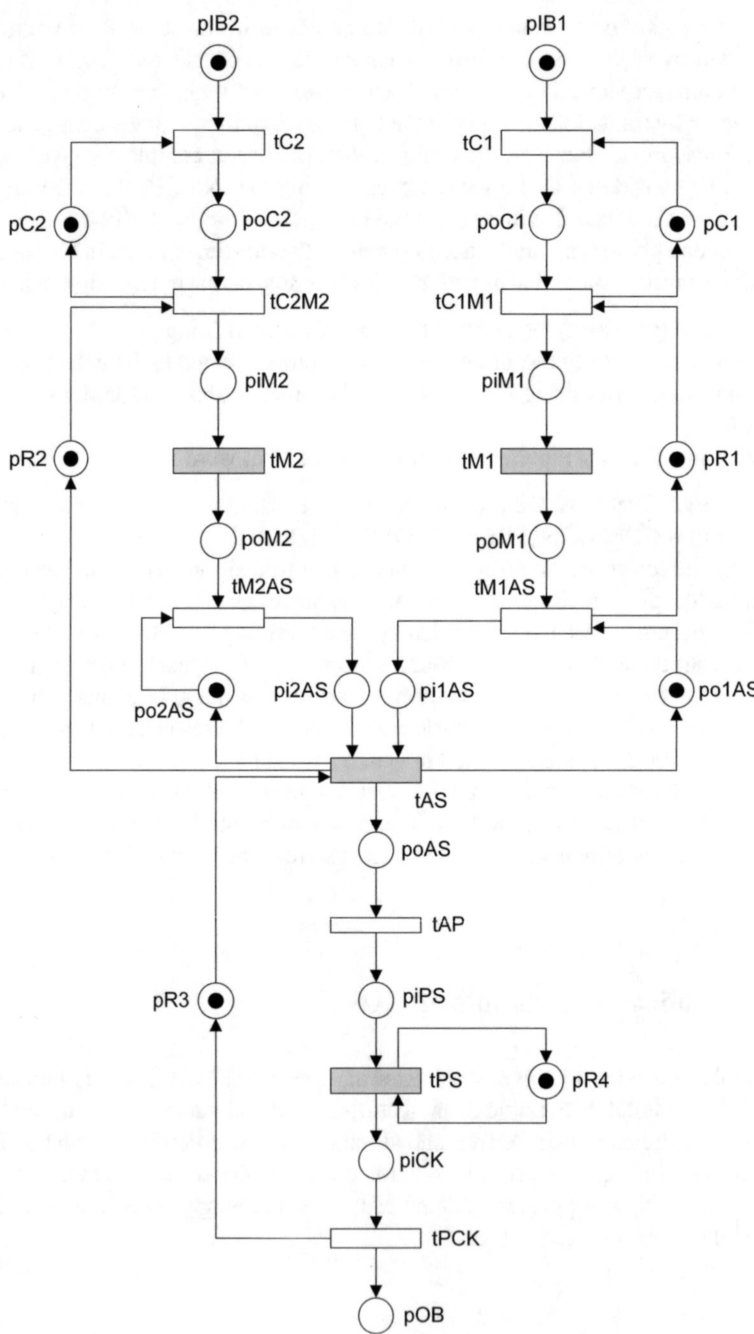

Fig. 10.2 The Petri net model of a flexible manufacturing system [5]

10.3.1 Phase-1: Creating the Static Petri Net Graph

Let the two conveyor belts, the two CNC machines, the assembly station, and the four robots are "utility resources". This means that in the first phase of the AOPN approach, which serves to create the static Petri net graph by taking an "activity-oriented view", only the activities and their precedence relationship between them will be seen in the model. The places representing the utility resources (the conveyor belts, the robots, and the machines) are not considered in Phase-1. Because of the absence of these resources (e.g., represented by places such as pC1, pC2, po1AS, po2AS, pR1, pR2, and so on) in the Petri net graph, along with all their connections (arcs) from these places to the transitions representing the activities, the resulting Petri net graph becomes smaller than the usual Petri net models. Figure 10.3 shows the resulting static Petri net graph by the AOPN approach.

10.3.2 Phase-2: Adding the Run-Time Dynamics

The second phase of the AOPN approach is the addition of the run-time dynamics on the static Petri net graph to make it the initial dynamic Petri net model. For example,

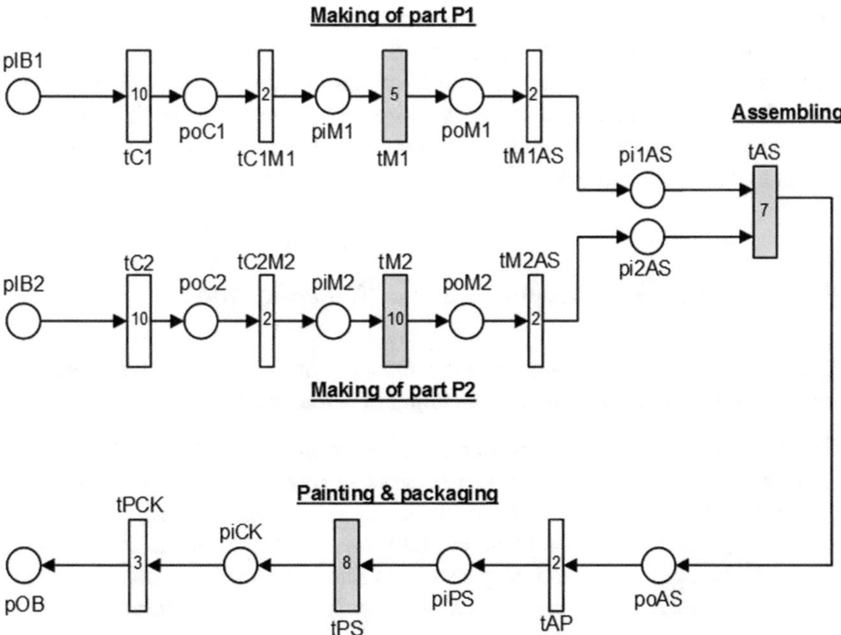

Fig. 10.3 The compact Static Petri net graph obtained by Phase-1

Table 10.1 The activities and the resources used by these activities

Transition	Resources required to start firing	Resources released after firing
tC1	C1	–
tC1M1	R1	C1 (acquired by **tC1)**
tM1	M1	M1
tM1AS	AS (one instance)	R1 (acquired by **tC1M1)**
tC2	C2	–
tC2M2	R2	C2 (acquired by **tC2**)
tM2	M2	M2
tM2AS	AS (one instance)	–
tAS	R3	R2 (acquired by **tC2M2)**, AS (one instance acquired by **tM1AS**), AS (one instance acquired by **tM2AS**)
tAP	–	–
tPS	R4	R4
tPCK	–	R3 (acquired by **tAS**)

the details about the activities requesting, using, and releasing a variety of resources are added in the second phase. The initial markings of the places and the firing times of the transitions are also added in the second phase. Table 10.1 given below, shows the activities and the resources used by these activities.

Figure 10.4 shows the Petri net model obtained after Phase-2 of the AOPN approach. The dynamic model shows the resources required by the different transitions and the resources released after firing. Also, shown in Fig. 10.4 are the initial markings of the places and the firing times of the transitions.

10.3.3 GPenSIM Functions for AOPN Realization

GPenSIM offers some functions for the realization of AOPN. First, some issues in realizing AOPN, especially in the scheduling of resources, is discussed:

- *Instances* of a resource: A resource can have many indistinguishable copies ("instances"), e.g., there are three operators in a lathe machine shop (resource "operator" has three instances). If all the three operators can handle the lathe machines, it does not make sense to prefer one operator over the others. In this case, all the operators could be generalized into a group, name this resource as "operator", and say that operator is a single resource with three instances.

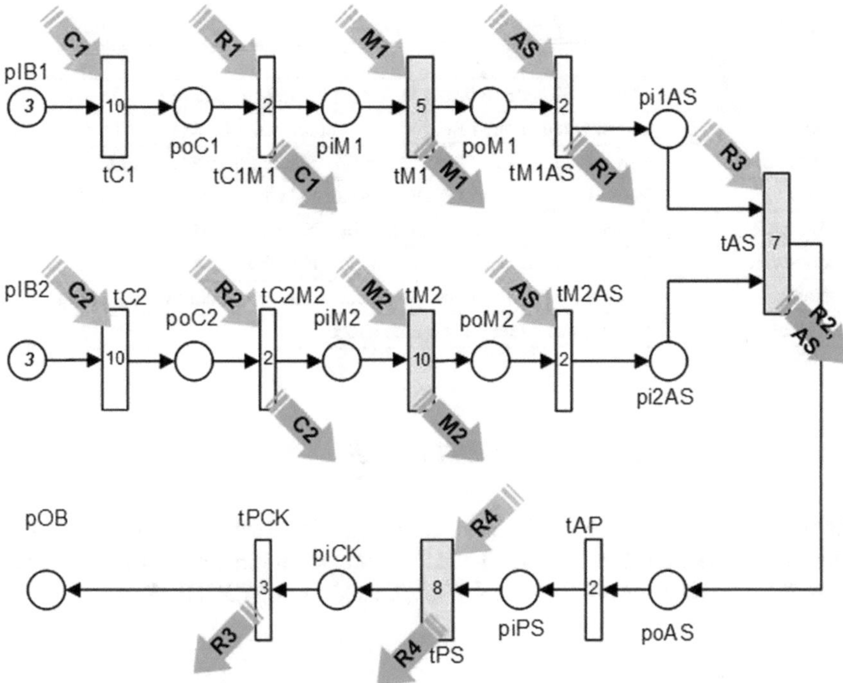

Fig. 10.4 The run-time Petri net model obtained by Phase-2 of the AOPN approach

- *Generic* resources: There are some "named" resources available, but all of them are the same for some specific applications, e.g., in a mechanical workshop, there are three mechanics named "Alan", "Bobby", and "Chan"; though they are specialists in some works, when it comes to engine repair, they all are the same. Thus, for engine repair, a generic mechanic could be chosen, without explicitly naming anyone.
- *Specific* resources: When the resources are named, specific (named) resources could be requested. For example, in the mechanical workshop, "Chan" is an electrician. Hence, for electrical fixing, the use of the specific resource "Chan" could be preferred.
- *Write Access*: When a resource has many instances, a transition may try to acquire one or many of these instances. Write access means that the resource will be locked, and all the instances will be made available to a requesting transition.

Table 10.2 shows the GPenSIM functions available for the modeling of resource scheduling.

Table 10.2 GPenSIM functions for AOPN realization

GPenSIM function	Purpose
availableInst	Check whether any instances are available in a resource
availableRes	Check whether any resources are available (not in use)
requestsSR	Request a number of instances from specific ("named") resources
requestGR	Request a number of resource instances, without naming any resource
requestAR	Request a number of resource instances among many alternatives
requestWR	Request all the instances of a specific resource (either all or none)
release	Release all the resources and resource instances held by a transition
prnschedule	Prints information on resource usage

10.3.4 Simulation of the AOPN Model

As usual, implementing a Petri net model using GPenSIM usually results in four files: the main simulation file (MSF), the Petri net Definition file (PDF), and the two common processor files (COMMON_PRE file and COMMON_POST file).

10.3.4.1 The PDF

The PDF file is shown in Fig. 10.5. The PDF defines the static Petri net graph by declaring the sets of places, transitions, and arcs of the AOPN model shown in Fig. 10.3.

10.3.4.2 The MSF

The MSF is shown in Fig. 10.6. In the MSF, firstly, the initial dynamics (e.g., initial tokens in places, firing times of transitions, available system resources) are declared. Then, the simulation iterations are started by calling the function "gpensim". When the simulation iterations are complete, the results are displayed. The MSF is shown in Fig. 10.6.

Note that in the MSF, only the resource **AS** (Assembly Station) is declared to have two instances, as the transitions **tM1AS** and **tM2AS** will require one instance of **AS** each, to start firing.

10.3.4.3 The COMMON_PRE

The common pre-processor file COMMON_PRE declares the resources required by the enabled transitions to start firing. The required resources by the different transitions are listed in the second column of Table 10.1. The COMMON_PRE is shown in Fig. 10.7.

```
% file: fms_AOPN_pdf.m: PDF
function [png] = fms_AOPN_pdf()

% name or label fo the model
png.PN_name  = 'AOPN model of a FMS';

% set of places
png.set_of_Ps = {...
    'pIB1','pIB2', 'pOB',...         % input and output buffers
    'poC1','poC2','piM1','piM2',... % intermediate buffers
    'poM1','poM2','pAS1','pAS2',... % intermediate buffers
    'poAS', 'piPS', 'piCK'};  % intermediate buffers

% set of transitions
png.set_of_Ts = {'tC1','tC2','tC1M1','tC2M2','tM1','tM2',...
    'tM1AS','tM2AS', 'tAS', 'tAP', 'tPS', 'tPCK'};

% set of arcs
png.set_of_As = {...
    'pIB1','tC1',1, 'tC1','poC1',1, ...      % tC1
    'poC1','tC1M1',1, 'tC1M1','piM1',1, ... % tC1M1
    'piM1','tM1',1, 'tM1','poM1',1,...       % tM1
    'poM1','tM1AS',1, 'tM1AS','pAS1',1,...  % tM1AS
    'pIB2','tC2',1, 'tC2','poC2',1, ...      % tC2
    'poC2','tC2M2',1, 'tC2M2','piM2',1,...  % tC2M2
    'piM2','tM2',1, 'tM2','poM2',1,...       % tM2
    'poM2','tM2AS',1, 'tM2AS','pAS2',1,...  % tM2AS
    'pAS1','tAS',1,'pAS2','tAS',1,'tAS','poAS',1,... % tAS
    'poAS','tAP',1, 'tAP','piPS',1,...       % tAP
    'piPS','tPS',1, 'tPS','piCK',1, ...      % tPS
    'piCK','tPCK',1, 'tPCK','pOB',1};        % tPCK
```

Fig. 10.5 The PDF of the AOPN model

10.3.4.4 The COMMON_POST

The common post-processor file COMMON_POST declares the resources released by the transitions when they complete firing. The resources released by the different transitions are listed in the third column of Table 10.1. The COMMON_POST is shown in Fig. 10.8.

```
% AOPN model of FMS
% MSF: 'fms_AOPN.m'
global global_info
global_info.STOP_AT = 300;

% PDF file
pns = pnstruct('fms_AOPN_pdf');

% initial markings
dp.m0 = {'pIB1',3,'pIB2',3};

% firing times
dp.ft = {'tC1',10,'tC2',10,'tM1',5,'tM2',10,...
     'tAS',7,'tPS',8,'tPCK',3,'allothers',2};

% declaration of resources
dp.re = {'C1',1,inf,'C2',1,inf,...
    'M1',1,inf,'M2',1,inf,...
    'AS',2,inf,...% NOTE: 2 instances, for tM1AS & tM2AS
    'R1',1,inf,'R2',1,inf,'R3',1,inf,'R4',1,inf};

% combine the static and the intial dynamics
pni = initialdynamics(pns, dp);

% run the simulations
sim = gpensim(pni);

% plot and print results
plotp(sim, {'pOB'});
prnschedule(sim); % print resource usuage
plotGC(sim);      % plot resource usuage
```

Fig. 10.6 The MSF of the AOPN model

10.3.4.5 Simulation Results

The simulation result is given in Figs. 10.9, 10.10, and 10.11. The simulation result is for the production of three units of products, as the simulation was started with three initial tokens in each of the places **pIB1** and **pIB2**.

The simulation result gives a very detailed analysis of resource usage. Figures 10.9 and 10.10 shows the resources and the resource instances that were used by transitions. Details such as which transition used the resources, how many times, and for how long, are also shown.

```
function [fire, transition] = COMMON_PRE(transition)

switch transition.name
    case 'tC1'   % conveyor belt "C1" required
        granted = requestSR({'C1',1});
    case 'tC2'   % conveyor belt "C2" required
        granted = requestSR({'C2',1});
    case 'tC1M1' % robot "R1" required
        granted = requestSR({'R1',1});
    case 'tC2M2' % robot "R2" required
        granted = requestSR({'R2',1});
    case 'tM1'   % machine "M1" required
        granted = requestSR({'M1',1});
    case 'tM2'   % machine "M2" required
        granted = requestSR({'M2',1});
    case 'tM1AS' % assembly station "AS" required
        granted = requestSR({'AS',1});
    case 'tM2AS' % assembly station "AS" required
        granted = requestSR({'AS',1});
    case 'tAS'   % robot "R3" required
        granted = requestSR({'R3',1});
    case {'tAP','tPCK'}    % nothing is required
        granted = true;
    case 'tPS'  % painting robot "R4" required
        granted = requestSR({'R4',1});
    otherwise
        error('Cant come here');
end % switch
fire = granted; % fire if the required resource is granted
```

Fig. 10.7 The common pre-processor COMMON_PRE

Figure 10.11 is a summary of the resource usage. If the transitions (activities) and resources were assigned costs (fixed costs and variable costs), then the summary will also show the final costs of the products; however, the costs are neglected (assigned zero value) in this example.

```
function [] = COMMON_POST(transition)
global global_info

switch transition.name
    case {'tC1', 'tC2', 'tAP', 'tM2AS'}
        % do not release any resources as they are
        % required by the subsequent transition
    case 'tC1M1'
        release('tC1'); % release "C1" acquired by tC1
    case 'tC2M2'
        release('tC2'); % release "C2" acquired by tC2
        release;         % also, release "R2" acquired by itself
    case 'tM1'
        release;     % release "M1" acquired by itself
    case 'tM2'
        release;     % release "M2" acquired by itself
    case 'tM1AS'
        release('tC1M1');% release "R1" acquired by tC1M1
    case 'tAS'
        release('tC2M2');% release "R2" acquired by tC2M2
        release('tM1AS');% release "AS-1" acquired by tM1AS
        release('tM2AS');% release "AS-2" acquired by tM2AS
    case 'tPS'
        release;          % release "R4" acquired by itself
    case 'tPCK'
        release('tAS');  % release "R3" acquired by tAP
    otherwise
        error('Cant come here');
end % switch
```

Fig. 10.8 The common post-processor COMMON_POST

10.3.5 Discussion: Advantage of AOPN Approach

The AOPN approach presented in this section can be used to simplify Petri net models of discrete event systems, especially ones with a large number of system resources. The AOPN approach can be used to obtain compact models, and the functions available in GPenSIM can be used for performance evaluation, inclusive of system resources.

To understand the advantage of the AOPN approach from the example given in this section, the two figures, Fig. 10.2 (Timed Petri net model) with Fig. 10.3 (AOPN model), are compared. Figure 10.4 shows the run-time model where the arrows labeled "C1" and "R1" show the transitions requesting and releasing resources during run-time. Again, by comparing Figs. 10.2 and 10.3, it is clear that the AOPN approach provides compact models.

```
RESOURCE USAGE:

RESOURCE INSTANCES OF ***** C1 *****
tC1 [0 : 12]
tC1 [12 : 24]
tC1 [24 : 36]
Resource Instance: C1:: Used 3 times. Utilization time: 36

RESOURCE INSTANCES OF ***** C2 *****
tC2 [0 : 12]
tC2 [12 : 24]
tC2 [24 : 36]
Resource Instance: C2:: Used 3 times. Utilization time: 36

RESOURCE INSTANCES OF ***** M1 *****
tM1 [12 : 17]
tM1 [24 : 29]
tM1 [36 : 41]
Resource Instance: M1:: Used 3 times. Utilization time: 15

RESOURCE INSTANCES OF ***** M2 *****
tM2 [12 : 22]
tM2 [24 : 34]
tM2 [36 : 46]
Resource Instance: M2:: Used 3 times. Utilization time: 30

RESOURCE INSTANCES OF ***** AS *****
(AS-1):   tM1AS [17 : 31]
(AS-2):   tM2AS [22 : 31]
(AS-1):   tM1AS [31 : 51]
(AS-2):   tM2AS [34 : 51]
(AS-1):   tM1AS [51 : 71]
(AS-2):   tM2AS [51 : 71]
Resource Instance: (AS-1):: Used 3 times.  Utilization time: 54
Resource Instance: (AS-2):: Used 3 times.  Utilization time: 46
```

Fig. 10.9 The simulation results (part-1)

The main advantage of the AOPN approach is the following. For the AOPN approach, as GPenSIM provides resource management support during simulations (managing resource reservations, allocations, and retrievals), a detailed analysis of the resource usage can be obtained. The details also include the costs (activity costs, resource costs, and the total cost), if the costs are added to the transitions and resources in the MSF.

```
RESOURCE INSTANCES OF ***** R1 *****
tC1M1 [10 : 19]
tC1M1 [22 : 33]
tC1M1 [34 : 53]
Resource Instance: R1:: Used 3 times. Utilization time: 39

RESOURCE INSTANCES OF ***** R2 *****
tC2M2 [10 : 12]
tC2M2 [22 : 24]
tC2M2 [34 : 36]
Resource Instance: R2:: Used 3 times. Utilization time: 6

RESOURCE INSTANCES OF ***** R3 *****
tAS [24 : 44]
tAS [44 : 64]
tAS [64 : 84]
Resource Instance: R3:: Used 3 times. Utilization time: 60

RESOURCE INSTANCES OF ***** R4 *****
tPS [33 : 41]
tPS [53 : 61]
tPS [73 : 81]
Resource Instance: R4:: Used 3 times. Utilization time: 24
```

Fig. 10.10 The simulation results (part-2)

10.4 When Not to Use AOPN

AOPN is invented for the sole purpose of simplifying Petri net model of a real-life system in which there are many utility resources. Utility resources refer to the resources that need not be shown in the Petri net model, such as resources that are always plenty and never fail.

However, AOPN cannot be used to make smaller state spaces. For example, if a Petri net model generates a huge state space (as usual), then AOPN cannot be used to slice this Petri net smaller so that the resulting state space will be also smaller. This assumption, slimmer the Petri net smaller the state space, is not correct [6]. On the contrary, AOPN usually makes the state space larger.

```
RESOURCE USAGE SUMMARY:
C1:  Total occasions: 3   Total Time spent: 36
C2:  Total occasions: 3   Total Time spent: 36
M1:  Total occasions: 3   Total Time spent: 15
M2:  Total occasions: 3   Total Time spent: 30
AS:  Total occasions: 6   Total Time spent: 100
R1:  Total occasions: 3   Total Time spent: 39
R2:  Total occasions: 3   Total Time spent: 6
R3:  Total occasions: 3   Total Time spent: 60
R4:  Total occasions: 3   Total Time spent: 24

*****  LINE EFFICIENCY AND COST CALCULATIONS: *****
  Number of servers:  k = 9
  Total number of server instances:  K = 10
  Completion = 84
  LT = 840
  Total time at Stations: 346
  LE = 41.1905 %
  **
  Sum resource usage costs: 0   (NaN% of total)
  Sum firing costs: 0   (NaN% of total)
  Total costs:  0
  **
```

Fig. 10.11 The simulation results: resource usage summary

References

1. Davidrajuh R (2011) Representing resources in Petri net models: Hardwiring or soft-coding? In: Proceedings of 2011 IEEE international conference on service operations, logistics and informatics. IEEE, pp 62–67
2. Davidrajuh R (2011) Scheduling using "activity-based modeling". In: 2011 IEEE international conference on computer applications and industrial electronics (ICCAIE). IEEE, pp 45–49
3. Davidrajuh R (2013) Realizing simple Petri net models for complex and large scheduling problems: An approach based activity-oriented Petri nets. pp 419–423
4. Davidrajuh R (2012) Activity-oriented Petri net for scheduling of resources. In: 2012 IEEE international conference on systems, man, and cybernetics (SMC). IEEE, pp 1201–1206
5. Davidrajuh R, Skolud B, Krenczyk D (2018) Performance evaluation of discrete event systems with gpensim. Computers 7(1):1–8
6. Davidrajuh R (2020) Experimenting with the static slicing of petri nets, pp 25–30

Part IV
Collaborating Modules

Chapter 11
Discrete Systems as Petri Modules

This chapter is about putting the Petri modules together in a modular Petri net. This chapter consists of three groups of sections. In the first section, nine blocks are introduced as the basic building blocks of a discrete system. The second section introduces six matrices, such as Adjacency, Laplacian, Reachability, Rader's, Connection, and Component matrices. The third section introduces the spanning tree and connected components of a graph. All the material introduced in this chapter will be used in the newer algorithms developed in the next chapter (Chap. 12 "Algorithms for Modular Networks").

Literature study that was done in Chap. 5 "Literature Review on Modular Petri Nets" indicates that most of the discrete systems can be modularized. Literature study also reveals that there are some basic building blocks of discrete systems [2, 3, 9–11]. Figures 11.4, 11.5, 11.6, 11.7, 11.8, 11.9, 11.10, and 11.11 shows the nine basic building blocks of discrete systems.

Assumption 11.1 (*A fundamental assumption of this book*) A modular system can be built by using one or more of the nine building blocks shown in Figs. 11.4, 11.5, 11.6, 11.7, 11.8, 11.9, 11.10, and 11.11. If part of the system cannot be composed by using one or more of the nine building blocks, then the system is pronounced non-modular and is out of the scope of this book.

The rest of this section discusses two simple and seeming obvious properties, namely, *timing* and *collaborativeness*. Then, these two properties are used to analyze the connectivity of modular Petri net models, to make sure whether the topology of connection can work either in a leader-followers, negotiating-peers, or Steiner-mode setting.

R. Davidrajuh, *Petri Nets for Modeling of Large Discrete Systems*, Asset Analytics,
https://doi.org/10.1007/978-981-16-5203-5_11

11.1 Module Abstraction

Figure 11.1 shows a simplified (abstracted) version of a module. This version will be used for the analysis of the basic building blocks. The input ports and the output ports are represented by one transition **tI** and another **tO**, respectively. A time delay **tD** represents the internal mechanism of the module.

Note:

1. This module abstraction can represent any module except a source module or a sink module (Fig. 11.11). A source module may not consume any tokens from outside. Hence, it may not need **tI**. It is the source module that itself produces tokens and sends those tokens through **tO** to the rest of the system. Whereas, a sink module may not possess a **tO**. This is because, in a sink module, the tokens that arrive through **tI** could be destroyed or saved inside the module. Thus, it may not need **tO**.
2. When the abstracted module is used in multiple numbers, the internals (time delay mechanism) will not be shown as displayed in the rest of the figures in this chapter.
3. In Figs. 11.4, 11.5, 11.6, 11.7, 11.8, 11.9, 11.10, and 11.11, the modules are connected by IMCs which are places. These places are again an abstraction. Between the two modules, there can be some places and transitions that can function as IMC. However, since the focus is on the modules and the topology of the connection between the modules, the IMCs can be abstracted away and be substituted by places.

11.1.1 Collaborativeness and Timing

A module m_i is defined as *collaborative* whenever a token enters the module through **tI**, it will cause a token to be ejected through **tO** after a finite time lap $\mathcal{T}_{m_i} \in \mathbb{R}^+$.

Definition 11.1 (*Collaborativeness of a module* ($\mathcal{C}_{m_i}$))

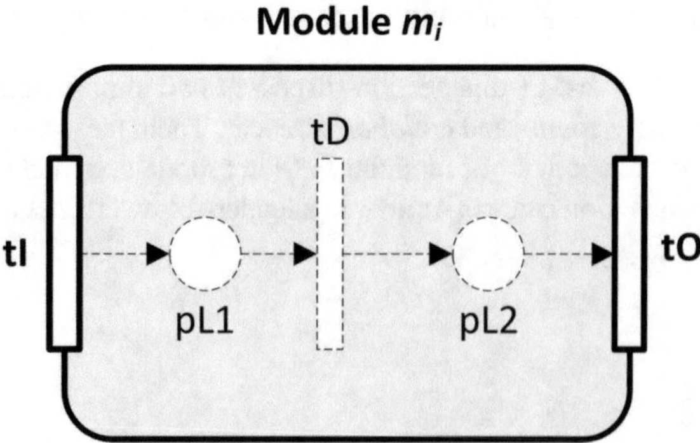

Fig. 11.1 A simplified module (abstraction)

$$\boldsymbol{M_0[tI\rangle \Rightarrow M'[tO\rangle, M' = M_0[f(t)\rangle}$$

In other words, if **tI** becomes enabled, then there will be series of firing $f(t)$ after which **tO** will become enabled to fire. □

Note: Some literature (e.g., [4, 5]) defines collaborativeness differently than that of Definition 11.1. For example, Liu and Jiang [4] defines collaborativeness as the characteristic of an individual process as well as a group of processes. In our definition (Definition 11.1), collaborativeness becomes the property of an individual module, an indicator of the module's ability or willingness to participate in a collaboration.

Definition 11.2 Timing of a module (T_{m_i}) is defined as the time it takes for an arriving token at **tI** and the resulting token to leave **tO**. More precisely, the time difference between the **tI** of m_i starts firing and the **tO** of m_i completes firing.

$$T_{m_i} = tO^{\downarrow} - tI^{\uparrow}$$

□

Figure 11.2 shows the timing of a module, assuming that the internal activities can be represented by a simple time delay tD. Figure 11.2a shows T_{m_i} as the time difference between $tO^{\downarrow}$ and $tI^{\uparrow}$. Alternatively, Fig. 11.2b shows T_{m_i} as the time difference between the time an input token is consumed from $pIMC_i$ by **tI** and the time an output token is deposited into $pIMC_{i+1}$ by **tO**.

11.1.2 Collaborative Module

Definition 11.1 defines the collaborativeness of a module. When a group of modules is about to start a collaboration, it is important to check whether a module is willing or able to participate in the collaboration. There can be several reasons for a module unwilling or unable to participate in a collaboration. Let us categorize these reasons in three cases:

- Case-1: No contacts with the module.
- Case-2: The module is under deadlock.
- Case-3: The module is under livelock.

Module-A in Fig. 11.3 symbolically shows the case-1. In this case, either the communication between the module and the rest of the system is not working. Or, the computer that is hosting this module is simply switched off.

Module-B in Fig. 11.3 shows the case-2. In case-2, the module is accessible in a sense the **tI** consumes a token (e.g., accepts a message) from the input IMC buffer (e.g., the communication channel). However, the module cannot send a token out of it, due to the deadlock (the token arrived at pBL0 can only be consumed by tBL1 or tBL2; thus, tBO would not have the two enabling tokens, one each in both pBL1 and

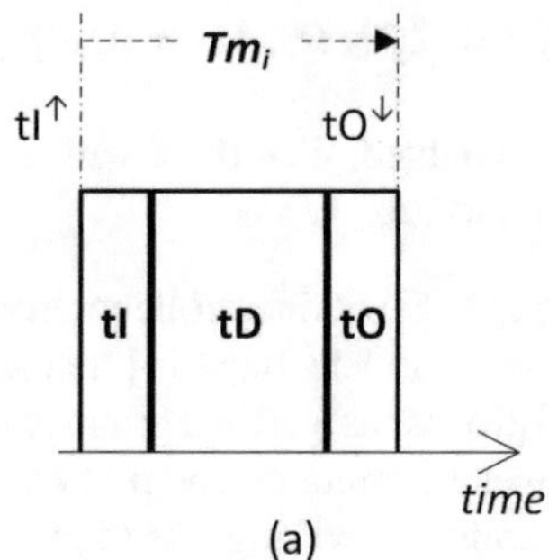

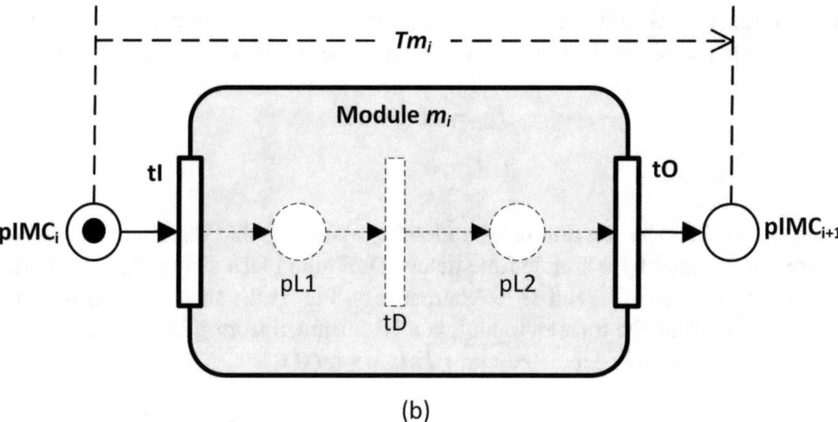

Fig. 11.2 Timing of a module

pBL2). In a deadlock, none of the transitions is enabled, due to the lack of enabling tokens. A deadlock situation usually arises due to the lack of resources.

Definition 11.3 (*Deadlock*) A module is said to be in deadlock if the following conditions are met:

1. $M_0[tI\rangle \wedge \overrightarrow{tI}$
2. $\forall M^{'} \in R, \; \forall t \in T, \quad \neg M^{'}[t\rangle$ □

Condition-1 states that if **tI** is enabled and has fired, then by condition-2, none of the transitions in any possible marking will be enabled.

Finally, Module-C in Fig. 11.3 shows the case-3, the livelock situation. Just like case-2 deadlock situation, a module under livelock consumes a token from the input IMC buffer. However, the module cannot send a token out of it due to its livelock. In a livelock, some transitions are enabled and fire. However, these transitions are involved in a cycle that is not breakable or cannot be terminated (in Module-C, if the token in pCL0 is consumed by tCL1, then tCL1 and pCL1 will make a cycle that will run forever). Thus, in this case too, the module is unable to send a token out

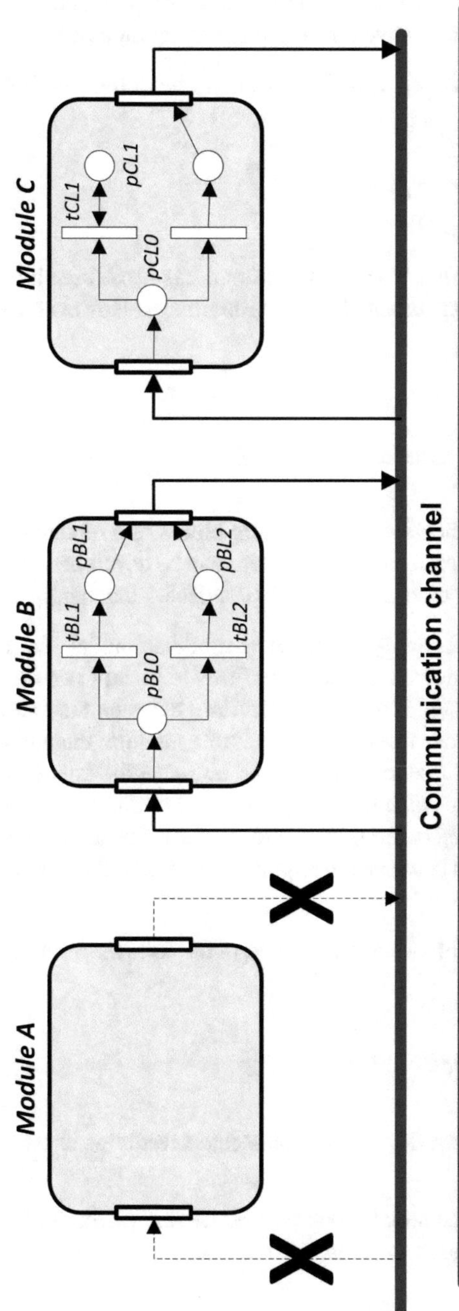

Fig. 11.3 Collaborative module: three cases

of the module, making this module not collaborative. A livelock situation usually means that a module is involved in an internal activity, and hence not able or willing to participate in a collaborative effort, with external modules.

Definition 11.4 (*Livelock*) A module is said to be in livelock if the following conditions are met:

1. $M_0[tI\rangle \ \wedge \ \overrightarrow{tI}$
2. $\forall M' \in R, \ \exists t \in T \quad M'[t\rangle$
3. $\forall M' \in R, \quad \neg M'[tO\rangle$ □

Condition-1 states that if **tI** is enabled and has fired, then by condition-2, there will be some transitions enabled in some markings. However, by condition-3, **tO** will never be enabled.

11.2 Loosely Connected Modules

This section presents the nine basic building blocks of a modular discrete system. A modular Petri net model of a discrete system can be developed by composing one or more of the nine basic blocks in a loosely connected manner.

Definition 11.5 In a **Loosely Connected** modular model, the modules are connected only through the well-defined interfaces (e.g., input and output ports). Also, the connection (e.g., Inter-Modular Connection) between the modules is passive, as the connection itself does not pass tokens into a module; the input port of the module must actively consume tokens from the buffer in the connection. Similarly, the connection itself cannot take output tokens from a module; it is the output port of the module that must eject the tokens into the buffer of the connection. Finally, the number of connections between the modules (inter-modular connections) is kept to a minimum. □

The basic building blocks are described in the following subsections.

11.2.1 Serial Block

In the serial block, the modules are connected serially as shown in Fig. 11.4. In a serial block:

- Timing: timing of the serial block will be he sum of the timing taken by all the modules that undergo in the connection.

$$\mathcal{T}_m = \sum_{i=1}^{n} \mathcal{T}_{m_i}$$

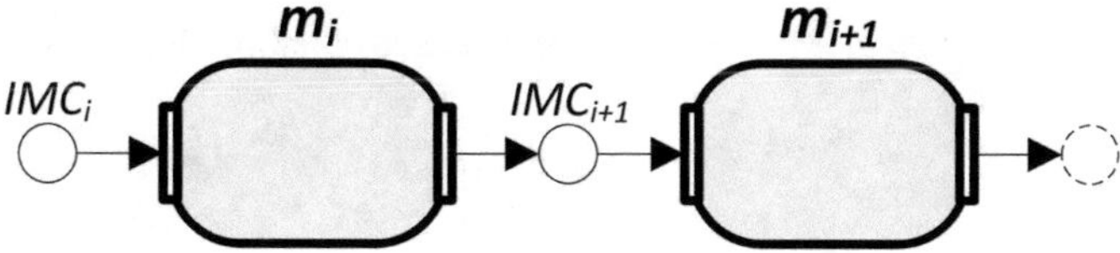

Fig. 11.4 Serially connected modules

- Collaborativeness: if all the modules are collaborative, then the block is also collaborative.

$$\mathcal{C}_m = \bigcap_{i=1}^{n} \mathcal{C}_{m_i}$$

11.2.2 Parallel Block

In the parallel block, the modules are connected in parallel as shown in Fig. 11.5. In a parallel block:

- Timing: timing of the parallel block will range between be the timing taken by the fastest module to the slowest module.

$$\mathcal{T}_m =< \mathcal{T}_{m_{min}}, \mathcal{T}_{m_{max}} >$$

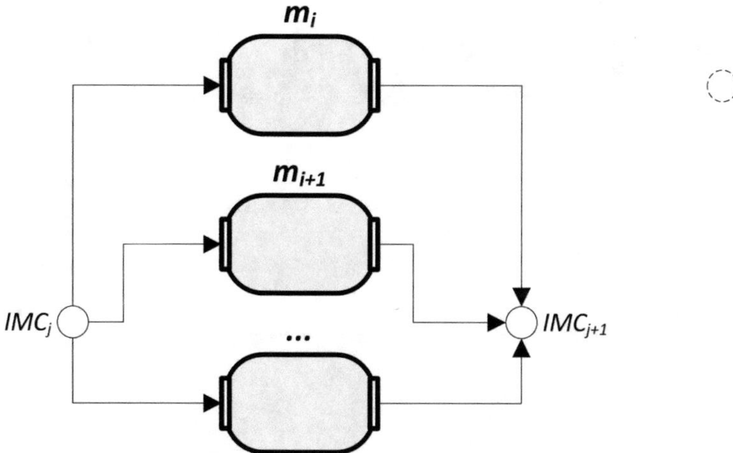

Fig. 11.5 Parallelly connected modules

- Collaborativeness: if at least one of the modules is collaborative, then the block is also collaborative.

$$\mathcal{C}_m = \bigcup_{i=1}^{n} \mathcal{C}_{m_i}$$

11.2.3 Cyclic (Iterating) Block

In the cyclic block, the modules are connected in a cyclic path. The cyclic block go through a number of iterations ***r***, determined by terminator module; see Fig. 11.6. Thus, in a cyclic block:

- Timing: timing of the block will be the number of iterations (***r***) multiplied by the sum of the timing of all the modules involved in the cyclic path.

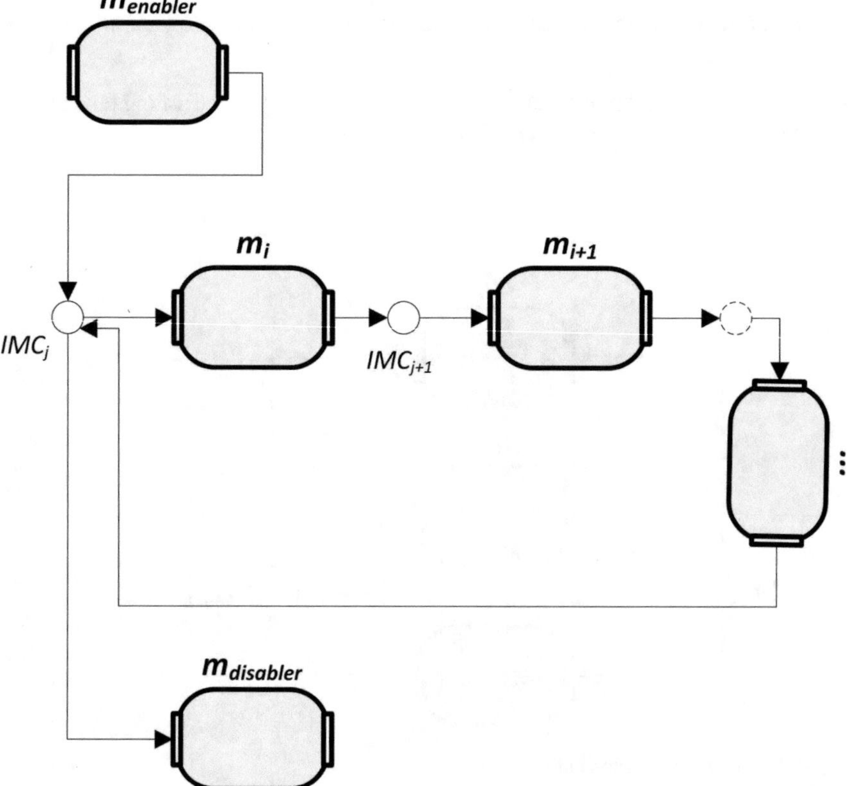

Fig. 11.6 Cyclically connected modules

$$\mathcal{T}_m = r \times \sum_{i=1}^{n} \mathcal{T}_{m_i}$$

- Collaborativeness: the block is collaborative as long as all the modules are collaborative as long as the iterations last.

$$\mathcal{C}_m = \bigcap_{i=1}^{n} \mathcal{C}_{m_i}$$

11.2.4 Alternating (Mutual-Exclusion) Block

In this block, the modules are enabled one at a time (mutually exclusive), see Fig. 11.7. Thus, in an alternating block:

- Timing: timing of the block will be either $\mathcal{T}_{m_i}$ or $\mathcal{T}_{m_j}$.

$$\mathcal{T}_m =< \mathcal{T}_{m_i}, \mathcal{T}_{m_j} >$$

- Collaborativeness: the block is collaborative as long as at least one of the module is collaborative.

$$\mathcal{C}_m = \mathcal{C}_{m_i} \cup \mathcal{C}_{m_j}$$

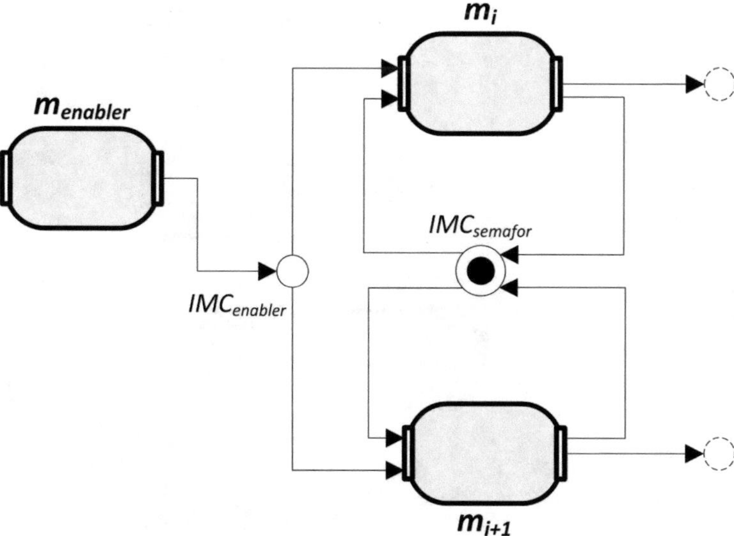

Fig. 11.7 Alternatively enabled modules

11.2.5 Independent Block

In the independent block (Fig. 11.8), the modules are not connected with each other in any way. Hence, the block timing cannot be computed from the timing of the individual modules. Similarly, the collaborativeness cannot be computed either.

11.2.6 Assembly Block

In the assembly block (Fig. 11.9), the assembler module will wait until all the proceeding modules are complete. Thus, in an assembly block:

- Timing: timing of the block will be the longest time taken by m_i or m_j, in addition to the timing of m_k.

$$\mathcal{T}_m = max(\mathcal{T}_{m_i}, \mathcal{T}_{m_j}) + \mathcal{T}_{m_k}$$

- Collaborativeness: the block is collaborative if and only if the assembly module all the blocks are collaborative.

$$\mathcal{C}_m = \mathcal{C}_{m_i} \cup \mathcal{C}_{m_j} \cup \mathcal{C}_{m_k}$$

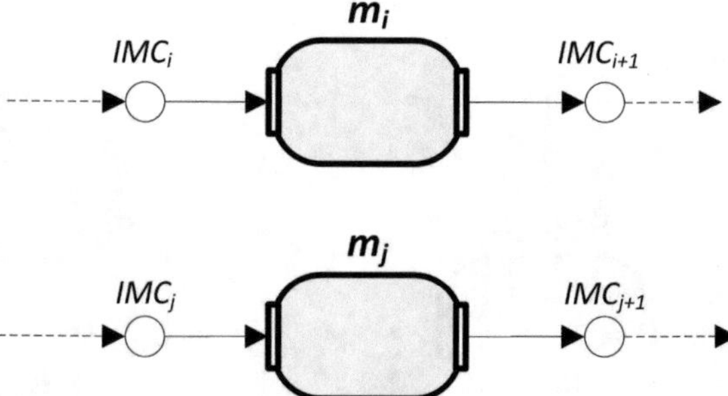

Fig. 11.8 Independent modules

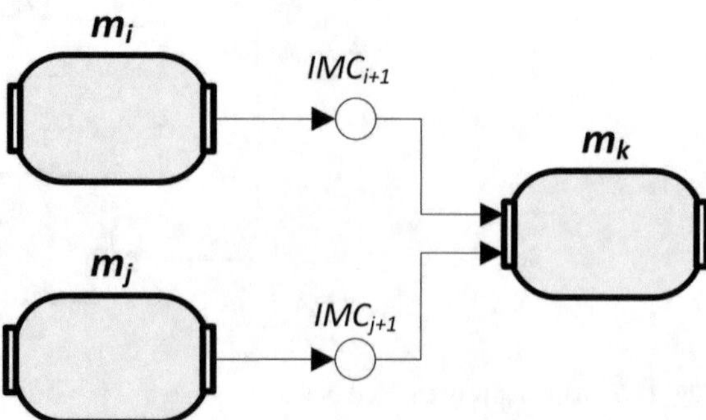

Fig. 11.9 Assembly modules

11.2.7 Disassembly Block

In the disassembly block (Fig. 11.10), the disassembler module will start modules in different branches. Thus, in a disassembly block:

- Timing: timing of the block will be the time taken by the disassembler module itself.

$$\mathcal{T}_m = \mathcal{T}_{m_i}$$

- Collaborativeness: the block is collaborative if disassembler module is collaborative.

$$\mathcal{C}_m = \mathcal{C}_{m_i}$$

11.2.8 Source Block and Sink Block

In simple terms, the source blocks produce tokens, whereas sink blocks absorb (consume and destroy) tokens (Fig. 11.11). Thus, in a source/sink block:

- Timing: timing of the block will be the time taken by the source/sink module.

$$\mathcal{T}_m = \mathcal{T}_{m_i}$$

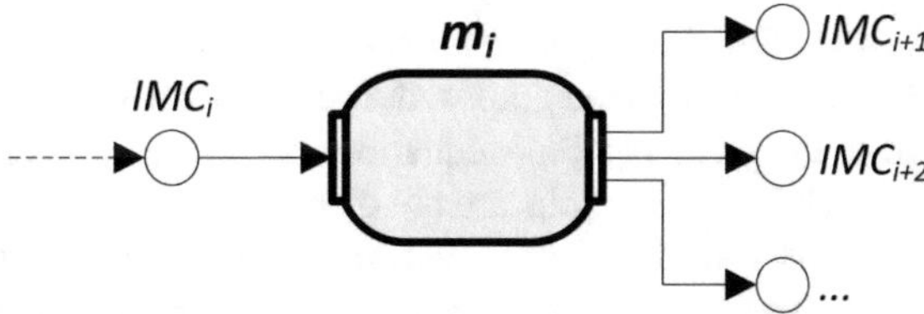

Fig. 11.10 Disassembly module

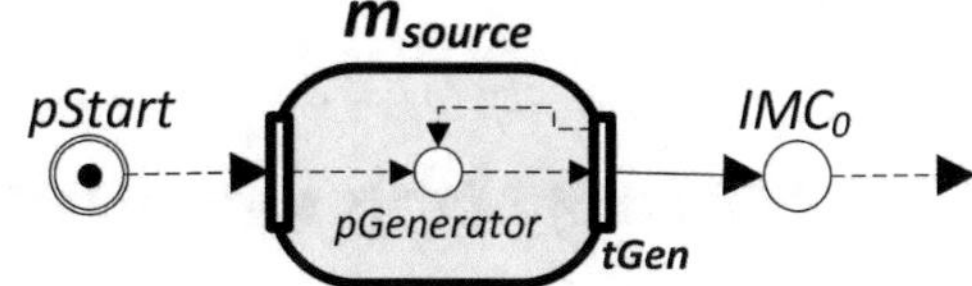

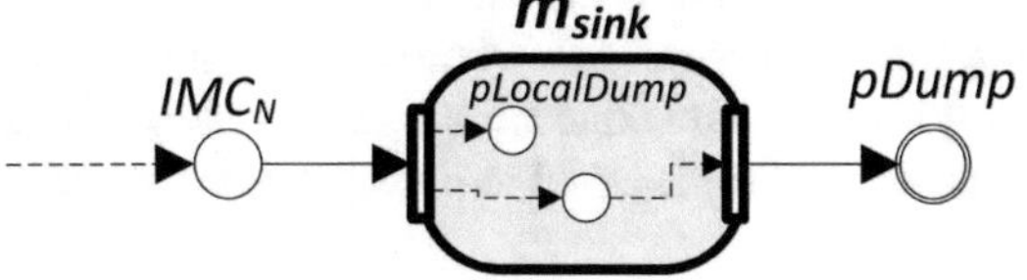

Fig. 11.11 Source module and sink module

- Collaborativeness: the block is collaborative if the source/sink module is collaborative.

$$\mathcal{C}_m = \mathcal{C}_{m_i}$$

11.3 Analysis: Connectivity of Modules

Before starting with the analysis of connectivity of modules, some basic graph algebraic definitions, functions, and equations are given in this section.

Why is this section relevant? A modular Petri net model can be developed in two possible ways:

- Legacy models: By applying the top-down approach, a monolithic Petri net can be decomposed into modules, and the modules can be connected to form the modular model.
- From scratch: By the bottom-up approach, start developing modules independently of each other, and finally connect the modules to form the overall model.

When the modular model is put into action, it may not function as expected. For example, some of the modules cannot be reached, or even if all the modules can be reached, some of the modules are not able to participate in negotiations. This section presents the graph algebraic solution to these problems. Network connectivity analysis is to find out whether the connections between the modules in a modular Petri net model will allow the model to work as it is supposed to.

Assumption 11.2 (*Fundamental assumption: all graphs are directed graphs*) As Petri nets are directed graphs, the connections between the modules are directed too. Thus, the graph algebraic equations presented in this section are for directed graphs only. Undirected graphs are not discussed in this section.

On the other hand, if needed, an undirected graph can be represented by a directed graph. This is possible by replacing each undirected edge with two directed edges with opposing directions.

11.4 Adjacency Matrix and Laplacian Matrix

Definition 11.6 **Adjacency matrix** (A) represents the connections in a directed graph $G = (V, E)$, V is the set of all the vertices and E is the set of all the edges. The dimensions of A is (m, m), where m is the number of vertices, $m = |V|$. $A(i, j) = a_{ij} = 0$ if there is no edge from v_i to v_j. $a_{ij} \neq 0$ if there is an edge from v_i to v_j, and the value of a_{ij} is equal to the arc weight of the edge from v_i to v_j. □

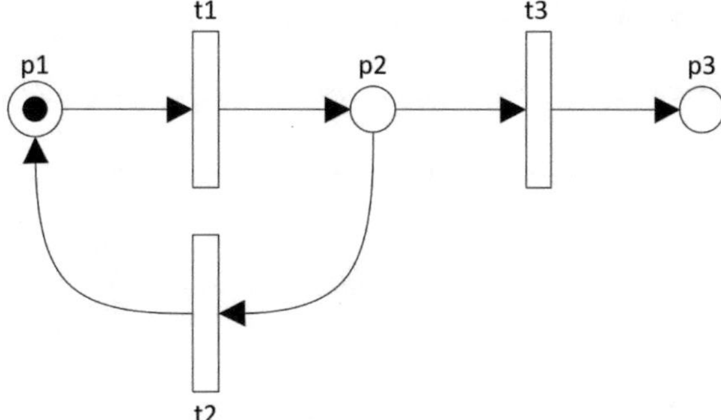

Fig. 11.12 A simple P-T Petri net

Definition 11.7 **Laplacian matrix** (L) is defined be the following equation:

$$L = D - A \tag{11.1}$$

where A is the Adjacency matrix and D is a diagonal matrix of elements, $d_{ii} = \sum_{j=i}^{n} a_{ij}$, $d_{ij} = 0$, if $i \neq j$. □

In other words, the diagonal element of D, d_{ii} is the **out-degree** of a vertex v_i, meaning sum of the weights of arcs going outwards from the vertex v_i.

Example 11.1 (**Adjacency and Laplacian matrices**) A simple P/T Petri net is shown in Fig. 11.12.

The adjacency matrix A and the Laplacian matrix L of the Petri net is given below

$$\mathbf{A} = \begin{array}{c} \\ p1 \\ t1 \\ p2 \\ t2 \\ p3 \\ t3 \end{array} \begin{array}{c} \begin{array}{cccccc} p1 & t1 & p2 & t2 & p3 & t3 \end{array} \\ \begin{pmatrix} 0 & 1 & 0 & 0 & 0 & 0 \\ 0 & 0 & 1 & 0 & 0 & 0 \\ 0 & 0 & 0 & 1 & 0 & 1 \\ 1 & 0 & 0 & 0 & 0 & 0 \\ 0 & 0 & 0 & 0 & 0 & 0 \\ 0 & 0 & 0 & 0 & 1 & 0 \end{pmatrix} \end{array}$$

$$\mathbf{L} = \begin{array}{c} \\ p1 \\ t1 \\ p2 \\ t2 \\ p3 \\ t3 \end{array} \begin{array}{c} \begin{array}{cccccc} p1 & t1 & p2 & t2 & p3 & t3 \end{array} \\ \begin{pmatrix} 1 & -1 & 0 & 0 & 0 & 0 \\ 0 & 1 & -1 & 0 & 0 & 0 \\ 0 & 0 & 2 & -1 & 0 & -1 \\ -1 & 0 & 0 & 1 & 0 & 0 \\ 0 & 0 & 0 & 0 & 0 & 0 \\ 0 & 0 & 0 & 0 & -1 & 1 \end{pmatrix} \end{array}$$

Lemma 11.1 *The diagonal elements of the adjacency matrix of a Petri net are zero.*

Proof Petri net is a bipartite graph. Therefore, there cannot be an arc from an element to itself. Thus, $a_{ii} = 0$. Hence, the diagonal elements of A are zero. □

Lemma 11.2 *The Laplacian matrix is singular.*

Proof Every row in the Laplacian matrix sums to zero.

$$\forall i \in (1:m), \quad L(i,:) = [-a_{i1}, -a_{i2}, \ldots, d_{ii}, -a_{i(i+1)}, \ldots,]$$

$$Sum(L(i:)) = -\sum_{j=1,\ j\neq i}^{n} a_{ij} + L_{ii}$$

Since $L_{ii} = d_{ii} = \sum_{j=1,\ j\neq i}^{n} a_{ij}$,

$$Sum(L(i:)) = 0, \quad \forall i \in (1:m)$$

Hence, the Laplacian matrix L is singular. □

Lemma 11.3 *The first eigenvalue of the Laplacian matrix L is zero.*

Proof Since L is singular, there must be a vector v s.t., $Lv = 0$. Thus, $Lv = \lambda v = 0$, meaning the eigen value is zero. □

The second eigenvalue λ_2 is known as the "**Algebraic Connectivity**" [6]. Algebraic connectivity is a very important property in determining the qualities of a networked system, as discussed in the next subsection.

11.5 Spanning Tree and Connectedness

Definition 11.8 A **Spanning Tree** (ST) of a directed graph $G = (V, E)$ is a subgraph in the form of a tree which includes all of the vertices of G. However, the tree must have minimum possible number of edges [1].

If the graph is strongly connected, then there can be several trees each starting with a different vertex as the source (root).

Strongly connectedness is already defined in Definition 1.12.

Example 11.2 (**Spanning Tree** and **Connected Components**) Considering the simple Petri net shown in Fig. 11.12, it has four spanning trees, each starting with the following nodes: p1, t1, p2, t2. The four spanning trees are shown in Fig. 11.13.

The Petri net is not strongly connected. Instead, it has three components, namely,
Component-1: {p1, t1, p2, t2}.
Component-2: {t3}.
Component-3: {p3}.

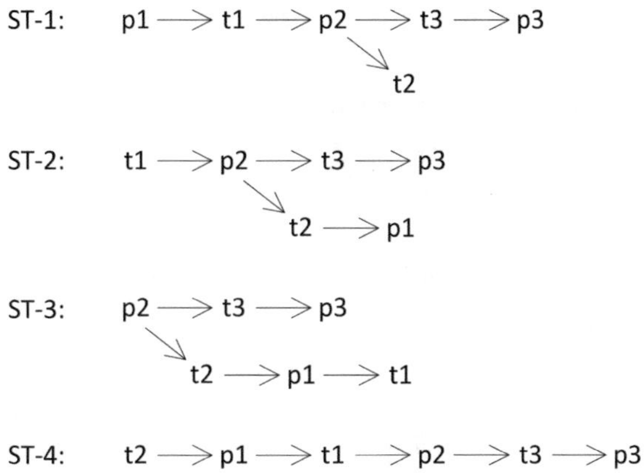

ST-1: p1 → t1 → p2 → t3 → p3
p2 → t2

ST-2: t1 → p2 → t3 → p3
p2 → t2 → p1

ST-3: p2 → t3 → p3
p2 → t2 → p1 → t1

ST-4: t2 → p1 → t1 → p2 → t3 → p3

Fig. 11.13 The four spanning trees

11.5.1 Spanning Tree and Connected Components

A Petri net is composed of one (in case of strong connectedness) or more connected components and may also possess Spanning Trees.

Lemma 11.4 *Let a Petri net has m number of places and n number of transitions. If the Petri net is strongly connected, then there are at least $(m + n)$ number of spanning trees, each starting with one of $(m + n)$ element as the* **root** *(aka* **source***) of the tree.*

Proof If the Petri net is strongly connected, then there is a path from one element in the graph to every other element. Thus, taking one element at a time as the source, there are $(m + n)$ number of spanning trees. □

Lemma 11.5 *Let a modular Petri net be composed of m number of modules and n number of inter-modular connectors. If the modular Petri net strongly connected, then there are at least $(m + n)$ number of spanning trees, each starting with one of m modules and n inter-modular connectors as the source of the three.*

Proof The proof is similar to the previous proof. In the previous proof, places are replaced with modules and transitions with inter-modular connector elements. □

Lemma 11.6 *If a directed graph is strongly connected, then there exists a spanning tree.*

Proof This lemma is a generalization of the previous two lemmas, Lemmas 11.4 and 11.5.

Theorem 11.1 *(The Algebraic Connectivity and the Spanning Tree) The Algebraic Connectivity λ_2 is non-zero, if and only if the graph has a spanning tree.* □

Proof The proof is given in [6].

11.6 The Four Matrices

Finally, there are four more matrices that are needed to be understood before the algorithms can be presented. The four matrices are:

1. Reachability Matrix.
2. Rader's Matrix.
3. Connection Matrix.
4. Component Matrix.

11.6.1 Reachability Matrix

The adjacency matrix A shows the immediate connections between two vertices. In each row-i, if a_{ij} is not zero, then element-i has an output to element-j. For example, in Fig. 11.14, the third row shows p2 has two outputs, to t2 and t3. Similarly, each column-j shows the inputs from other elements to the element-j. In Fig. 11.14, the fourth column shows t2 has one input from p2. Hence, matrix A is about one-step, from which element one can move another element in one-step.

Matrix A^2 $(= A \times A)$ is about two-steps. If $a^2_{ij} \in A^2$ is not equal to zero, then there is a path from element-i to element-j in two-steps. Also, the value of a^2_{ij} indicates how many different paths are there from element-i to element-j in two-steps. For example, if $a^2_{ij} = 1$, there is only one two-steps path between the elements i and j.

Similarly, matrix $A^r = A \times A \times A \cdots = \prod_{i=1}^{r} A$ is about r-steps. If $a^r_{ij} \in A^r$ is not equal to zero, then there is a path from element-i to element-j in r-steps. Also, the value of a^r_{ij} indicates how many different paths are there from element-i to element-j in r-steps. For example, if $a^r_{ij} = l$, there are l-number of r-steps paths between the elements i and j.

The **reachability matrix** R is defined by the following equation ($|E|$ represents the total number of edges):

$$\mathbf{A} = \begin{array}{c} \\ p1 \\ t1 \\ p2 \\ t2 \\ p3 \\ t3 \end{array} \begin{array}{c} \begin{array}{cccccc} p1 & t1 & p2 & t2 & p3 & t3 \end{array} \\ \begin{pmatrix} 0 & 1 & 0 & 0 & 0 & 0 \\ 0 & 0 & 1 & 0 & 0 & 0 \\ 0 & 0 & 0 & 1 & 0 & 1 \\ 1 & 0 & 0 & 0 & 0 & 0 \\ 0 & 0 & 0 & 0 & 0 & 0 \\ 0 & 0 & 0 & 0 & 1 & 0 \end{pmatrix} \end{array}$$

Fig. 11.14 The adjacency matrix

$$R = I \cup A \cup A^2 \cup A^3 \cup \ldots \cup A^{|E|-1} = \cup_{i=1}^{|E|-1} A^i \tag{11.2}$$

where, I represents the identity matrix and $\cup$ is the logical-OR operator. This means, the reachability matrix represents the possibility of starting from one element and reaching other elements in any number of steps. For example, if $a_{ij} \in R$ is not zero, then from element-i, it is possible to reach element-j in a number of steps.

Example 11.3 (reachability matrix (R)) Given below is the reachability matrix of the Petri net shown in Fig. 11.12.

$$\mathbf{R} = \begin{array}{c} \\ p1 \\ t1 \\ p2 \\ t2 \\ p3 \\ t3 \end{array} \begin{array}{c} \begin{array}{cccccc} p1 & t1 & p2 & t2 & p3 & t3 \end{array} \\ \begin{pmatrix} 1 & 1 & 1 & 1 & 1 & 1 \\ 1 & 1 & 1 & 1 & 1 & 1 \\ 1 & 1 & 1 & 1 & 1 & 1 \\ 1 & 1 & 1 & 1 & 1 & 1 \\ 0 & 0 & 0 & 0 & 1 & 0 \\ 0 & 0 & 0 & 0 & 1 & 1 \end{pmatrix} \end{array}$$

In the reachability matrix, all the elements in the first row are non-zero. This indicates that, from p1, it is possible to reach all other vertices. All the elements in the second, third, and fourth rows are also non-zero. This means, from the vertices t1, p2, and t2, all other vertices can be reached in an undisclosed number of steps.

The fifth row representing the vertex p3 has all zero elements but $r_{p3,p3}$. This means only p3 can be reached from p3. Finally, the sixth row has only two non-zero elements, $r_{t3,p3}$ and $r_{t3,t3}$. This means, from t3, only t3 and p3 can be reached.

11.6.2 Rader's Matrix

In the previous subsection, the reachability matrix R was computed iteratively. Since multiplying $A_{(|V| \times |V|)}$ by $A_{(|V| \times |V|)}$ costs $\mathcal{O}(|V|^3)$ operations, computing R iteratively costs a running time of $\mathcal{O}(|V|^3 \times |E|)$.

Rader's method [7] provides a short-cut. Let α be a small value, e.g., $\alpha = 0.5$ and I be the identity matrix. Rader's matrix D is give by the following equation:

$$D = (I - \alpha \times A)^{-1} \tag{11.3}$$

D would possess exactly the same non-zero elements as in R. In other words, $r_{ij} = 0$, *iff* $d_{ij} = 0$, and $r_{ij} \neq 0$, *iff* $d_{ij} \neq 0$.

Running Time of Rader's method: If the matrix inversion is done by the Gauss-Jordan elimination, the inversion takes a running time of $\mathcal{O}(|V|^3)$ [8]. Thus, the resulting running time of Rader's method will be:

- $\mathcal{O}(|V|^3)$ for computing $E = (I - \alpha \times A)$
- $\mathcal{O}(|V|^3)$ for computing inversion of E

Hence, the running time of Rader's method is equal to $\mathcal{O}(|V|^3) + \mathcal{O}(|V|^3) = \mathcal{O}(|V|^3)$.

Considering that D requires only one compound matrix operation, and has a smaller running time, computing D is a faster and elegant alternative to computing R. Hence, in the algorithms that are presented in Chap. 12 "Algorithms for Modular Connectivity", it is assumed that the reachability matrix R is always computed by the Rader's method and not by the iterative method.

Example 11.4 (**Rader's matrix** (D)) For the Petri net shown in Fig. 11.12 represented by the Adjacency matrix A

$$\mathbf{D} = \begin{array}{c} \\ p1 \\ t1 \\ p2 \\ t2 \\ p3 \\ t3 \end{array} \begin{array}{c} \begin{array}{cccccc} p1 & t1 & p2 & t2 & p3 & t3 \end{array} \\ \begin{pmatrix} 1.0667 & 0.5333 & 0.2667 & 0.1333 & 0.0667 & 0.1333 \\ 0.1333 & 1.0667 & 0.5333 & 0.2667 & 0.1333 & 0.2667 \\ 0.2667 & 0.1333 & 1.0667 & 0.5333 & 0.2667 & 0.5333 \\ 0.5333 & 0.2667 & 0.1333 & 1.0667 & 0.0333 & 0.0667 \\ 0 & 0 & 0 & 0 & 1.0000 & 0 \\ 0 & 0 & 0 & 0 & 0.5000 & 1.0000 \end{pmatrix} \end{array}$$

if the non-zero values of D are replaced by 1, then

$$|\mathbf{D}| = \begin{array}{c} \\ p1 \\ t1 \\ p2 \\ t2 \\ p3 \\ t3 \end{array} \begin{array}{c} \begin{array}{cccccc} p1 & t1 & p2 & t2 & p3 & t3 \end{array} \\ \begin{pmatrix} 1 & 1 & 1 & 1 & 1 & 1 \\ 1 & 1 & 1 & 1 & 1 & 1 \\ 1 & 1 & 1 & 1 & 1 & 1 \\ 1 & 1 & 1 & 1 & 1 & 1 \\ 0 & 0 & 0 & 0 & 1 & 0 \\ 0 & 0 & 0 & 0 & 1 & 1 \end{pmatrix} \end{array}$$

which is the same as R.

11.6.3 Connection Matrix

The third matrix is the connection matrix C. It is now evident that the reachability matrix $R = |X|$ represents the reachability of the individual vertex. For example, if $r_{ij} \neq 0$ means from vertex-i (the "source"), it is possible to reach vertex-j (the "destination") in a number of steps. What does the transpose of R (R^T) mean? R^T represents the travel back to the source from the destination. In other words, $r^T_{ij} \in R^T \neq 0$ means, it is also possible to travel from the destination vertex-j back to the source vertex-i.

The connection matrix C is given by the following equation:

$$C = R \cap R^T \tag{11.4}$$

where $\cap$ represents the logical-AND operator. Connection matrix C represents the reachable groups. For example, $c_{ij} \in C \neq 0$ *iff* there is a path from vertex-i to vertex-j, and also from vertex-j to vertex-i. On the other hand, $c_{ij} = 0$ *iff* the vertices i and j are not reachable in both directions. As a result, each row in C shows the vertices involved in a particular reachable group. For example, if row-i of C possess non-zero elements in the columns $\{k, l, andm\}$, then the vertices k, l, and m make up a reachable group.

Example 11.5 (**Connection matrix** (C)) For the Petri net shown in Fig. 11.12 the Connection matrix C

$$\mathbf{C} = \begin{array}{c} \\ p1 \\ t1 \\ p2 \\ t2 \\ p3 \\ t3 \end{array} \begin{array}{c} \begin{array}{cccccc} p1 & t1 & p2 & t2 & p3 & t3 \end{array} \\ \begin{pmatrix} 1 & 1 & 1 & 1 & 0 & 0 \\ 1 & 1 & 1 & 1 & 0 & 0 \\ 1 & 1 & 1 & 1 & 0 & 0 \\ 1 & 1 & 1 & 1 & 0 & 0 \\ 0 & 0 & 0 & 0 & 1 & 0 \\ 0 & 0 & 0 & 0 & 0 & 1 \end{pmatrix} \end{array}$$

In C, the first row states that p1 is in a reachable group involving t1, p2, and t2. The second row states that t1 is in a reachable group involving p1, p2, and t2. The third row states that p2 is in a reachable group p1, t1, and t2. Hence, the first four rows report the same reachable group involving the same set of vertices {p1, t1, p2, t2}. The reachable group is, of course, the strongly connected component. The fifth row states that p3 is the sole member of another strongly connected component. Finally, the sixth row states that t3 is the sole member of another strongly connected component. Hence, according to C, there are three strongly connected components namely, {p1, t1, p2, t2}, {p3}, and {t3}; this is already stated previously, in the Example 11.2 "Spanning Tree and Connected Components".

11.6.4 Component Matrix

From the example shown above, each row in the Connection matrix C states a strongly connected component. However, these rows maybe not be unique as different rows depict the same strongly connected component. If the duplicate rows are purged from C, then the resulting filtered C is called the component matrix $\check{C}$. The component matrix $\check{C}$ would have a number of rows equal to the number of strongly connected components, and each row represents a strongly connected component.

Example 11.6 (**Component matrix** ($\check{C}$)) Considering the Connection matrix C shown in the previous example

$$\check{C} = \textbf{unique\_rows(C)} = \begin{matrix} \\ p1 \\ p3 \\ t3 \end{matrix} \begin{matrix} p1 & t1 & p2 & t2 & p3 & t3 \\ \end{matrix} \! \begin{pmatrix} 1 & 1 & 1 & 1 & 0 & 0 \\ 0 & 0 & 0 & 0 & 1 & 0 \\ 0 & 0 & 0 & 0 & 0 & 1 \end{pmatrix}$$

The first, second, and third rows of $\check{C}$ identify the strongly connected component {p1, t1, p2, t2}, {p3}, and {t3}, respectively.

11.7 Algorithms for Modular Connectivity

Based on the material presented in this chapter, five new algorithms are presented in the next chapter, for analyzing network connectivity in the modular Petri net models of discrete systems.

References

1. Beineke LW, Wilson RJ, Gross JL, Tucker TW (2009) Topics in topological graph theory. Cambridge University Press, Cambridge
2. Der Jeng M (1997) A Petri net synthesis theory for modeling flexible manufacturing systems. IEEE Trans Syst Man Cybern Part B (Cybern) 27(2):169–183
3. Fridgen G, Stepanek C, Wolf T (2015) Investigation of exogenous shocks in complex supply networks—a modular Petri net approach. Int J Prod Res 53(5):1387–1408
4. Liu G, Jiang C (2016) Petri net based model checking for the collaborativeness of multiple processes systems. In: 2016 IEEE 13th international conference on networking, sensing, and control (ICNSC). IEEE, pp 1–6
5. Liu G, Zhou M, Jiang C (2017) Petri net models and collaborativeness for parallel processes with resource sharing and message passing. ACM Trans Embed Comput Syst (TECS) 16(4):1–20
6. Lunze J (2019) Networked control of multi-agent systems: consensus and synchronisation, communication structure design, self-organisation in networked systems, event-triggered control. Bookmundo
7. Rader CM (2011) Connected components and minimum paths. In: Graph algorithms in the language of linear algebra. SIAM, pp 19–27
8. Raz R (2002) On the complexity of matrix product. In: Proceedings of the thiry-fourth annual ACM symposium on theory of computing, pp 144–151
9. Righini G (1993) Modular Petri nets for simulation of flexible production systems. Int J Prod Res 31(10):2463–2477
10. Tsinarakis GJ, Tsourveloudis N, Valavanis KP (2005) Modular Petri net based modeling, analysis, synthesis and performance evaluation of random topology dedicated production systems. J Intell Manuf 16(1):67–92
11. Tsinarakis GJ, Valavanis KP, Tsourveloudis N (2003) Modular Petri net based modeling, analysis and synthesis of dedicated production systems. In: 2003 IEEE international conference on robotics and automation (Cat. No. 03CH37422), vol 3. IEEE, pp 3559–3564

Chapter 12
Algorithms for Modular Connectivity

This chapter presents five new algorithms for analyzing the network connectivity in the modular Petri net models. These algorithms are simple yet powerful enough to solve fundamental networking problems in modular Petri net models of large discrete event systems (e.g., discrete manufacturing systems). The algorithms are designed with Industry 4.0 in mind, meaning the modules are intelligent enough to choose with whom they may communicate, in case some of the modules are not communicating, mute, or simply not functioning.

The five Algorithms:

1. Algorithm 2 "Existence of Spanning Tree" is to check whether a modular model has a spanning tree.
2. Algorithm 3 "Source of Spanning Tree" is an extension of Algorithm 4, in a sense, this algorithm also proposes a set of elements that can function as the sources of the spanning trees.
3. Algorithm 4 "Functional Spanning Tree" is also an extension of Algorithm 4. This algorithm is applicable when a network does not possess a spanning tree. In this case, this algorithm proposes a *functional* spanning tree, with which most of the modules can be reached, at the expense of some other modules.
4. Algorithm 5 "Existence of Connected Components" is to check whether a modular model is strongly connected, and if not, how many strongly connected components are there.
5. Algorithm 6 "Steiner Spanning Tree" is to find a spanning tree that connects the set of selected modules (known as "terminals") together.

In summary, Algorithms 4–6 determine the spanning tree of a modular model. Algorithm 7 deals with strongly connected components in the modular model. Finally, Algorithm 8 deals with establishing a spanning tree that connects only a selected group of modules (terminals).

R. Davidrajuh, *Petri Nets for Modeling of Large Discrete Systems*, Asset Analytics,
https://doi.org/10.1007/978-981-16-5203-5_12

In the final section of this chapter, the five algorithms are applied for the three different types of networking of modules. The three different types of networking are:

1. Leader-Followers networking.
2. Negotiating-Peers networking.
3. Steiner-mode networking.

12.1 Algorithm: Existence of Spanning Tree

Algorithm 4 is to check whether a modular model has a spanning tree, reaching all the modules. First, this algorithm computes the Laplacian matrix L. Then, from L, it computes the algebraic connectivity λ_2. If $\lambda_2 \neq 0$, then there exists a spanning tree, from a source module, reaching all other modules.

Algorithm 2: Existence of a Spanning Tree.

input : Adjacency Matrix A
output: Boolean value $true$ or $false$
output: Laplacian matrix L

1 **compute Laplacian matrix** L
2 **compute Algebraic connectivity matrix** λ_2
3 **if** $\lambda_2 \neq 0$ **then**
4 | **return** (*true, L*) `% spanning tree exists`
5 **else**
6 | **return** (*false, []*) `% spanning tree does not exist`

Running time of the algorithm: the algorithm is dominated by two operations namely, computation of the Laplacian L (line-1, takes $\mathcal{O}(n^3)$) and finding the eigen values of L (line-2) also takes $\mathcal{O}(n^3)$ [12]. Thus, the running time of the algorithm is $\mathcal{O}(n^3)$.

12.2 Algorithm: Source of a Spanning Tree

Algorithm 5 behaves in two ways. If a source node is given as an input parameter, the algorithm will verify (in lines 8–16) whether there is a spanning tree starting with this source node or not. On the other way, if a source node is not given as input, then the algorithm will scan the net (lines 18–19) and propose a source node from which all other nodes can be reached.

Algorithm 3: Source of a Spanning Tree.

```
input  : Adjacency Matrix A
input  : (Optional input): Source node v_s
output: Boolean value
output: (if optional source node is given): then potential source node will be the second
        output

1  if not(ExistenceOfSpanningTree(A)) then
2  |   % spanning tree does not exist
3  |_  return (false, 0)
4
5  % Spanning tree exists
6  compute reachability matrix R
7  % if source node is given optionally
8  if v_s given then
9  |   extract the row of v_s in R
10 |   if all elements in the row are non-zero then
11 |   |   % spanning tree exists for
12 |   |   % the given source v_s
13 |   |   return (true, v_s) % return true
14 |   else
15 |   |_  return (false, v_s) % return false
16 else
17 |
18 |   find row-i of R with all non-zero elements
19 |_  return (true, i)
```

Running time of the algorithm: Line-1 checks the existence of a spanning tree using Algorithm 4; thus, this operation takes $\mathcal{O}(n^3)$ time. In line-6, computing the reachability matrix R takes another $\mathcal{O}(n^3)$ time.
If the source node is given as an input, lines 9–10 take $\mathcal{O}(n)$ time. Otherwise, processing R to find an all non-zero row (line-18) takes $\mathcal{O}(n^2)$ time. Hence, the running time of the Algorithm 5 finding the "sources of spanning tree" is $\mathcal{O}(n^3)$.

12.3 Algorithm: Functional Spanning Tree

This algorithm is also an extension of Algorithm 2. This algorithm is applicable when a network does not possess a spanning tree. In this case, this algorithm proposes a functional spanning tree, with which most of the modules can be reached at the expense of some other modules.

Algorithm 4: Finding a functional Spanning Tree.

input : Adjacency Matrix A
output: index of the source module i
output: number of modules in the spanning tree n_{max}

1 **compute reachability matrix** R
2 **Find row-**i **of** R **with maximum number of non-zero elements** (n_{max})
3 **if** (n_{max} **== 1**) **then**
4 `% maximum number of non-zero elements == 1, in any row, meaning all modules are isolated`
5 **return** (*0*, *NaN*)
6 **else**
7 `% 1 <=` n_{max} `<= N`
8 **return (source=**i**, modules_in_tree=**n_{max}**)**

Running time of the algorithm: Since this algorithm is all about line-1 computing matrix R and line-2 analysis of R, it takes $\mathcal{O}(n^3)$ time.

12.4 Algorithm: Existence of Connected Components

This algorithm is to check whether a modular model is strongly connected. If not, the number of connected components in the net will be returned.

Algorithm 5: Existence of Connected Components.

input : Adjacency Matrix A
output: number of strongly connected components n
output: purged connected matrix $\check{C}$

1 **compute reachability matrix** R
2 **compute connection matrix** $C, C = R \wedge R^T$
3 `% purge the duplicate rows of C`
4 **compute components matrix** $\check{C}$ = **unique rows of** C
5 **return (**n**=number of rows of** $\check{C}$**, matrix** $\check{C}$ **)**
6 `% n==1: strongly connected`

In this algorithm, line-1 computes the reachability matrix R with which the connection matrix C is computed in line-2. Further, C is purged of duplicate rows to create the component matrix $\check{C}$ in line-4. The number of rows n of $\check{C}$ is equivalent to the number of strongly connected components in the graph; this means, if $n = 1$, then the graph is strongly connected.

Running time of the algorithm: This algorithm computes three different matrices in the three lines, line-1 to 4. All three computation takes $\mathcal{O}(n^3)$ time, each. Thus, the running time of the algorithm is $\mathcal{O}(n^3)$.

12.5 Algorithm: Steiner Spanning Tree

Algorithms 2 and 3 determines a spanning tree in which *all* the modules must participate (connected in the spanning tree). Algorithm 4 is about developing a *functional* spanning tree. A functional spanning tree means in case, not all the nodes can be connected in a tree, then the functional spanning tree connects most of the modules in the network, as many modules as possible. However, Steiner spanning tree is different.

Steiner spanning tree is different in the sense that the tree needs to connect only a set of selected modules known as the **terminals**. In a Steiner spanning tree, all the terminal modules must participate. However, to connect the terminal modules together, some other connecting modules are also used, as the terminal modules *alone* cannot form a tree. The connecting modules that are not terminal modules but happen to participate in the tree only to establish the tree are known as "Steiner modules".

12.5.1 Steiner Spanning Tree: The Basics

Definition 12.1 Steiner Spanning Tree: Given a directed graph $G = (V, E)$, weight of each edge $\forall e \in E, \quad w(e) \in \mathbb{Z}^+$, there is a set of vertices $V_T = v_i \in V, \quad V_T \subseteq V$ known as the Terminals. The objective is to find a sub-tree $T, T \subseteq G$ that span all the terminals and the total weight of T (sum of arc weights of vertices $v_i \in V_T$) is minimal [16].

Example 12.1 (Steiner Spanning Tree):

Figure 12.1 shows a graph with nine vertices. Three of those vertices, A, C, and G, are the terminals. Figure 12.2 shows the (minimum) spanning tree of the network. Since there are nine nodes ($|V| = 9$), eight arcs are needed ($|V| - 1 = 8$) to connect all the nodes together as the spanning tree (spanning tree consists of the arcs AB, BC, CD, CF, CI, DE, FG, and GH, shown in bold line). However, the spanning tree is not of interest at this moment, rather the Steiner Spanning Tree. Figure 12.3 shows a possible Steiner spanning tree that connects the terminals together. The Steiner spanning tree includes the obligatory terminal nodes (A, C, and G), and also the vertices B and F as Steiner nodes.

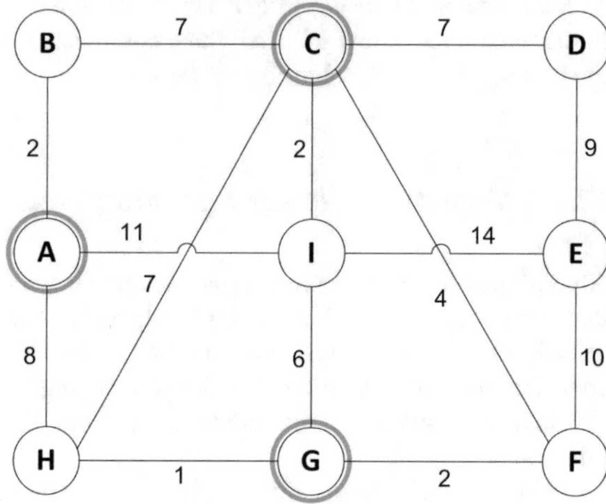

Fig. 12.1 Graph with three terminal nodes A, C, and G

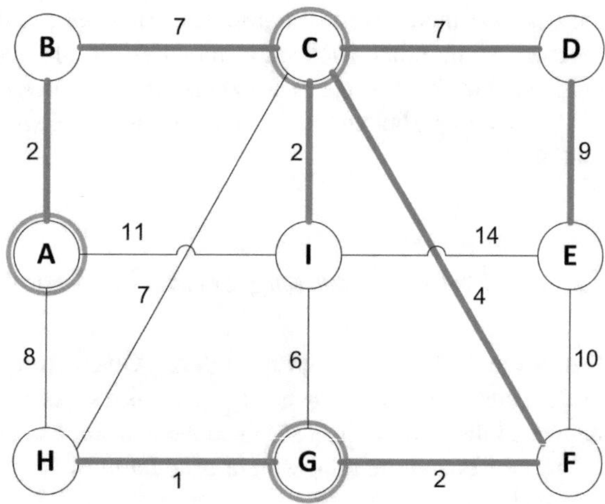

Fig. 12.2 Graph with three terminal nodes (A, C, and G): Minimum Spanning Tree superimposed

Developing a Steiner Spanning tree is an NP-complete problem [3]. Thus, it takes a brute-force approach to find the optimal solution, taking a non-polynomial time. However, there exist approximation algorithms taking polynomial timing [8, 15, 17].

Note that the Steiner spanning tree shown in Fig. 12.3 is an optimal solution as it takes a total arc weight of 15. Another optimal tree is $A - H - G - F - C$, as it also takes a total arc weight of 15. Also, note that these two spanning trees are basically paths than trees.

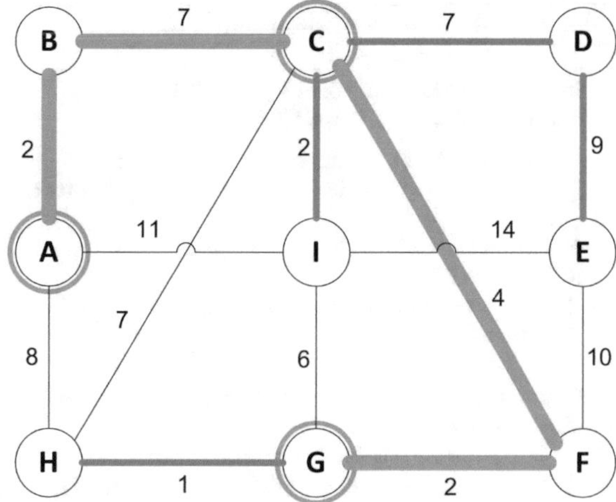

Fig. 12.3 A Steiner Spanning Tree connecting the three terminal nodes

12.5.2 Steiner Spanning Tree: The Algorithm

This algorithm is to establish a Steiner spanning tree given a set of terminal nodes. The algorithm is shown in Algorithm 6.

The algorithm is divided into four cases:

- Case-I (lines-5 to 7): This case is a trivial case as the number of nodes in the set of terminal nodes is one ($|V_T| == 1$). In this case, a tree of one node is the node itself. Hence, the terminal node is returned as the Steiner spanning tree.
  The running time of this case: $\mathcal{O}(1)$, a constant time.
- Case-2 (lines-10 to 16): This case is a special case as the number nodes in the set of terminal nodes is two, ($|V_T| == 2$), a source and a destination. In this case, at first, a single-source-shortest-path (SSSP) is run from the source node. In the resulting tree, the shortest path from the source node to the destination node is extracted. This shortest path is returned as the Steiner Spanning Tree.
  The running time of this case: there are several algorithms for finding SSSP [1]; e.g., Bellman-Ford (takes $\mathcal{O}(V \times E)$ time [4]), Dijkstra's algorithm ($\mathcal{O}(E\ log\ V)$ [2]), and directed acyclic graphs (DAG, $\mathcal{O}(V + E)$ [5]). In addition, extracting the shortest path between the two terminal nodes would take $\mathcal{O}(E)$ time. Hence, assuming DAG algorithm for SSSP, the running time of this case is $\mathcal{O}(V + E)$.
- Case-3 (lines-19 to 23): This case is also a special case as all the nodes of the graph are terminal nodes, ($|V_T| == |V|$). In this case, minimum spanning tree is run from any node, and the resulting tree is returned as the Steiner Spanning Tree. Running time of this case: running minimum spanning tree by Kruskal's algorithm ([9]) or Prim's algorithm ([13]) takes $\mathcal{O}(E\ log\ V)$ time [14].
- Case-4 (lines-26 to 33): This case is the general case where the number of terminal nodes is less than the number of nodes in the graph, ($|V_T| < |V|$). In this case, the minimum spanning tree algorithm is run from any of the terminal nodes, say from

Algorithm 6: Steiner Spanning Tree.

```
input : Graph G = (V, E)
input : set of terminal nodes V_T, V_T ⊆ V
output: SST = (V_s, E_s), SST ⊆ G

Let N = |V|  % N: number of nodes in G
% the algorithm is divided into 4 cases

% Case-1: trivial case: just one terminal node
if |V_T| == 1 then
    % just return the terminal node
    return (V_T)

% Case-2: special case: number of terminal nodes == 2
else if |V_T| == 2 then
    % run single-source-shortest-path from terminal-1
    sssp = SingleSourceShortestPath(G, terminal-1)
    % return the shortest path between
    % terminal-1 and terminal-2
    sst = shortestPath(sssp, terminal-2)
    return (sst)

% Case-3: special case: all the nodes are terminal nodes,
  V_T = V
else if |V_T| == N then
    % find the minimal spanning tree (MST) of G
    % Steiner is the same as MST
    mst = MinimumSpanningTree(G)
    return (mst)

% Case-4: the usual case, V_T ⊂ V
else
    % step-1: run minimum spanning tree from terminal-1
    mst = MinimumSpanningTree(G, terminal-1)
    % step-2: the loop: as long as a steiner node
    % v_s exists with one degree of connection
    while (∃ v_s s.t. (| • v_s| + |v_s • | == 1) ) do
        remove the steiner node v_s from mst
    return (mst)
```

terminal-1. The resulting tree would consist of terminal nodes and Steiner nodes. Iteratively, as long as there are any Steiner nodes as leaves of the tree, (in other words, Steiner nodes with only one degree of connection), these Steiner nodes will be removed from the tree.

Running time of this case: running the minimum spanning tree by Kruskal's algorithm or Prim's algorithm takes $\mathcal{O}(E \log V)$ time. As there could be a maximum of $|V| - |V_T|$ Steiner nodes, removing the Steiner leaves would take another $\mathcal{O}(|V| - |V_T|) = \mathcal{O}(V)$ time. Hence, the running time of this case is $\mathcal{O}(E \log V + V)$ time, which can be approximated by $\mathcal{O}(E \log V)$.

12.6 Applications of the Algorithms

The five algorithms are applied for the creation of three types of networks that connect collaborating Petri modules. The three types of networks are:

1. Leader-Followers network.
2. Negotiating-Peers network.
3. Steiner-mode network.

The following scenario will be considered to show the creation of three types of networks.

12.6.1 Scenario for Creation of Networks

Figure 12.4 shows a group of Petri modules that functions as specialized controllers. Each of these modules controls a specific manufacturing entity. The buffering places between the modules represent the communication channel.

Figure 12.4 represents Reconfigurable Manufacturing System (RMS) which is characterized by dedicated serial lines for material and part flow and flexible manufacturing system [7]. The advantage of RMS is that product and production rate can be quickly changed to respond to changing market conditions. Also, RMS is economical as the different entities can be manipulated individually [7].

In Fig. 12.4, the internal details of the Petri modules that function as specialized controllers are ignored, and the focus is on the interfaces (inter-modular connections).

Let us assume that the RMS that is shown in Fig. 12.4 is for a pull-production system.[1]

12.7 Leader-Followers Networking (LFN)

Let us start with a lemma:

Lemma 12.1 *Leader-followers network* $\Longrightarrow$ *existence of a Spanning Tree*

Proof In a leader-follower network $G = (V, E)$, the leader module v_0 makes the decision and passes it to all other follower modules. The decisions go to the immediate neighbors of the leader first and then propagate to others via the immediate neighbors.

[1] Pull production is a production control method by which the downstream activities (e.g., the module "Finishing") signal their needs to upstream activities (e.g., "Conveyor Belt-1" and "Machining-1"). Pull production is to eliminate overproduction and buffering of products. Also, in pull production, nothing is produced by the upstream activities until the downstream activities signal their needs [11].

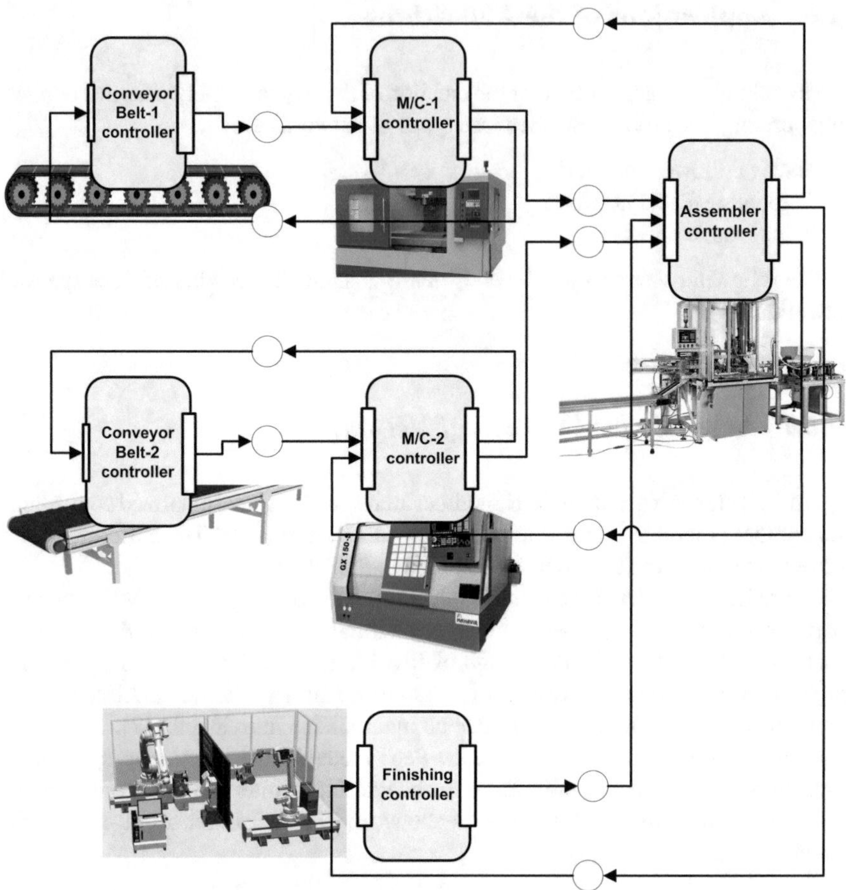

Fig. 12.4 The abstract modules of RMS

In other words, the decisions pass through all the vertices of the graph in a tree-like manner.
$\forall v_i \in V, i \neq 0, \exists$ directed path $v_0 \rightsquigarrow v_i$ from v_0 to v_i.

(This lemma is stated as an assumption in [10] and [6], without proof).

12.7.1 Algorithm for Creation of LFN

Algorithm 7 shows the algorithm for the creation of Leader-Follower networking. This algorithm uses the algorithm "SourceOfSpanningTree" and the collaborativeness of the modules.

Algorithm 7: Algorithm for creation of Leader-Followers Networking.

input : Modular Petri net MPN
input : Source module m_S
output: Boolean value

```
if not(SourceOfSpanningTree(MPN,m_S)) then
    % No spanning tree exist with m_S as the source
    % Thus, networking not possible
    return (0)

% spanning tree exists:
% check collaborativeness C_mi of all the modules
if (∏ C_mi) ≠ 1 then
    % some modules in spanning tree
    % are not collaborative
    return (0) % leader-followers not possible
else
    % leader-followers networking is possible
    % with module m_S as the leader
    return (1)
```

12.7.2 *Example for Creation of LFN*

Referring to the RMS shown in Fig. 12.4: Let us say that, whenever the output buffer for finished products is nearing its full capacity, the controller in the module "Finishing" signals all other modules (e.g., either to stop production or to slow down). This means module "Finishing" (the leader) needs to inform all other modules (the followers), and there is no need for the leader to get any information back from the followers.

Figure 12.5 shows that the controller "Finishing" making use of Leader-Followers networking. Starting with the module "Finishing" as a source, if there is a spanning tree covering all the modules, and if all the modules are collaborative, then the leader-followers networking can be used for warning about the stoppage.

12.8 Steiner-Mode Networking (SMN)

At first, the algorithm for the creation of a Steiner-Mode Network is given. Then, an application of Steiner-Mode Networking is given.

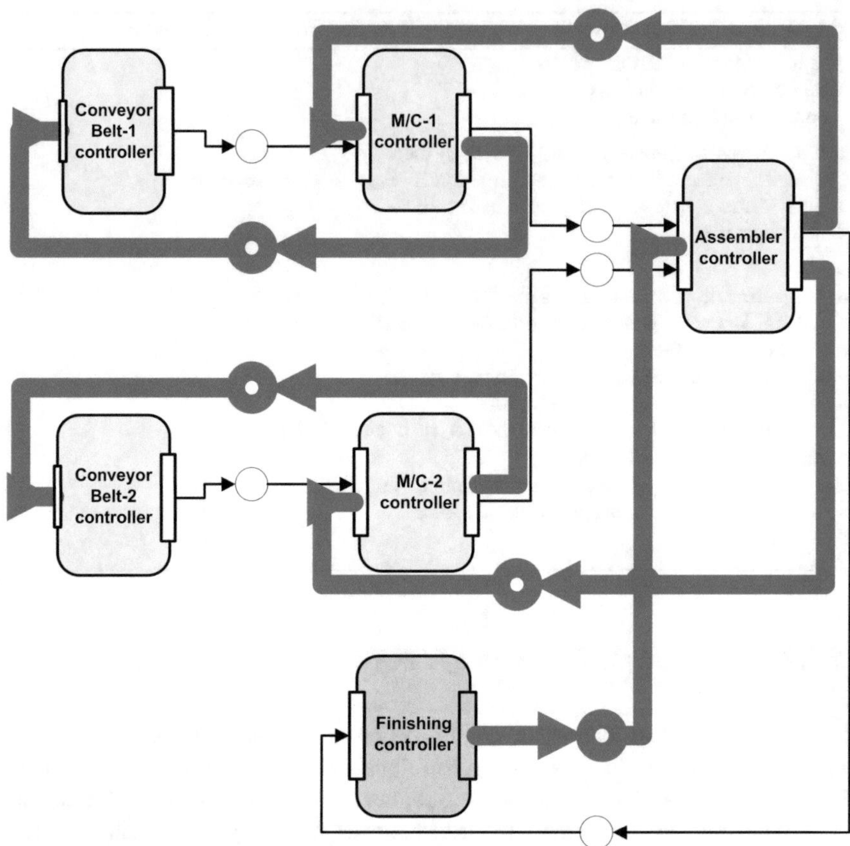

Fig. 12.5 Leader-Followers Networking in action

12.8.1 Algorithm for Creation of SMN

Algorithm 8 is for creating a Steiner-Mode network. This algorithm is also an application of the algorithm "SteinerSpanningTree".

12.8.2 Example for Creation of SMN

Let us visit the scenario displayed in Fig. 12.4. Let us assume that some defects are detected by the controller "Finishing" under the inspection of the products at the finishing station. Also, the defects stem from the part manufactured by machine-2 (M/C-2). Also, perhaps, the defects are due to the low-quality input material that is brought in by the conveyor belt-2. Hence, the controller module "Finishing" is

Algorithm 8: Algorithm for creation of Steiner-Mode Networking.

```
input : Modular Petri net MPN
input : Set of Terminals T_S
output: Boolean value
% first, check whether terminals are
% willing to communicate
for all the terminals in T_S
if ((∏ C_mi) ≠ 1) then
    % some terminals are not collaborative
    return (false) % Steiner-mode not possible

% find a Steiner Tree with the terminals
[SST] = SteinerSpanningTree(MPN, T_S)
if (SST is empty) then
    % Steiner-Mode not possible
    return (false)

% finally, check whether all the
% Steiner modules in SST are
% willing to communicate too
for all the Steiner modules in SST
if ((∏ C_mi) == 1) then
    return (true) % Steiner-mode network is possible
else
    % some Steiner modules not responding
    return (false)
```

to send a signal to the controller modules "M/C-2" and "Conveyor Belt-2" to stop immediately. Since "Finishing" does not have a direct connection with "M/C-2" and "Conveyor Belt-2", the "Assembler" is used as a Steiner node intermediary to create the network. Figure 12.6 shows the resulting Steiner-Mode Network.

12.9 Negotiating-Peers Networking (NPN)

Again, let us start with a lemma

Lemma 12.2 *In a directed graph $G = (V, E)$, if every vertex $v_i \in V$ as a source has a spanning tree iff the graph is strongly connected.*

Proof In a strongly connected graph, there is a directed path from every vertex to all other vertices, making spanning trees. On the other hand, if a vertex v_i has a spanning tree, then there is a directed path from the vertex to all other vertices. Since

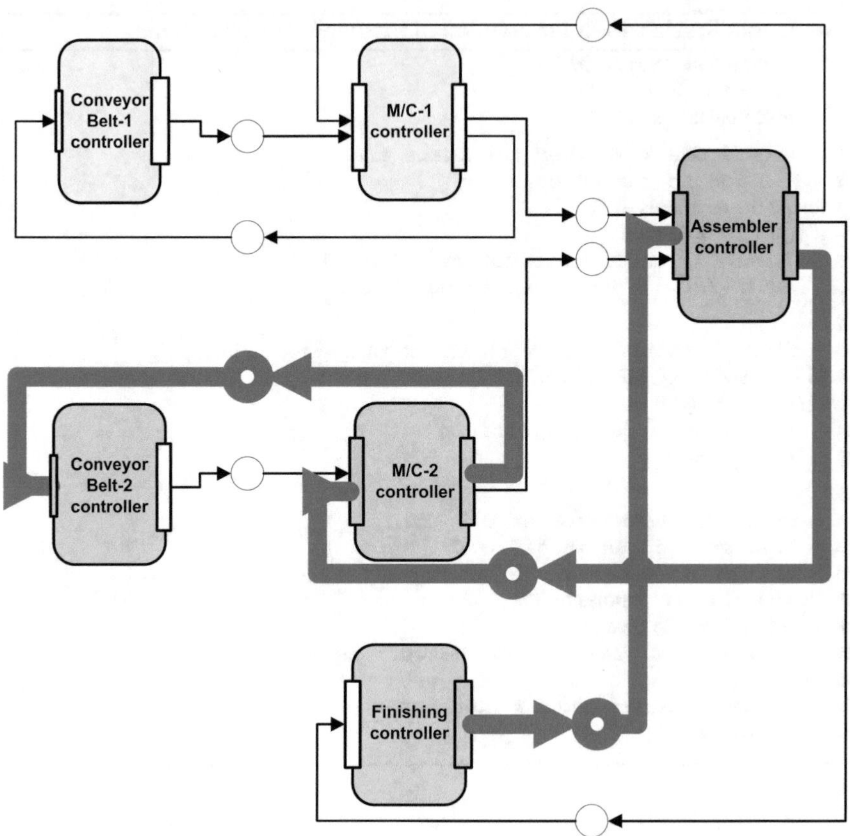

Fig. 12.6 Steiner-Mode Networking in action

the other vertices also have spanning trees, there is a directed path from these vertices back to v_i effectively forming cycles involving all the vertices. Thus, the vertices are strongly connected. Thus, (strongly connected graph $\Longleftrightarrow$ spanning tree from every $v_i \in V$).

12.9.1 Algorithm for Creating NPN

Algorithm 9 is for creating a Negotiating-peers Network. This algorithm is an application of the algorithm "ExistenceOfComponents".

Algorithm 9: Algorithm for creating a Negotiating-Peers Network.

input : Modular Petri net MPN
output: Boolean value

```
[n, Č] = ExistenceOfComponents(MPN)
if (n ≠ 1) then
    % the network is not strongly connected
    % hence, negotiating-peers not possible
    return (0)

% if the network is strongly connected,
% then check collaborativeness C_mi of all modules
if ((∏ C_mi) ≠ 1) then
    % some modules are not collaborative
    return (0) % negotiating-peers not possible

% all modules are connected & collaborative
% hence, negotiating-peers networking is possible
return (1)
```

12.9.2 Example for Creation of NPN

Referring back to Fig. 12.4, for normal operation, all the modules must be strongly connected so that a module can pass its status to all other modules in both the upstream and downstream. Also, if *any* module has a problem, then all other modules can be warned.

Let us assume that due to external conditions, the production rate has to be increased. Also, the speed of the input conveyor belts can be increased to any level. In this case, all the controllers except the input conveyors have to negotiate with each other about increasing the production rate to eliminate the unwanted buildup of materials in buffers. In other words, a Negotiating-Peers Networking is to absorb all the controller modules (except the controllers for conveyor belts) into collaboration. Figure 12.7 shows negotiating-peers networking in action.

12.10 Chapter Summary

This chapter presents five new algorithms that find spanning trees, strongly connected components, and Steiner spanning trees. With these five algorithms, three network algorithms are proposed that allow collaborating modules to function as intelligent agents to solve problems in the Industry 4.0 era. With the help of these network algorithms, the modules themselves can align into collaboration.

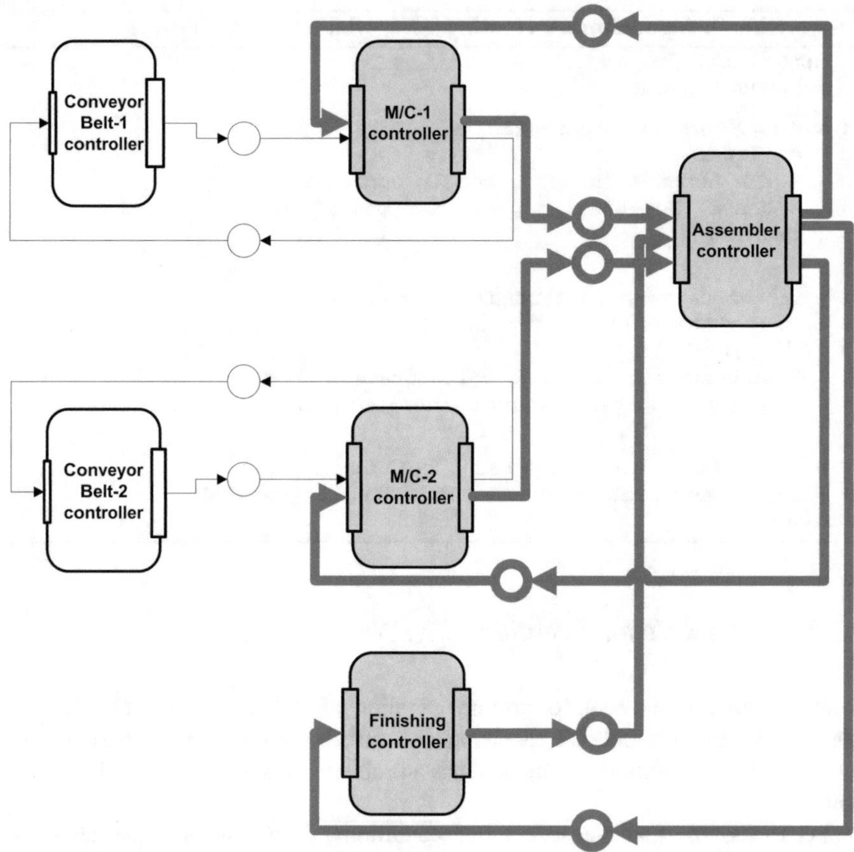

Fig. 12.7 Negotiating-Peers Networking in action

In Chap. 13 "Model Checking for Collaborativeness" an architecture (or simply, a structure) of a module is presented that can assist collaboration. This structure is generalized in Chap. 14 "Generic Petri Module". Modules developed with this generic structure can invite other modules into collaboration; also, these modules are capable of accepting the invitation from other modules.

References

1. Cormen TH, Leiserson CE, Rivest RL, Stein C (2009) Introduction to algorithms, 3rd edn. The MIT Press
2. Dijkstra EW et al (1959) A note on two problems in connexion with graphs. Numerische mathematik 1(1):269–271
3. Garey MR, Johnson DS (1979) Computers and intractability, vol 174. freeman San Francisco

4. Goldberg A, Radzik T (1993) A heuristic improvement of the bellman-ford algorithm. Technical report, Stanford Univ CA Dept of computer science
5. Hopcroft J, Tarjan R (1973) Efficient algorithms for graph manipulation. Communications of the ACM 16(6):372–378
6. Hu J, Feng G (2010) Distributed tracking control of leader-follower multi-agent systems under noisy measurement. Automatica 46(8):1382–1387
7. Koren Y, Gu X, Guo W (2018) Reconfigurable manufacturing systems: principles, design, and future trends. Front Mech Eng 13(2):121–136
8. Kou L, Markowsky G, Berman L (1981) A fast algorithm for steiner trees. Acta informatica 15(2):141–145
9. Kruskal JB (1956) On the shortest spanning subtree of a graph and the traveling salesman problem. Proc Am Math Soc 7(1):48–50
10. Li Z, Liu X, Ren W, Xie L (2012) Distributed tracking control for linear multiagent systems with a leader of bounded unknown input. IEEE Trans Autom Control 58(2):518–523
11. Marchwinski C, Shook J (2003) Lean lexicon: a graphical glossary for lean thinkers. Lean Enterprise Institute
12. Pan VY, Chen ZQ (1999) The complexity of the matrix eigenproblem. In: Proceedings of the thirty-first annual ACM symposium on Theory of computing, pp 507–516
13. Prim RC (1957) Shortest connection networks and some generalizations. The Bell Syst Tech J 36(6):1389–1401
14. Tarjan RE (1983) Data structures and network algorithms, vol 44. Siam
15. Vazirani VV (2003) Bin packing. Springer, Approximation algorithms, pp 74–78
16. Wu BY, Chao K-M (2004) Spanning trees and optimization problems. CRC Press
17. Zhou H (2003) Efficient steiner tree construction based on spanning graphs, pp 152–157

Chapter 13
Model Checking for Collaborativeness

This chapter focuses on the property of collaborativeness. Collaborativeness is a property of a module, indicating whether the module is willing or be able to participate in collaboration with the other modules. This chapter applies the theories and techniques developed in the previous chapters of this book to solve the problem of model checking for collaborativeness. The literature study suggests the use of external tools, off-line, for model checking of collaborativeness. However, this chapter proposes using an online technique that is tailor-made for the GPenSIM environment.

13.1 The Problem

Collaborativeness of a module is already introduced in Sect. 11.1 "Module Abstraction", with the help of definitions and examples. In short, collaborativeness of a module indicates whether the module can participate in collaboration as it is free from any internal deadlocks or livelocks.

Literature study on "model checking for collaborativeness" provides a few works (such as [5–7, 12]). All these works suggest a straightforward approach for model checking for collaborativeness; the approach involves three steps:

- Step-1: Generate the state space (Reachability Graph) of the module.
- Step-2: Transform the reachability graph to the language of a model checker (such as SPIN [10], INA [13], and nuSMV [4]).
- Step-3: Perform the model checking using the model checker.

The tools (model checkers) that are available for model checking are for off-line use only. The state space of a Petri net has to be translated into the particular language of the model checker so that the model checker can process it. Some other tools (e.g., [14]) provide translators that convert the state spaces generated by some Petri nets software (e.g., TINA [1] and CPN Tools) to the language of the model

R. Davidrajuh, *Petri Nets for Modeling of Large Discrete Systems*, Asset Analytics,
https://doi.org/10.1007/978-981-16-5203-5_13

checker NuSMV. In both cases, model checking can be done only on an off-line mode. It is apparent that the three-step approach is **static**, as it is **not possible to check collaborativeness online and in real time**.

What is interesting is **an approach that can be used on-line and real-time**. For instance, when a large number of modules are active and running on different computers, can a module, on its own, evaluate its collaborativeness in a much simpler and faster way?

13.2 Towards a New Approach

This section works towards an approach that can be a substitute for the static and off-line approaches that use standard model checkers. The proposed approach is especially for the GPenSIM environment, as it is based on **Petri modules** implemented and executed on the GPenSIM platform. The process of model checking consists of three steps inside a 5-step approach. Before proceeding any further to the steps, let us make a fundamental assumption.

Assumption 13.1 (*A Petri module for model checking is a bounded net*) The purpose of a Petri module is to make sure that it is compact and easy to simulate. Hence, it can be safely assumed that during the design process, the designers made structural adjustments to make the Petri module a bounded Petri net. There exist some algorithms (e.g., [2]) that can make structural adjustments to a Petri net to make it become structurally bounded.

Definition 13.1 (*Bounded Petri net*) A Petri net is called k-bounded, $k \in \mathbb{N}^+$, if all of the places, in all reachable markings (including the initial marking), does not contain more than k tokens. If $k = 1$ (1-bounded), then the Petri net is said to be safe. A Petri net graph (static Petri net) is called structurally bounded if it is bounded for every possible initial marking [9]. □

A bounded Petri module provides compact state space. For example, for a smaller value of k, a k-bounded Petri module that consists of M-number of places, the number of states in the state space could reach up to M^k.

The following five sections present the five steps of the approach (for model checking for collaborativeness).

13.3 Step-1: Identifying the Group of Modules

Using a top-down approach, the first step is to identify a group of Petri modules for the collaboration to perform a specific job. Let us assume that a new collaboration is to be started for this job. For example:

- A job involving cyclic operations: A group of modules is needed to perform the operation cyclically; see Fig. 11.6. In this case, all the modules that involve in the cycle must be invited for collaborations. And, to start the job, all of these modules must indicate their willingness to collaborate.
- A job that can be done by alternative modules: For some types of jobs, several modules can perform these jobs. This case starts by inviting the first module, and will continue until one of them is collaborative; see Fig. 11.7.
- A job that consists of serial operations: When a job has to be performed by a series of modules, each performing a specific task or operation of the job, all these modules must be invited for collaboration. And, all these modules must be collaborative. See Fig. 11.4.
- Section 11.2 "Loosely Connected Modules" presents a detailed study of the groups of modules (known as blocks) and their collaborativeness.

13.4 Step-2: Inviting a Module

Figure 13.1 suggests a structure for the module to handle incoming invitations for collaboration. The invitation is the start of model checking for collaborativeness.

When a module receives an invitation (through the TCP/IP socket), the input port **tI** will deposit a token with color "mcc" (mcc stands for model checking for collaborativeness) into pLI. tMCC will consume the token (the token with color "mcc") and start the process of model checking for collaborativeness (if there are some other transitions that also have pLI as an input place, these transitions are prevented consuming the token with color "mcc"). The process involves two more steps, step-3 "Creating the state space", and step-4 "Analyzing the state space".

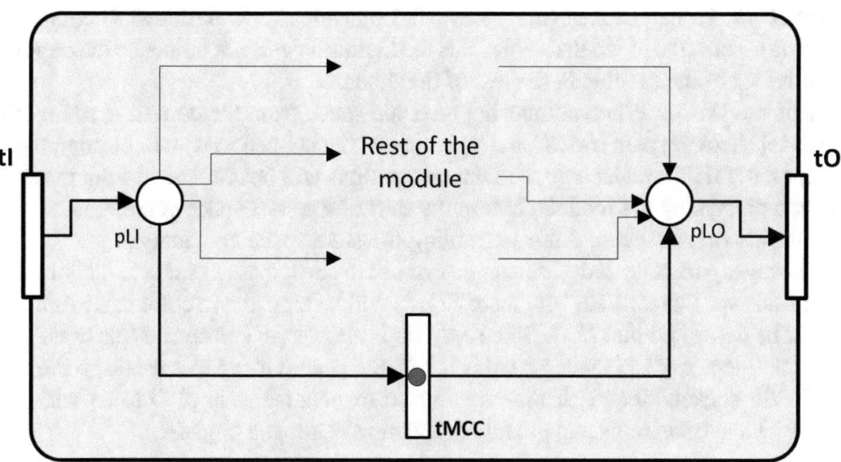

Fig. 13.1 The structure of a module highlighting the model checking path

It is highly likely that a module is involved with some other activity when an invitation arrives (a message arrives through TCP/IP socket). Even so, the model checking path "input port **tI**—pLI—tMCC—pLO—output port **tO**" make sure that model checking for collaborativeness can be done in parallel to whatever activity the module was occupied with.

Even if the module is paralyzed by an ongoing blockage (such as a livelock or a deadlock), the path for model checking will be free from the blockage, and therefore, the module can always reply to the inviter. Only when the communication with the outside world is broken, a module will not be able to respond to an invitation.

13.5 Step-3: Generating the State Space

Transition tMCC performs three operations. Let us focus on the first two operations:

1. Get the current state of the module (using the GPenSIM function "current_state"). E.g.,
   ```
   m0 = current_state();
   ```
2. Compose the state space (GPenSIM function "cotree"), using the current state as the initial marking. E.g.,
   ```
   StateSpace = cotree(Sys, m0);
   ```

It is important to note that the current state and the generated state space, are not influenced or affected by the modeling checking path (tMCC and its input and out connections):

- Invisible input token: When tMCC invokes the function "current_state", in the resulting current state, there will not be any trace of the token that arrived in pLI representing the invitation. This is because this token is already consumed by tMCC as the input token (the token will be inside tMCC until tMCC completes firing). Thus, the token that represents the invitation will not influence the ongoing activities of the module in the rest of the module.
- Invisible tMCC: When composing the state space from the current marking, the model checking path (tMCC and its input and out connections) will be completely ignored. tMCC and its input and out connections will be eliminated from the Petri net representing the module, before the start of the state space generation.
- Invisible output token: After generating the state space and analyzing it for any blockages, tMCC will decide whether or not to participate in a new collaboration. The answer ("mcc: YES" or "mcc: NOx") will be tagged as a color to a token that will be deposited into pLO. Since *only* **tO** is allowed to consume a token with the color "mcc: xxx", **tO** will grab this token and send it away as a message through TCP/IP socket. Hence, there is no chance for this token in pLO to be taken by some local transitions and get into circulation inside the module.

Keeping the model checking (token representing the invitation, tMCC that makes the decision, and the output token carrying out the decision) away from the normal activities of a module is crucial. This separation is essential, as what is needed is the study of the current situation and future situations of the module from the state space, without any influence of the model checking process.

Generating the state space:
Reachability graph algorithm is used to create the state space. The reachability graph algorithm implemented in GPenSIM is almost similar to the original algorithm invented by Karp and Miller [11], which is generalized by Finkel [8] and presented in [3].

13.5.1 Terminal State and Terminal Transition

Firstly, let us define the **terminal states** and **terminal transitions** of a state space. The formal definition of the state space is given in Definition 1.5 on page 6.

Definition 13.2 A **terminal state** ($M_{\dashv}$) of a state space (RG), $RG = (R, T_l, A)$: $M_{\dashv} \in R$ is defined as a terminal state if: $\forall t \in T_l, \nexists M_i \in R \mid M_{\dashv}[t\rangle M_i$. □

In other words, terminal states are the leaves of the state space, as there are no transitions that can change a terminal state to another state.

Definition 13.3 A **terminal transition** ($t_{\dashv}$) of a state space (RG), $RG = (R, T_l, A)$: For each terminal state $M_{\dashv} \in R, \exists t_{\dashv} \in T_l, \exists M_i \in R, \mid M_i[t_{\dashv}\rangle M_{\dashv}$. □

In other words, a terminal transition is the one that creates a terminal state from some other state.

The following three subsections look into three simple modules to check whether they suffer from blockages such as deadlocks or livelocks, by studying the generated state spaces. What is interesting to look for in these state spaces is the following:

- **Existence of deadlock**: there is a terminal state in the state space that is created by the firing of a terminal transition that is **not tO**.
- **Existence of livelock**: there is a cycle in the state space that can not be terminated.
- **Free from deadlock or livelock**: all the terminal states in the state space are created exclusively by the firing of **tO**. In other words, **tO is the only terminal transition.** Also, there are no cycles that cannot be terminated.

13.5.2 Possibility for Deadlocks

As described earlier, the arrival of an invitation for collaboration means the following: the arrival of a message through TCP/IP, **tI** downloads this message and deposit it as a token with color "mcc" into pLI, and eventually, this token is consumed by tMCC, triggering the computation of the state space.

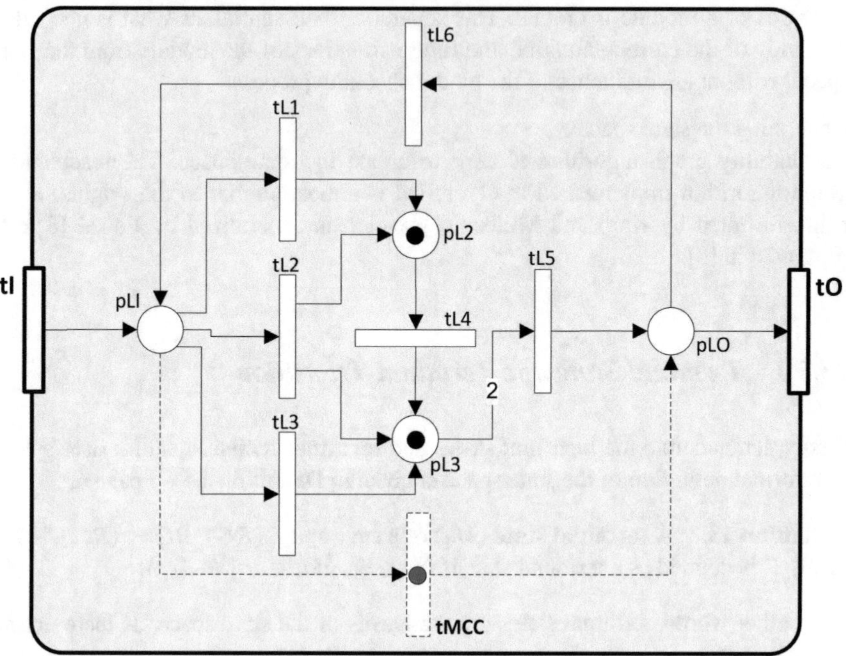

Fig. 13.2 Module-A: possibility for deadlocks?

Figure 13.2 shows a module (module-A) after the arrival of an invitation (tMCC has already consumed the colored token). Figure 13.3 shows the generated state space with the current state {pL2, pL3} as the initial marking. The generated state space is shown in graphic format, and it is only for human consumption. When tMCC invokes the function "cotree", a GPenSIM structure will be returned as the state space.

The state space shown in Fig. 13.3 reveals the following:

- A path to **tO**: it is clear that there is a sequence of firing {tL4, tL5} that leads to a token in pLO. Thus, enabling **tO** to fire.
- A cycle but not livelock: There is also a cycle consisting of the firing of {tL4, tL5, tL6, and tL2}. However, this cycle is not a livelock as the cycle can be terminated whenever **tO** choose to fire when a token is in pLO.
- A deadlock: There are deadlocks visible in the state space: from the initial marking of {pL2, pL3}, the firing of the sequence {tL4, tL5, tL6} will lead to the state of {pLI}. From this state:
  - If tL1 fires, followed by the firing of tL4, state {pL3} results in which a terminal state (none of the transitions is enabled). Since the terminal transition is tL4 and not **tO**, the system is deadlocked.
  - tL3 fires, the resulting state will be again {pL3}, a terminal state. Since the terminal transition is tL3 and not **tO**, it is a deadlock.

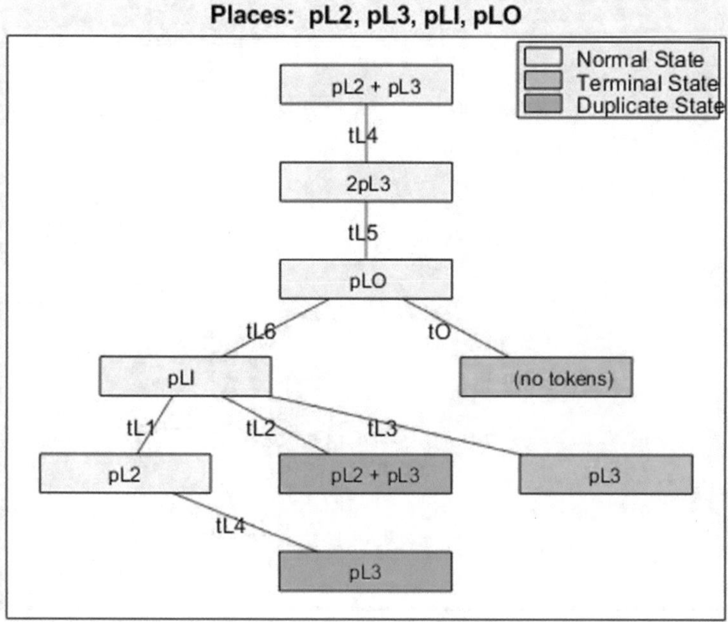

Fig. 13.3 Module-A: the state space showing deadlocks

- If tL2 fires, the cycle will start again with the state {pL2, pL3}, which is the initial state.

In summary, the system is **prone to deadlock**.

13.5.3 Possibility for Livelocks

Figure 13.4 shows another module (module-B) after the arrival of an invitation. Figure 13.5 shows the generated state space with the current state {pL5} as the initial marking. Though the module seems complicated with some connections, the generated state space seems rather simple, consisting of just two cycles:

- The first cycle: from the initial marking of {pL5}, the firing sequence {tL5, tL4} creates a cycle involving the two states {pLI, pLO} and {pL5}.
- The second cycle: from the initial marking of {pL5}, a single firing of tL5 leads to the state of {pLI, pLO}. From this state, there is a firing sequence of {tL1, tL3} that creates the cycle involving the two states {pLI, pLO} and {pL2}.

The state space consists of just two cycles. And **these cycles are livelocks** as there is no way to terminate these cycles. In other words, there is no way **tO** can be

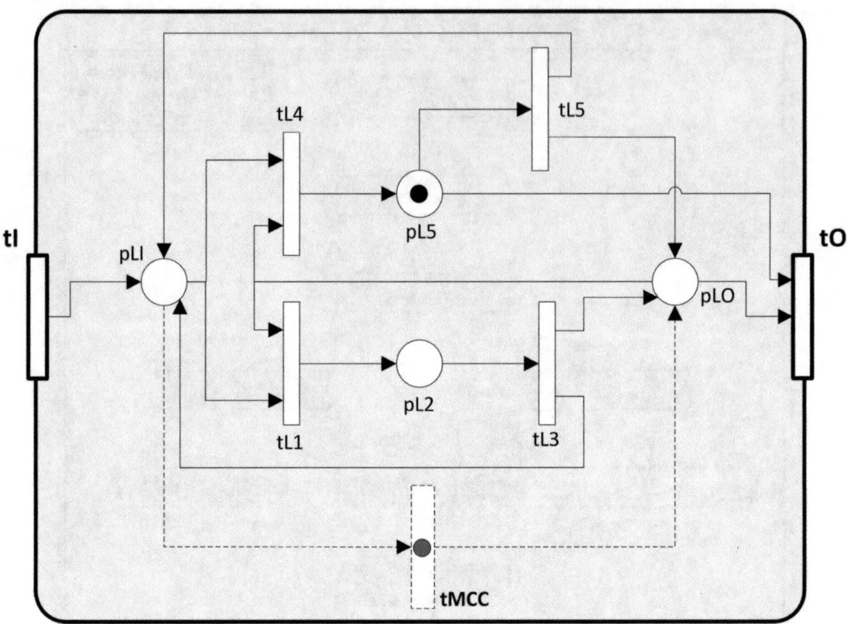

Fig. 13.4 Module-B: possibility for livelocks?

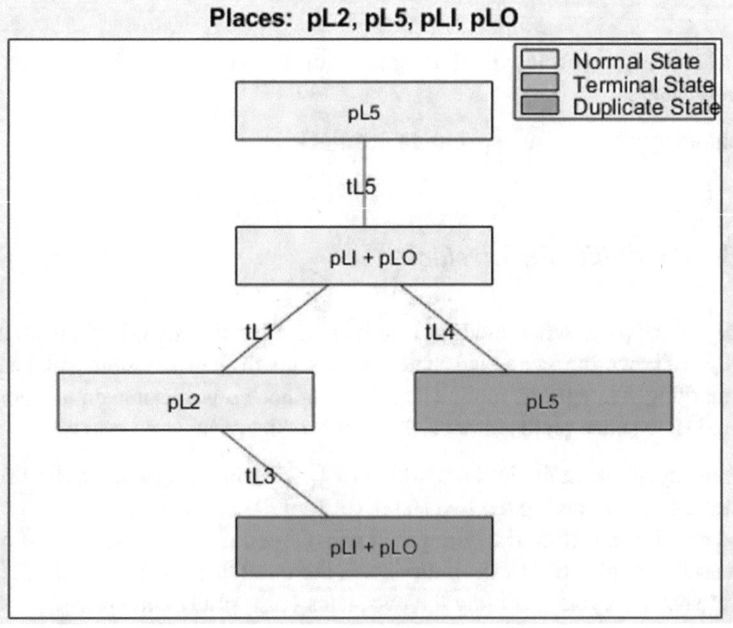

Fig. 13.5 Module-B: the state space showing livelocks

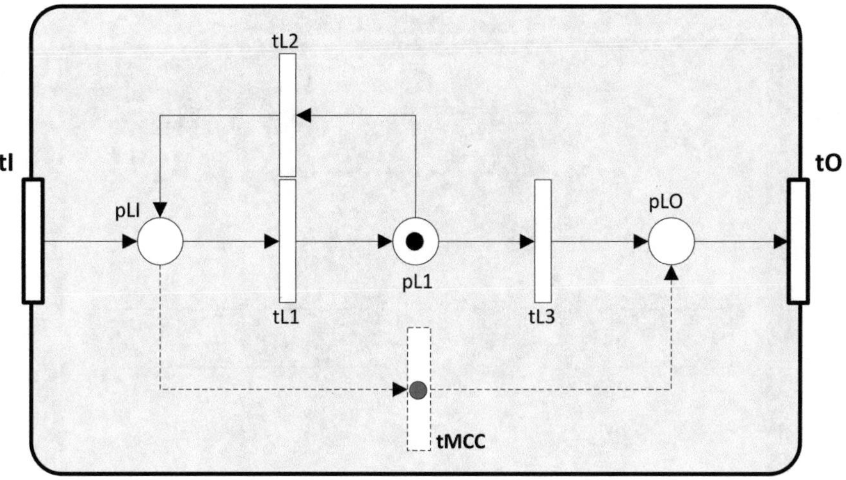

Fig. 13.6 Module-C: free from livelocks and deadlocks?

enabled eventually, as **tO** needs a token each in pLO and pL5 at the same time. This will never happen with the given initial marking of {pL5}.

13.5.4 Free from Livelocks and Deadlocks

Figure 13.6 shows yet another module (module-C). Figure 13.7 shows the generated state space with the current state {pL1} as the initial marking.

In the state space, there is a cycle involving the firing sequence of {tL2, tL1}. However, this cycle is not a livelock as when the token arrives in pL1, this token can be simply snatched away by tL3. Thereby, breaking the cycle. tL3 also deposits an output token into pLO enabling **tO** to fire. Hence, **tO** is the only terminal transition that creates a terminal state.

It is clear from the state space that there are no deadlocks or livelocks.

13.6 Step-4: Analyzing the State Space

The previous subsection presented three simple modules and their state spaces. The previous section also presented analyses of these state spaces, to verify whether these systems suffered from any deadlocks or livelocks when an invitation for collaboration arrived. From these observations, the following conclusions can be made. **A Petri module is**:

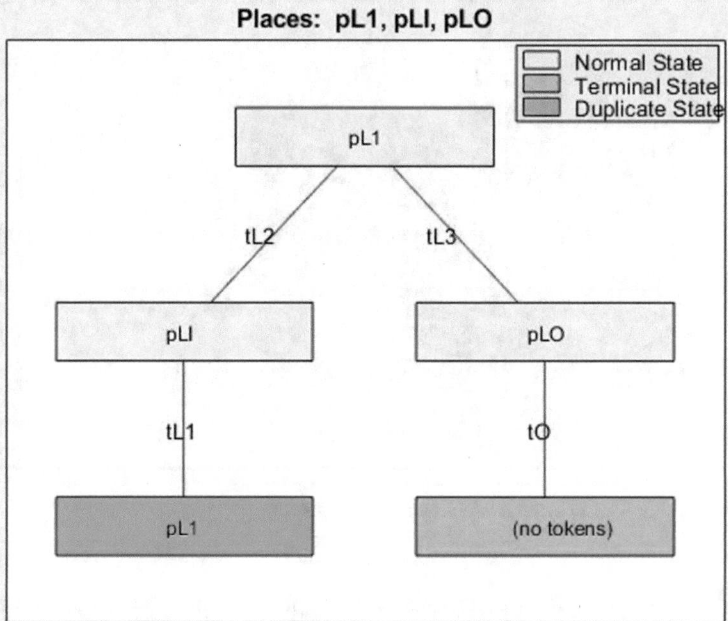

Fig. 13.7 Module-C: the state space shows that the system is free from livelocks and deadlocks

- **deadlocked: if there exists a terminal transition that is not the output port tO.**
- **livelocked: if there are cycles that can not be terminated.**
- **ready for collaboration: free from deadlocks and livelocks.**

13.6.1 Making a Decision on Collaborativeness

Making a decision on the collaborativeness of a module is also the task of the transition tMCC. Decision-making on collaborativeness is the third task of tMCC (the first and second tasks are finding the current state and generating the state space, respectively, as discussed before). To make the process of decision-making simpler, let us assume the following rules. tMCC will:

- say **NO** to collaboration, if there are livelocks or deadlocks, either going on right now, or possibly in future. In this case, tMCC will tag the color "mcc: NOx" to the token that is deposited into pLO.
  The "x" in the "mcc: NOx" represents the reason for declining the invitation:
  - x = 1: The module is under a deadlock.
  - x = 2: The module is under a livelock.

Table 13.1 Outcome of the model checking for collaboration

Tag	Diagnostic information
mcc:YES	(agreed for collaboration)
mcc:NO1	The module is under a deadlock
mcc:NO2	The module is under a livelock
mcc:NO3	(module neither under a deadlock or livelock). However, It is busy with a heavy ongoing computation. Thus, will not be disturbed in the near future
mcc:NO4	(module neither under a deadlock or livelock). The module is set (has agreed) for another collaboration
mcc:NO5–mcc:NO8	(*not used*)
mcc:NO9	The collaboration is denied for unspecified/unknown reasons

- x = 3–4: The module neither under a deadlock or livelock. However:
  * x = 3: It is busy with a heavy ongoing computation. Thus, will be not disturbed in the near future.
  * x = 4: The module is set (has agreed) for another collaboration.
- x = 9: The collaboration is denied for unspecified/unknown reason.

tMCC will say **YES** to collaboration, if the module is free from livelocks and deadlocks, and also not tied up with heavy computation either at present or planned in future. In this case, tMCC will tag the color "mcc: YES" to the token that is deposited into pLO.

Table 13.1 summarizes the outcome of the model checking for collaboration. The first row shows that property specification for collaboration is satisfied. The rest of the rows present the diagnostic information when the property specification for collaboration is not satisfied.

13.7 Step-5: Establishing the Connectivity

After finding a group of modules for collaboration (the modules that are willing to collaborate), the connection between the modules must be established. The modules may not be directly connected with each other. In this case, a Steiner Network that includes some Steiner modules as intermediaries becomes necessary. Section 12.5.2 "Steiner Spanning Tree" presents an algorithm for establishing a Steiner Network.

13.8 The New Approach

Figure 13.8 shows the new approach that involves five steps. As clearly shown in Fig. 13.8, only steps 2–4 are considered as model checking for collaborativeness (partial verification). Steps 1 and 5 are about planning and forming a network of collaboration.

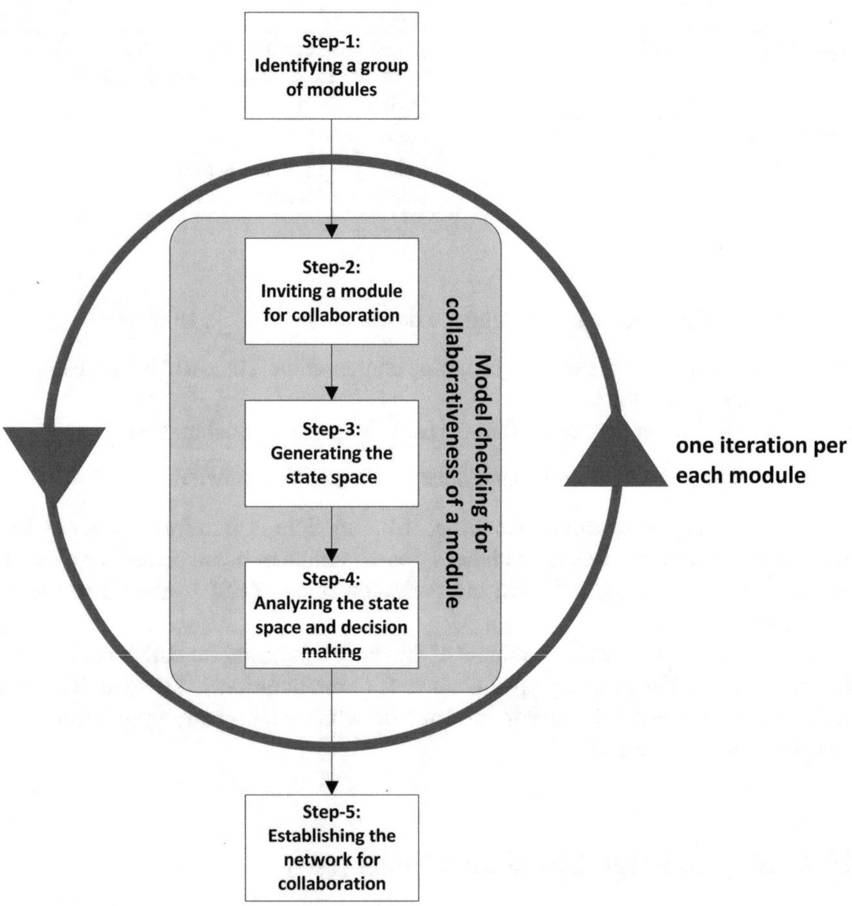

Fig. 13.8 Model checking for collaborativeness of a module

13.9 Application Example

A short summary of the networking of collaborating partners: there are two types of networking depending on one-way (command passing) or two-way (negotiation) communication:

1. One-way: Leader-Followers Network (LFN).
2. Two-way: Negotiating-Peers Network (NPN).

If the collaborating modules are not directly connected, the Steiner-mode Networking (SMN) is utilized (for one-way or two-way).

One module is needed to initiate the collaboration. For example, if the example for the creation of LFN (Sect. 12.7.2) is considered, the controller module "Finishing" is the initiator. In the example for the creation of NPN, it is logical to assume either "Assembler" of "Finishing" as the initiator. However, any of the modules that are going to be part of the networking can be the initiator, and even an outside module can be so. The initiator performs the following steps:

1. Compute all the collaborating modules.
2. Find out the proper network for the collaboration.
3. Invite all the partners, one by one.
4. For all the invited module, if $\bigcap(mcc.YES)_i = 1$, then collaboration is set in place.

In the example for the creation of LFN (section 12.7.2), "Finishing" will send the invitation to all five modules ("Conveyer Belt-1", "Conveyer Belt-2", "M/C-1", "M/C-2", and "Assembler"). If all these modules agree for collaboration, then the collaboration can start.

$$\begin{aligned} Start = (mcc.YES)_{CB-1} \cap (mcc.YES)_{CB-2} \cap \\ (mcc.YES)_{M/C-1} \cap (mcc.YES)_{M/C-2} \cap \\ (mcc.YES)_{Assembler} \end{aligned} \tag{13.1}$$

On the decision-making power: The decisions taken by a module whether to collaborate on a new collaboration, is mainly based on the existence of deadlocks or livelocks. Even if deadlocks or livelocks do not exist, some iterations inside the module may take a load of time as the module is already busy or loaded with some heavy (time consuming) task. If the historical data is available on the time taken for various types of jobs, tMCC (the decision maker on collaborativeness) may use these data too for decision-making. However, this enhanced decision-making power is not discussed in the algorithms given in this chapter and is earmarked as further work.

13.10 Chapter Summary

The proposed approach (for model checking for collaborativeness) answers the two difficulties in model checking, namely, state explosion and online applicability. The model checker that is proposed in this chapter is for an online approach; meaning model checking can be done while the model is executing. Also, model checking is not affected by the state explosion problem as the state spaces of the modules are compact. And the approach is specially designed for GPenSIM environment, making use of the Petri modules.

It must be emphasized that the approach described in this chapter takes a pragmatic approach and it cannot be used to solve all the model checking problems. What is proposed in this chapter is known as **partial verification**; partial verification focuses on the verification of the most important property for a specific application.

Finally, it must also be emphasized that the goal of the book is to develop a new modular Petri net that is capable of modeling, simulation, and control large discrete manufacturing systems. Model checking is only taken as a case study; model checking is not the focus of this book.

References

1. Berthomieu B, Ribet P-O, Vernadat F (2004) The tool tina-construction of abstract state spaces for Petri nets and time Petri nets. Int J Prod Res 42(14):2741–2756
2. Carmona J, Cortadella J, Kishinevsky M, Kondratyev A, Lavagno L, Yakovlev A (2008) A symbolic algorithm for the synthesis of bounded Petri nets. In: International conference on applications and theory of Petri nets. Springer, pp 92–111
3. Cassandras CG, Lafortune S (2009) Introduction to discrete event systems. Springer Science & Business Media
4. Cimatti A, Clarke E, Giunchiglia E, Giunchiglia F, Pistore M, Roveri M, Sebastiani R, Tacchella A (2002) Nusmv 2: an opensource tool for symbolic model checking. In: International conference on computer aided verification. Springer, pp 359–364
5. Conghua Z, Zhenyu C (2006) Model checking workflow net based on Petri net. Wuhan Univ J Nat Sci 11(5):1297–1301
6. Dai G, Bai X, Zhao C (2007) A framework for model checking web service compositions based on bpel4ws. In: IEEE international conference on e-business engineering (iCEBE'07). IEEE, pp 165–172
7. Feller AL, Wu T, Shunk DL, Fowler J (2009) Petri net translation patterns for the analysis of e-business collaboration messaging protocols. IEEE Trans Syst Man Cybern Part A Syst Humans 39(5):1022–1034
8. Finkel A (1987) A generalization of the procedure of karp and miller to well structured transition systems. In: International colloquium on automata, languages, and programming. Springer, pp 499–508
9. Furia CA, Mandrioli D, Morzenti A, Rossi M (2012) Modeling time in computing. Springer Science & Business Media
10. Holzmann GJ (2004) The SPIN model checker: primer and reference manual, vol 1003. Addison-Wesley Reading
11. Karp RM, Miller RE (1969) Parallel program schemata. J Comput Syst Sci 3(2):147–195

12. Liu G, Jiang C (2016) Petri net based model checking for the collaborative-ness of multiple processes systems. In: 2016 IEEE 13th international conference on networking, sensing, and control (ICNSC). IEEE, pp 1–6
13. Starke PH, Roch S (1992) INA: integrated net analyzer. Reference Manual
14. Szpyrka M, Biernacka A, Biernacki J (2014) Methods of translation of Petri nets to NuSMV language. In: CS & P, pp 245–256

Chapter 14
Generic Petri Module

This chapter presents a generic three-layered architecture for Petri modules that can participate in collaboration while performing some useful function on their own. This chapter starts with a crude structure for Petri modules and discusses the necessity of using colored Petri net. Finally, the generic architecture is presented.

14.1 Structure of Petri Module for Collaboration

Figure 14.1 shows the structure of a module that is capable of initiating a network as well as being invited for collaboration. The module consists of three parts, namely:

- Part-I: Host.
- Part-II: Local Implementation.
- Part-III: Guest.

The upper part of the module (Part-I: Host) is for initiating collaboration. The cold start transition[1] tINV is the one that will perform the first three steps of an initiator (mentioned in Sect. 13.9; the steps are computing the modules for collaboration, inviting the modules, and find out a proper network). When the invited modules respond, their messages are collected by the transition tNWC (stands for network creator). tNWC is responsible for running the Eq. 13.1 shown in page 209.

The middle part of the module (Part-II: Local Implementation) is the one that is performing the application for the module. For example, if the module is a controller, then this part consists of places and transitions that realize (or execute) the control logic; if the module is an Adder, then it would have places and transitions that compute the results of addition.

[1] A cold start transition is a transition with no input places. Since input tokens do not restrict this transition, this transition is always enabled.

R. Davidrajuh, *Petri Nets for Modeling of Large Discrete Systems*, Asset Analytics,
https://doi.org/10.1007/978-981-16-5203-5_14

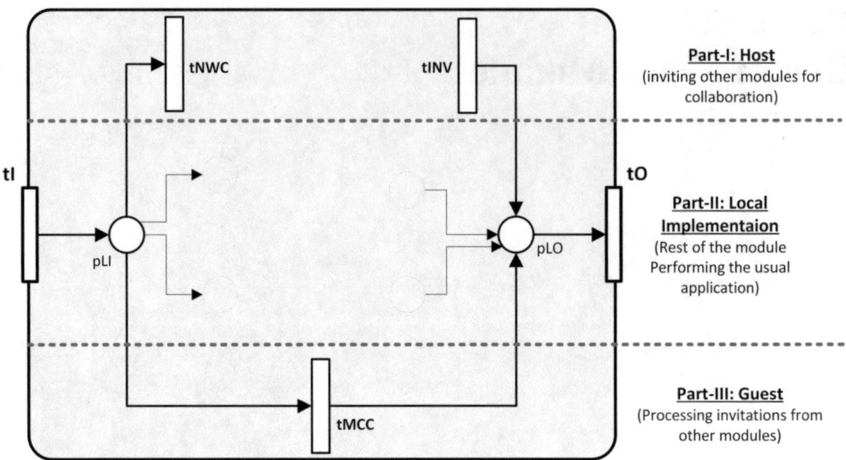

Fig. 14.1 Petri module for collaboration

The bottom part of the module (Part-III: Guest) is for processing the invitations. The function of tMCC is generating and analyzing the state space for any deadlocks and livelocks; Sects. 13.5 and 13.6 describe the functions of tMCC.

14.2 Colored Petri Module

Figure 14.1 clearly shows that without colored Petri net, the module will not work:

- When tINV sends invitations to modules, it will tag the color "inv:xxx" on the token deposited into pLO. Only the transition **tO** can consume a token tagged with color "inv:". Thus, this token cannot be consumed by any internal transitions. **tO** will send this token as a TCP/IP message to the module identified by the "xxx".
- When the receiving module (invited module) receives the TCP/IP message, the **tI** of the receiving module deposit a token with color "mcc" into pLI. Only the transition tMCC can consume this token. After making a decision, tMCC will deposit a token with color "mcc:YES" or "mcc:NOx" into pLO, as discussed in Sect. 13.6. Here again, only **tO** can consume a token with color "mcc:XXX" from pLO. **tO** will dispatch this message to the inviting module.
- When the message reaches the invitee, **tI** will deposit this message as a color "inv:YES" or "inv:NOx" on the token, and this token will be consumed by tNWC.

Due to brevity, a detailed discussion on Colored Petri net is not given in this book. However, GPenSIM Manual on Colored Petri net, authored by the author of this book ([1]) gives complete information. Also, many worked examples on Colored Petri nets are given in this manual.

14.3 Generic Petri Module

In Fig. 14.1, for simplicity, only one input port **tI** and one output port **tO** is shown. However, for non-trivial applications, there can be many input ports and output ports. This is because a Petri module can interface with three types of external entities:

1. Communication channel: For example, TCP/IP socket for receiving and sending messages to the other modules.
2. External sensors and actuators: There may be some external sensors that feed data into the module. Also, some external actuators that can be fed with instructions and control command from the modules.
3. The other Petri modules that run on the same computer: Buffering places can interface these modules.

Hence, a generic architecture for Petri module should possess three types of interfaces (input and output ports):

- **Communication Interface**: Usually, all the interactions with communication channel (e.g., downloading and uploading TCP/IP messages) are done by a single **tIC** and **tOC**, as shown in Fig. 14.1.
- **Machine Interface**: If the module has external sensors directly attached to it that feed sensor data to the module, then it is ideal to have specific **tIM** for each sensor. Similarly, if the module sends signals to external actuators that are directly connected to it, then a specific **tOM** for each actuator.
- **Application Interface**: If many modules that are running (hosted on) the same computer, the IMC between these modules will be buffering places. In this case, dedicated **tIA** (resp. **tOA**) should be provided to consume (resp. deposit) tokens from (resp. to) these buffering places.

Figure 14.2 shows the generic architecture of a Petri module with multiple input ports and output ports.

Figure 14.2 shows the transitions function as the input and output ports of the generic module. Figure 14.2 also shows local places functioning as the buffer between the three layers of the module. However, local transitions can also function as the gates between the layers. It is a good idea to maintain a clear separation of the three layers with the use of buffering places or transitions.

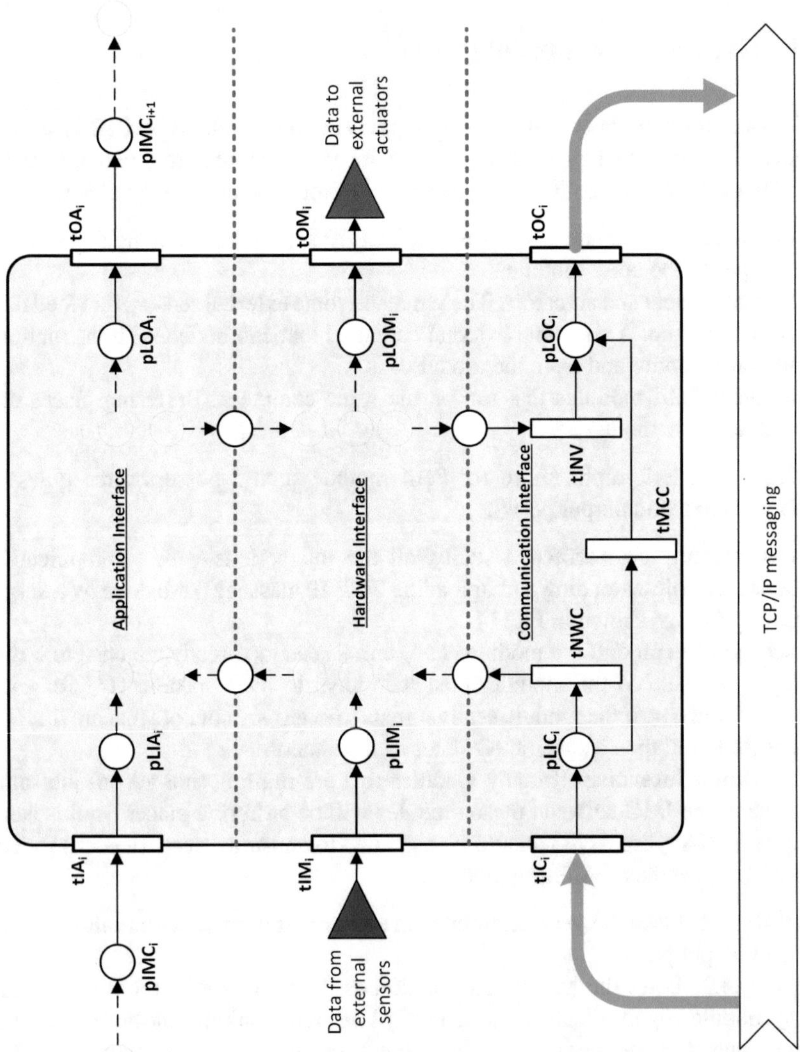

Fig. 14.2 Generic Petri module

Reference

1. GPenSIM (2019) General-purpose Petri net simulator, Technical report. http://www.davidrajuh.net/gpensim. Accessed 20 July 2020

Appendix A
GPenSIM Webpage

GPenSIM is developed by the author of this book. GPenSIM can be freely downloaded from: http://www.davidrajuh.net/gpensim/ (Fig. A.1).

R. Davidrajuh, *Petri Nets for Modeling of Large Discrete Systems*, Asset Analytics,
https://doi.org/10.1007/978-981-16-5203-5

A book by Springer published with the GPenSIM version 10 (Newest and stable version).

The book:
Davidrajuh, Reggie (2018) "Modeling discrete-event systems with GPenSIM: An introduction." Springer, ISBN: 978-3-319-73101-8

Online Extras for this book:
GPenSIM v.10 Software + Installation Guide + 38 Worked Examples

NEW! Online Addendum to the book:
Addendum-1: Implementing Colored Petri Nets in GPenSIM + Examples 39-49
Addendum-2: Using GPenSIM Resources + Examples 50-56
Addendum-3: Cost Calculations in Petri Nets + Examples 57-60
Addendum-4: Creating Modular Petri Net model

Fig. A.1 GPenSIM webpage

Index

R. Davidrajuh, *Petri Nets for Modeling of Large Discrete Systems*, Asset Analytics,
https://doi.org/10.1007/978-981-16-5203-5

Printed in the United States
by Baker & Taylor Publisher Services